The Atoning Priesthood
of
Jesus Christ

Frank B. Holbrook, M.Th.

Adventist Theological Society Publications
Berrien Springs, Michigan 49103

Acknowledgements

Scriptures quoted from NASB are from the *New American Standard Bible,* ©The Lockman Foundation 1960, 1962, 1963, 1968, 1971, 1972, 1973, 1975, 1977.

Scriptures quoted from NEB are from *The New English Bible,* copyright © The Delegates of the Oxford University Press and the Syndics of the Cambridge University Press 1961, 1970. Reprinted by permission.

Scriptures quoted from NIV are from the *Holy Bible, New International Version,* copyright © 1973, 1978, 1984, International Bible Society. Used by permission of Zondervan Bible Publishers.

Scriptures quoted from NKJV are from The New King James Version, copyright © 1979, 1980, 1982, Thomas Nelson, Inc., Publishers.

Scriptures quoted from NRSV are from the New Revised Standard Version Bible, copyright © 1989, by the Division of Christian Education of the National Council of the Churches of Christ in the U.S.A. Used by permission. All rights reserved.

Scriptures quoted from RSV are from the Revised Standard Version Bible, copyright © 1946, 1952 by the Division of Christian Education of the National Council of the Churches of Christ in the U.S.A. Used by permission.

Notice: The italicizing of key words and phrases in citations from the above translations is for the purpose of emphasis by the author. The italics are not to be regarded as a part of the text as published in the above translations.

Unless otherwise indicated, all scriptural quotations are from the Revised Standard Version, 1946, 1952 editions.

———— ◆ ————

The author assumes full responsibility for the accuracy of all quotations cited in this book.

Copyright ©1996 by Frank B. Holbrook

Ventura Desktop Typesetting and Design by Martha Lunt, using Times Roman, 11/13.

Printed by Review & Herald Publishing Association
Hagerstown, Maryland

Printed in U.S.A.
ISBN 0-925675-16-4

Dedicated to the memory of
Edward Heppenstall
under whose tutelage I began to grasp
the centrality of the cross of Christ
and to the memory of
Gerhard F. Hasel
my long-time friend and colleague
who encouraged and arranged for
the writing of this volume.

Table of Contents

ABBREVIATIONS

Translations

AB	Anchor Bible
ARV	American Revised Version
JB	Jerusalem Bible
KJV	King James Version
MLB	Modern Language Bible (Berkeley)
NASB	New American Standard Bible
NEB	The New English Bible
NIV	The New International Version
NKJV	The New King James Version
NRSV	New Revised Standard Version
RSV	Revised Standard Version
TEV	Today's English Version (Good News Bible)

Reference Works

AG   William F. Arndt and F. Wilbur Gingrich. *A Greek-English Lexicon of the New Testament* (Chicago: The University of Chicago Press, 1957).

AUSS   *Andrews University Seminary* Studies. Nancy J. Vyhmeister, ed. (Berrien Springs, MI: Andrews University Press).

BDB   Francis Brown, S. R. Driver, Charles A. Briggs. *A Hebrew and English Lexicon* (Boston/New York: Houghton Mifflin Company, 1907).

DARCOM   *Daniel & Revelation Committee Series.* Frank B. Holbrook, ed. (Silver Spring, MD: Biblical Research Institute, General Conference of Seventh-day Adventists, 1982-1992), 7 vols.

Volume 1 *Selected Studies on Prophetic Interpretation* (William H. Shea).

Volume 2 *Symposium on Daniel.*

Volume 3 *The Seventy Weeks, Leviticus, and the Nature of Prophecy.*

Volume 4 *Issues in the Book of Hebrews.*

Volume 5 *Doctrine of the Sanctuary: A Historical Survey (1845-1863).*

Volume 6 *Symposium on Revelation,* Book 1.

Volume 7 *Symposium on Revelation,* Book 2.

DB	*Dictionary of the Bible.* James Hastings, ed., rev. ed. Frederick C. Grant and H.H. Rowley, eds. (New York: Charles Scribner's Sons, 1963).
ExpBC	*Expositor's Bible Commentary, The.* Frank E. Gaebelein, ed. (Grand Rapids, MI: Zondervan Publishing House, 1976-1992), 12 vols. Used by permission of Zondervan Publishing House.
EGT	*Expositor's Greek Testament, The.* W. Robertson Nicoll, ed. (Grand Rapids: Wm. B. Eerdmans Publishing Company, 1961), 5 vols.
IDB	*Interpreter's Dictionary of the Bible.* George A. Buttrick, ed. (New York/Nashville: Abington Press, 1962) 5 vols.
ISBE	*International Standard Bible Encyclopedia.* Geoffrey W. Bromiley, ed., rev. ed. (Grand Rapids, MI: William B. Eerdmans Publishing Company, 1979-1988), 4 vols .
LXX	Septuagint, Alfred Rahlfs, ed. (New York: American Bible Society, 1959).
NICNT	*New International Commentary on the NT, The.* Gordon Fee, ed. (Grand Rapids: William B. Eerdmans Publishing Company, 1964).
NIDCC	*New International Dictionary of the Christian Church, The.* J. D. Douglas, ed., rev. ed. (Grand Rapids: Zondervan Publishing House, 1974, 1978).
NT	New Testament
QOD	*Seventh-day Adventists Answer Questions on Doctrine* (Washington, DC: Review and Herald Publishing Association, 1957).
OT	Old Testament
PC	*Pulpit Commentary, The.* H.D.M. Spence and Joseph S. Excell, eds. (Chicago: Wilcox & Follett Company, nd), 52 vols.
PFF	LeRoy E. Froom. *Prophetic Faith of Our Fathers, The* (Washington, D.C.: Review and Herald, 1946-1954), 4 vols.
SA[1]	*Sanctuary and the Atonement, The.* Arnold V. Wallenkampf and W. Richard Lesher, eds. (Washington, D.C.: Biblical Research Committee, General Conference of Seventh-day Adventists, 1981).
SA[2]	*Sanctuary and the Atonement, The.* Abridged. Frank B. Holbrook, ed. (Silver Spring, MD: Biblical Research Institute, 1989).

SDABC   *Seventh-day Adventist Bible Commentary, The.* Francis D.
          Nichol (Washington, D.C.: Review and Herald Publishing As-
          sociation, 1953-1957), 7 vols.

SDABD   Siegfried H. Horn, et al. *Seventh-day Adventist Bible Dictionary*
          (Washington, D.C.: Review and Herald Publishing Association,
          1960).

TDNT   *Theological Dictionary of the New Testament (Kittel)* Geoffrey
          W. Bromiley, trans. and ed. (Grand Rapids, MI: William B.
          Eerdmans Publishing Company, 1962), 10 vols.

Ellen G. White Writings

AA   *Acts of the Apostles, The.* (Mountain View, CA: Pacific Press
          Publishing Association, 1911).

BE   *Bible Echo* (Australia).

CH   *Counsels on Health* (Mountain View, CA: Pacific Press Publish-
          ing Association, 1923).

COL   *Christ's Object Lessons* (Washington, D.C.: Review and Herald
          Publishing Association, 1900).

DA   *Desire of Ages, The.* Mountain View, CA: Pacific Press Publish-
          ing Association, 1898).

Ed   *Education* (Mountain View, CA: Pacific Press Publishing Asso-
          ciation, 1903).

Ev   *Evangelism* (Washington, D.C: Review and Herald Publishing
          Association, 1946).

GC   *Great Controversy, The* (Mountain View, CA: Pacific Press
          Publishing Association, 1911).

GW   *Gospel Workers* (Washington, D.C.: Review and Herald Pub-
          lishing Association, 1915, 1944).

LS   *Life Sketches of Ellen G. White* (Mountain View, CA: Pacific
          Press Publishing Association, 1915).

MB   *Thoughts from the Mount of Blessing* (Mountain View, CA:
          Pacific Press Publishing Association (1900, 1928, 1943).

ML   *My Life Today* (Washington, D.C.: Review and Herald, 1952).

MYP   *Messages to Young People* (Nashville, TN: Southern Publishing
          Association, 1930).

PP   *Patriarchs and Prophets* (Mountain View, CA: Pacific Press
          Publishing Association, 1890, 1913).

RH   *Review and Herald* (SDA church paper).

SC	*Steps to Christ* (Mountain View, CA: Pacific Press Publishing Association, 1908).
SD	Sons and Daughters of God (Washington, D.C.: Review and Herald, 1955).
SG	*Spiritual Gifts,* Vols. 1-4, Facsimile Reproduction (Washington, D.C.: Review and Herald Publishing Association, 1944).
SL	*The Sanctified Life* (Washington, D.C.: Review and Herald Publishing Association, 1937).
SM	*Selected Messages* (Washington, D.C.: Review and Herald Publishing Association, 1958, 1980), 3 books.
T	*Testimonies for the Church* (Mountain View, CA: Pacific Press Publishing Association, 1948), 9 vols.

Note: For those readers who may have an interest in key words in the original languages, it should be observed that they have been occasionally transliterated and inserted in parentheses in the cited passages. If the passage is in the OT, the word transliterated is Hebrew/Aramaic; if in the NT, it is Greek.

To the Reader

My father, reared a Roman Catholic, united in his early, adult years with the Methodist church, the childhood faith of his fiancée. Thus, it was my good fortune to be reared in a Christian home and to attend for the first eight years of my life the Sunday School and other services of a large Methodist congregation in Washington, D.C.

As I attended Sunday School and learned more about Jesus, some questions began to form in my young mind. Since Jesus was so good and kind and helped so many people, why did He return to heaven? Why did He stay such a short time on earth? What was He doing in heaven? In spite of their many years of association with other Christians, my parents had never heard a sermon on the subject of Christ's second coming, much less any discussion on why Jesus ascended to heaven, or what His present activity might be!

Not until my parents began to study seriously the teachings of the Seventh-day Adventist Church did they discover the wonderful truth about the priesthood of Jesus Christ in the heavenly sanctuary. Suddenly, the light began to dawn on our minds. Since there were definite links between the earthly and heavenly sanctuaries (type and antitype), a knowledge of the former would shed light on the nature of the Saviour's heavenly ministry in the latter! Such a concept brought heaven close to earth, and for the first time the silent heavens which hid the Saviour from our view, as it were, began to speak! By careful study we could now trace in the typical rituals of the earthly sanctuary the actual saving activities of our High Priest in the realities above!

Continuing study of the living, exalted Christ as our High Priest has held a central interest in our family ever since. Fifteen years of teaching on this subject at Southern Missionary College, Collegedale, Tennessee, and another decade functioning as the secretary of the Daniel and Revelation Committee of the General Conference of Seventh-day Adventists has only served to deepen my interest in this vital truth of Christ's priesthood. It is the writer's prayer that in the following pages the reader may share his interest and may find his/her faith in Christ's saving ministrations in heaven enriched and confirmed. "Holy brethren, who share in a heavenly call, consider Jesus, the apostle and high priest of our confession" (Heb 3:1).

Inasmuch as the viewpoints of higher-critical study of the Bible have left the ivory-towers of learning to become more commonplace among Christians in general, it may be helpful to state for the reader the premises upon which this present study on the atoning priesthood of Jesus Christ rests. We note five points:

1. The unity of the Christian Scriptures. "In many and various ways *God spoke of old to our fathers by the prophets;* but in these last days *he has spoken to us by a Son*" (Heb 1:1, 2).

It is the same God who speaks to us in either the OT (the witness of the prophets) or the NT (the apostolic witness to Jesus Christ). The *same* God speaking the *same* message of salvation from sin is the central subject in both Testaments. Before the cross the Gospel of salvation by faith in a divine Redeemer to come was taught by types and rituals; after the cross, by the actual life events of that Redeemer. The religion of the Holy Scriptures is one.

2. The Holy Spirit's Authorship of the Scriptures. "All *scripture is inspired by God* and profitable for teaching, for reproof, for correction, and for training in righteousness "(2 Tim 3:16). "The prophets prophesied . . . by the Spirit of Christ within them" (1 Pet 1:10, 11). The human writers of Scripture were the Spirit's penmen. The Holy Spirit does not contradict Himself. What He reveals on a given topic in one passage of Scripture will be in agreement with what He reveals on the same topic elsewhere in the Scriptures.

3. The Scriptures are their own Interpreter. This simply means that one passage of Scripture on a given subject will shed light on another passage dealing with the same subject. Very few biblical teachings—if any—are fully summarized in all their details in one passage. Consequently, biblical doctrines are constructs, arrived at by comparing what the Holy Spirit has said through the different writers on the *same* subject.

Jesus Himself followed this procedure to prove His Messiahship to two of His disciples: "And beginning at Moses and all the prophets, he interpreted to them in all the scriptures the things concerning himself" (Luke 24:27). Later, that same day, He reaffirmed this approach to the apostles: "These are my words which I spoke to you, while I was still with you, that everything written about me in the law of Moses and the prophets and the psalms must be fulfilled" (Luke 24:44).

Some disparage this method of Scripture study, calling it "proof-texting." This is a misleading charge; it opens the door to unsound interpretations. Unless we permit the Scriptures to explain Scripture—as Jesus did—we will find ourselves reading *into* Scripture our own human interpretations.

4. The Israelite sanctuary was designed as a ritual parable to teach the plan of salvation. "For we [Christians] *also* have had the gospel preached to us, just as *they* [Israelites of the Exodus] did" (Heb 4:2, NIV). Since it is positively declared that the Israelites in their trek from Egypt had the same gospel that Christians receive, it is safe to infer they received it through the rituals of the sanctuary system.

These rituals, as we shall see, illustrate in a typical manner the sacrifice and priestly ministry of the Messiah, including the final judgment—all major aspects of Heaven's plan of salvation. Consequently, it is legitimate to draw in other portions of Scripture dealing with these same subjects to illumine this ritual parable. It is really a two-way street. The sanctuary types illustrate basic truths in the plan of salvation, and other portions of Scripture shed light on the typical rites. The result is a fuller, clarified understanding of Jesus Christ and the divine plan for saving sinners.

5. The Historicist Method of Interpreting Daniel and Revelation. If, by way of illustration, we think of the actual incarnation of God the Son, His sinless life and atoning death, resurrection, and priesthood as putting real "sinews" and "flesh" on the "bones" of the sanctuary rites (so to speak), it is Bible prophecy that breathes life and animation into them!

The prophecies of Daniel foretold the exact time for the appearing of the Messiah, His mission and atoning death, and the inauguration of His priesthood, as well as the exact time for the beginning of His closing priestly ministration. The prophecies of Revelation color in more of the picture of His heavenly priesthood.

The historicist interpretation rests on the premise that Daniel and Revelation are *revelations of God's foreknowledge,* and that their predictions (like a scroll) unroll in historical events from the times of the prophets (Daniel/John) up to and embracing the establishment of God's eternal kingdom.

Finally, we may say that one important reason for another study on the priesthood of Christ as reflected in the Israelite sanctuary is the fact that the true backdrop for the NT's portrayal of our Lord's atoning work is the OT's sacrificial system. His life and death and subsequent activity are presented at times even in the very terminology of the sanctuary. The more thoroughly we understand that system, the more fully—and at times more correctly—will we understand our wonderful Saviour and the divine plan of salvation.

———— ◆ ————

To assist the reader in understanding the intent of this study a few remarks should be made in regard to the sequence of the following chapters. Our study is an exploration of the biblical teaching of the atoning priesthood of Jesus Christ. Consequently, it is not the aim of our search to present a detailed analysis of the Israelite sanctuary. Rather, we intend to examine the major truths which the sanctuary types—supported by the Scriptures elsewhere—

contribute to our understanding of Christ's important, priestly ministrations.

For that reason we begin with His inauguration as our King-Priest shortly after His ascension. Since priests function in connection with temples, we next review the Scriptural teaching about the heavenly temple-sanctuary where Christ ministers. According to the Scriptures the heavenly temple-sanctuary relates to the earthly, Israelite sanctuary in a type-antitype relationship. Thus, it is necessary for the Bible student to employ sound principles of interpretation, if he/she is to understand correctly the earthly types. In this manner—by examining the typical sanctuary system—we may grasp with better understanding the nature and importance of Christ's priestly ministrations in heaven.

The plan of salvation, as it is laid out in the sanctuary ritual—and as it is carried out in reality by Christ, is the Godhead's response to the origin and course of sin in the created universe. Hence, we move to a chapter devoted to the great estrangement which the entrance of sin among the angels and our first parents brought about in a once-harmonious universe.

We then move to the heart of our study: the three great emphases the sanctuary types teach about the Deity's endeavor to save sinners and to resolve the rebellion; namely, an atoning sacrifice, priestly mediation, and final judgment. These activities—described in the types—become the subjects of prophetic forecasts and finally as realities, as Christ fulfills both the types and the predictions one by one. Our study closes with brief answers to a few pertinent questions that are commonly asked about our Lord's priesthood.

Readers unacquainted with the Israelite sanctuary and its function will obtain more benefit from this study if they will first read Appendix C which presents a summary sketch of the Israelite sanctuaries. Bible dictionaries and Bible encyclopedia articles on the Tabernacle/Temple will give further details. Since the sanctuary types deal with the plan of salvation from sin, some readers may find helpful "The ABCs of Personal Salvation" in Appendix A. The year-day principle is an important key in the interpretation of the prophecies of Daniel and Revelation. It is discussed in Appendix B. Appendix D provides a few charts to assist readers in visualizing the prophecies of Daniel 7-9 and the phases of the final judgment which are covered by the typical Day of Atonement rite in the Israelite sanctuary.

Frank B. Holbrook
Dalton, Georgia

1

Christ's Inauguration As King-Priest

The sacrificial death of Jesus Christ on Calvary and His subsequent priesthood in heaven form an indivisible whole. From a scriptural viewpoint these two "events" cannot, indeed, *must not be separated.* Christ's death has no atoning significance for the individual sinner apart from Christ's priestly intercession. On the other hand our Lord's priesthood would be meaningless if He lacked the merits of His atoning death to mediate. "For every high priest is appointed to offer gifts and sacrifices; hence it is *necessary* for this priest [Christ] also to have something to offer" (Heb 8:3).

Although it is evident that Christ's priesthood is as essential to Heaven's plan of salvation as is His death, many modern Christians remain in ignorance of His priestly activity; hence, the reason for this present study. It is our purpose to explore the truth about Christ's atoning priesthood—foretold in prophecy, illustrated by the Israelite sanctuary, and illuminated by various portions of the inspired Scriptures. In so doing we invite the reader to establish a renewed relationship with the *living* Christ who is engaged in a vital ministry for him/her.

Exalted Victor

The priesthood of Jesus Christ began in heaven fifty days after His resurrection from Joseph's tomb. In the midst of "innumerable angels" the Saviour of the world was "crowned [*stephanoō*] with glory and honor" (Heb 2:9). Here begins our Lord's saving ministry as humanity's High Priest (cf. Rom 5:10), and the apostle's allusion to the *stephanos*—the chaplet bestowed on the victor of an athletic contest—rather than to the kingly *diadēma* (diadem) discloses the excitement and rapturous joy all Heaven experienced on this occasion to celebrate the *victory* of our Lord over the forces of evil!

Because God the Son had previously "humbled himself" through His amazing willingness to assume on a permanent basis our human nature, and because He "became obedient unto death, even death on a cross," God "*highly exalted* [*huperupsoō*] him and bestowed on him the name which is above every name, that at the name of Jesus every knee should bow, in heaven and on earth and under the earth, and every tongue confess that Jesus Christ is Lord, to the glory of God the Father" (Phil 2:8-11).

Christ's heavenly exaltation presupposed His earthly exaltation or "lifting up [*hupsoō*]" on the cross for "the expiation . . . of our sins" (1 John 2:2).[1] Jesus had explained to Nicodemus, "As Moses *lifted up* the serpent in the wilderness, so must the Son of man *be lifted up*" (John 3:14). Near the end of His life He made a similar statement to the Greeks who had sought an interview in the court of the Temple: " 'I, when I *am lifted up* from the earth, will draw all men to myself,' He said this," John adds, "to show by what death he was to die" (John 12:32, 33). In a very real sense Christ's atoning death on the cross, though it appeared at first to be a terrible defeat, was truly the "lifting up"—the exaltation—of a victor! The Father's enthronement of Christ at Pentecost acknowledged His Son's magnificent accomplishment (Acts 2).

Glorified Redeemer

Christ's heavenly exaltation is also described by the apostles as His glorification. Peter declared to the crowd in Solomon's Porch that God had "*glorified* [*doxazō*] his servant Jesus" whom they had denied (Acts 3:13 cf. 2:33). John comments that in the days of Jesus' ministry, "The Spirit had not been given [a reference to Pentecost], because Jesus was not yet *glorified*" (John 7:39). He also observes that the apostles' understanding of their Master's life (involving the prophecies about it) was clarified after "Jesus *was glorified*" (John 12:16).

The Father glorified Jesus—that is, honored the incarnate Christ by appointing Him "the heir of all things" (Heb 1:2). In addition, He conferred on Christ "all authority [*exousia*] in heaven and on earth" (Matt 28:18), recognizing Him as "the *head* over all things for the church" (Eph 1:22).[2] All the attributes of kingly majesty, dignity, and splendor were bestowed upon Christ. Holy angels and the representatives of the unfallen worlds honored the Redeemer and submitted willingly to His sovereignty (cf. Job 1:6; 1 Pet 3:22).

The book of Revelation symbolizes the enthronement of the exalted Christ under the figure of a lamb standing "in the midst" of God's throne "as though it had been slain" (Rev 5:6; 7:17). Twenty-eight times throughout the Apocalypse Christ is referred to as "the Lamb," and the throne of God's universal dominion receives the title, "the throne of God and of the Lamb" (cf. Rev 3:21; 22:1, 3).

Revelation 5:6 is the first visionary description of Christ's enthronement beside the Father. The emphasis of the scene is upon the Redeemer's atoning sacrifice. "Worthy art thou," exclaim the living creatures and elders, "for thou wast slain and by thy blood didst ransom men for God from every tribe and tongue and people and nation" (Rev 5:8, 9).

The ascription of praise and honor to the Lamb is repeated and enlarged upon by the myriads of angels who joyfully exclaim, "Worthy is the Lamb who was slain, to receive power and wealth and wisdom and might and honor and glory and blessing!" (Rev 5:11, 12).

This particular scene, symbolizing Christ as a once-slain—but again living—lamb standing at the throne of God, carries a significant truth (Rev 5:6). The tense of the verb ("had been slain") in the original language (a perfect, passive, participle) denotes that Christ had been slain in the past, but the *results* obtained by His death remain and are always available for the redemption of repentant sinners.[3] The horns and eyes of the symbol indicate the glorified Christ's absolute power and wisdom. But the Apocalypse's repeated emphasis on Christ's title, "the Lamb," and the underscoring by the Greek perfect tense of the continuous efficacy of His sacrifice, clearly mark out the heavenly sanctuary as the command center from which the glorified Redeemer will now carry forward to a successful conclusion all aspects of the plan of salvation.[4]

Enthroned King

Upon Christ's ascension to the heavenly realm, God "made him sit at his right hand" (Eph 1:20). Sharing the eternal throne of universal dominion (Rev 3:21), Christ occupies a kingship "far above all rule and authority and power and dominion, and above every name that is named, not only in this age but also in that which is to come" (Eph 1:21). In this position God "has put all things under his feet" (Eph 1:22)—and continues to do so until His messianic reign is accomplished (cf. 1 Cor 15:24-28).

The expression, "to sit at his [God's] right hand" occurs (with slight variations) 20 times in the NT (if we count Gospel parallels and citations of

Psalm 110:1).[5] The NT statements are all based on Psalm 110, a Davidic writing. "The *Lord [Yahweh]* says to *my lord [Adonî]*: 'Sit at my right hand, till I make your enemies your footstool' " (vs. 1). It is evident from His discussion with the Pharisees that both Jesus and the scribes understood the personage addressed as "my lord" to be the Messiah or Christ.[6]

Since the NT writers accept Jesus of Nazareth as the fulfillment of all the messianic prophecies, they recognize His enthronement as co-ruler with the Father as the direct fulfillment of Psalm 110:1. The expression, "at my right hand," connotes *a position* of honor (that is, at God's side), but is in no wise intended to locate the whereabouts of Christ's physical presence in the heavenly sanctuary.

"To sit at God's right hand" is a figurative phrase, indicating the Saviour's new, exalted dignity, full authority and majesty, His rank and preeminence over the created universe. Christ Himself speaks of the glorified redeemed in a similar manner when He promises that they will sit on His throne as He Himself sat on His Father's throne (Rev 3:21). Obviously, the phrasing speaks of their dignity as "fellow heirs with Christ" (Rom 8:17) and not of a sitting on a single, literal throne which would be impossible for the millions of redeemed persons.

In what manner does Christ now "reign"? What is the nature of His kingdom? When Christ stood before Pilate, He plainly indicated He sought no earthly empire to rule. "My kingship is not of this world; if my kingship were of this world, my servants would fight, that I might not be handed over to the Jews; but my kingship is not from the world' " (John 18:36).

The advent of "the kingdom of God," which Christ early on announced as imminent, was the kingdom of His grace. Repentance from sin and faith in Him as Saviour were the requirements for entrance (Mark 1:15). The Holy Spirit would work in the heart to bring about an entirely new life (John 3:3-8; cf. 2 Cor 5:17). Many of Christ's parables taught the characteristics of that spiritual kingdom and of those who would become its subjects.

When the Pharisees, who thought only in terms of political rule, challenged Him about "when" the announced kingdom was coming, He replied, "The kingdom of God is not coming with signs to be observed; nor will they say, 'Lo, here it is!' or 'There!' for behold, the kingdom of God is within you" (Luke 17:21, margin). Those who accept Christ as Saviour and Lord not only obtain "redemption, the forgiveness of sins" from the Father, but are also "delivered . . . from the dominion of darkness *and transferred . . . to the kingdom of his beloved Son*" (Col 1:13, 14).

In this age (the messianic age) Christ reigns from "the *throne of grace*" in the heavenly sanctuary (Heb 4:16). The NT writers view the previous ages from Adam to the Messiah as moving toward "the climax of history" (Heb 9:26, NEB)—literally, "[the] completion of the ages." Thus, the era in which Christ's first advent, death, resurrection, and subsequent reign from heaven take place is viewed as "these last days" (Heb 1:2) or "the last days" (Acts 2:17).[7] The present era of Christ's reign of grace *also* has its end-time events that will culminate in our Lord's *second* advent to take His people to Himself (Matt 24:32, 33; Heb 9:28).

The reign of Christ from the "throne of grace" is not something mystical or intangible. Through the agency of His church He is extending the borders of His kingdom throughout the world. Just as He once said to the Jewish leaders—"My Father is working until now, and I Myself am working: (John 5:17, NASB)—so now He rules in the nations of this world to carry out "the eternal purpose" (Eph 3:11) to bring the plan of salvation to a triumphant conclusion and to terminate the rule of sin.

"Then comes the end, when he [Christ] delivers the kingdom to God the Father *after destroying every rule and every authority and power. For he [Christ] must reign* until he [God the Father] has put all enemies under his feet" (1 Cor 15:24, 25). When, at the end of the age—at the end of Christ's reign of grace—the seventh angel blows his trumpet, "the kingdom of the world [will] become the kingdom of our Lord and of his Christ!" At that point Christ moves into the rulership of the kingdom of glory, "and he shall reign for ever and ever" (Rev 11:15) upon "his glorious throne" (literally, "upon his throne of glory" (Matt 25:31).

But Christ's kingship will always be subordinate to that of the Father. Just as in the incarnation, God the Son condescended to take humanity's nature so as to be our representative head, just so He volunteers to remain in that position eternally. "And when all things are subjected to Him, then the Son Himself also will be subjected to the one who subjected all things to Him, that God may be all in all" (1 Cor 15:28, NASB).

Invested High Priest

In his speech to the Jews assembled in Jerusalem to celebrate the Feast of Pentecost, Peter explained that the Joel-predicted outpouring of the Holy Spirit, which they were witnessing, was Heaven's announcement that Jesus of Nazareth had been enthroned at God's right hand as Lord and Christ.

"This Jesus God raised up, . . . *Being therefore exalted at the right hand of God,* and having received from the Father the promise of the Holy Spirit, *he has poured out this which you see and hear.* For David did not ascend into the heavens; but he himself says, '*The Lord said to my Lord, Sit at my right hand,* till I make thy enemies a stool for thy feet.' Let all the house of Israel therefore know assuredly that God has made him both Lord and Christ, this Jesus whom you crucified" (Acts 2:32-36).

But Peter understood Christ's heavenly enthronement to involve more than kingship. A few weeks later he proclaimed in the Temple courts that Jesus "is the one whom God exalted to His right hand as *Prince* and *Savior,* to grant [*didōmi,* give] repentance to Israel, and forgiveness of sins" (Acts 5:31, NASB). In this declaration Peter combines the princely or kingly rule of Christ with that of priesthood. In Israel it was the priesthood (the high priest and his associate priests) who dealt with the issues of sin, repentance, and forgiveness.

The apostolic author of Hebrews sums up the argument of the first half of his epistle with an affirmation similar to Peter's: "Now the point in what we are saying is this: *we have such a high priest, one who is seated at the right hand of the throne* of the Majesty in heaven, *a minister in the sanctuary and the true tent* which is set up not by man but by the Lord" (Heb 8:1, 2).

Thus, it is evident that in the mind of Peter and his brethren Pentecost (Acts 2) marked not only the enthronement of the exalted and glorified Christ as King, but also His investiture as high priest. He was inaugurated to be a royal priest on heaven's highest throne. Whereas in Israel, kingship and priesthood were separated (inherited by descendants of Judah and Levi respectively), in Jesus Christ the two roles are united.

But Christ is not merely occupying an impersonal position. He is *humanity's* king-priest, *our* royal high priest, forever linked to us through His incarnation so that He may minister in our behalf the salvation the Deity has devised. "Therefore he had to be made like his brethren in every respect, so that he might become a merciful and faithful high priest in the service of God, *to make expiation for the sins of the people.* For because he himself has suffered and been tempted, he is able to help those who are tempted" (Heb 2:17, 18).

The blood of Jesus Christ is heaven's currency in its business of salvation. That is, the *merits* of His sinless life and atoning death are what He pleads before God in behalf of every repentant sinner who comes seeking forgiveness and acceptance. As John writes, "We *have an advocate with the Father,* Jesus Christ the righteous; and he is the expiation for our sins, and not for ours only but also for the sins of the whole world" (1 John 2:1, 2). And the writer of Hebrews adds, "Consequently he is able for all time to save those who draw near to God through him, since he always lives to make intercession for them" (Heb 7:25).

It is fitting, as Christians, that we should continually look back to Calvary, for there the basis of our salvation was achieved. Every communion service recalls the central fact of the Christian faith: Christ's atoning death (1 Cor 11:26). And it is equally fitting that we eagerly anticipate His second coming, the grand consummation of the plan of redemption (Heb 9:28). But it is also a Christian's great privilege to focus his/her faith and life's energies in this present era upon *the living Christ* in the heavenly sanctuary ministering "in the presence of God on our behalf" (Heb 9:24)!

We approach the living Christ—our high priest—through the medium of prayer. And we can do this with confidence. He bears our humanity; He has experienced our pain and sorrows. He understands our fears, our hurts, our griefs. "Since therefore we have a great high priest who has passed through the heavens, Jesus the Son of God, let us hold fast to the religion we profess. For ours is not a high priest unable to sympathize with our weaknesses, but one who, because of his likeness to us, has been tested every way, only without sin. Let us therefore boldly approach the throne of our gracious God, where we may receive mercy and in his grace find timely help" (Heb 4:14-16, NEB).

Prophetic Portrayals of Priesthood

King-Priest Like Melchizedek (Ps 110:1, 4)

While the Levitical system foreshadowed the priesthood of Christ, certain OT prophecies plainly stated the fact. David wrote the most ancient of these predictions in Psalm 110, the same prophecy that foretold the enthronement of the Messiah at God's right hand (vs. 1). After this opening statement, God continues speaking to the Messiah, "The Lord has sworn and will not change his mind, 'You are a priest for ever after the order of Melchizedek' " (vs. 4).

This divine commission provides the biblical argument for the apostle in the book of Hebrews to prove that the typical, Levitical priesthood with its sacrificial rituals and festivals had come to an end with the Father's appointment of Jesus Christ to a priesthood like Melchizedek's.[8] "Christ did not exalt himself to be made a high priest, but was appointed by him who said to him, . . . 'Thou art a priest for ever, after the order of Melchizedek' " (Heb 5:5, 6; cf. 7:11-19).

Melchizedek was an Amorite king whom Abraham met during his sojourn in the land of Canaan sometime during the first quarter of the second millennium, B.C. Evidently, the king ruled over a city-state, Salem (known later as Jerusalem, cf. Ps 76:2). Melchizedek was a priest of "God Most High" as well as a king (Gen 14:17-20). This brief allusion to the Deity indicates that the worship of the true God, originally held by the immediate descendants of Noah, had not died out entirely. Apparently a genuine faith in the Creator still existed in some family lines other than Abraham's, and the patriarch did not hesitate to give this priestly believer a tenth (tithe) of the spoils of war.[9]

Several hundred years later the Holy Spirit selected the Salem king as a type of the coming Messiah, bidding David to write, "You [the Messiah] are a priest for ever *after the order* of Melchizedek" (Ps 110:4). The focus of the prediction is on "the order" or the "nature of" (*taxis,* Heb 5:6) the ruler's priesthood. That is, the Messiah would assume a priesthood similar to Melchizedek's.[10] Thus, approximately a thousand years before Christ's advent, Inspiration foretold that the Messiah would rule from God's throne as a king-priest! Christ would unite in His person the roles of kingship and priesthood and would rule and minister in this double capacity.

Ministry of Intercession (Isa 53:11, 12)

The prophet Isaiah (eighth century B.C.) often referred to as the "gospel prophet," wrote of the Messiah's priestly ministry. The reference is recorded among what are commonly known as the "Servant Songs." The central personage in the fourth song (Isa 52:13–53:12) is sometimes designated "the Suffering Servant." He graphically portrays the Saviour's substitutionary death for the sins of humanity.

Liberal scholarship rejects the identification of the "Suffering Servant" with Jesus of Nazareth, but Jesus applied the prophecy to Himself on the night of His betrayal. Citing a key line in Isaiah 53:12, He said, "I will tell you that this scripture must be fulfilled in me, 'And he was reckoned with the transgressors'; for what is written about me has its fulfillment" (Luke 22:37). The early Christians were in full agreement with this identification (cf. 1 Pet 2:24; Acts 8:30-35).

Although the main focus of the song is on the Messiah's substitutionary sufferings, the last two verses make a clear reference to His future, priestly intercession.

"He [the Messiah] shall see the fruit of the travail of his soul and be satisfied; by his knowledge shall the righteous one, my servant [the Messiah], *make many to be accounted righteous* [*sdq*];[11] and he shall bear their iniquities. . . . he poured out his soul to death, and was numbered with the transgressors; yet he *bore* the sin of many, and made intercession [*pg'*][12] for the transgressors" (Isa 53:11, 12).

When joined together, the last lines of each verse (vss. 11, 12) seem to form a literary chiasm in themselves:

A   The righteous one, my servant, [shall] make many to be accounted
    righteous;
B   He shall bear their iniquities (vs. 11).
B' He bore the sin of many,
A' He made intercession for the transgressors (vs. 12).

In this arrangement the statements of A and A' and B and B' form two
couplets, the lines of each couplet being parallel. Lying at the center, B and B'
emphasize the sin-bearing aspect of the Messiah's death. On the other hand
the intercession of the Messiah stated in A' implies how He intercedes the
merits of His sinless life and death to cause repentant sinners "to be accounted
righteous" as stated in line A.

These verses describe the ministry of a priest. It is the work of a priest
(1) to bear sin (Lev 10:17) and to make atonement/expiation for it (Heb 2:17),
and (2) to intercede in behalf of repentant sinners who seek forgiveness and
acceptance with God (cf. Heb 7:25; 9:24) on the basis of the merits of that
atonement/expiation.

Tucked away in this ancient prophecy was the most marvelous truth: One
day a *righteous* Messiah would bear the penalty "for the sins of the whole
world" (1 John 2:2) by dying in behalf of humanity, and in His priestly
intercessions for repentant sinners would secure for them not only forgiveness,
but would *cause* (Hebrew, hiphil-causative) His own righteousness to be
accounted to them so that they would stand fully accepted before God![13]

Crowned Levitical High Priest (Zech 6:9-15)

A third announcement of the Messiah's priesthood was made in Judea after
the return of the exiles from Babylon in the last quarter of the sixth century
B.C. Sixteen difficult years had ensued and the building on the Temple
eventually was suspended. However, in the second year of the Persian king,
Darius I (520 B.C.), the prophets Haggai and Zechariah encouraged the leaders and people with promises from the Lord to start the work again on the
Temple and to complete the project (cf. Ezra 5:1, 2; 6:14, 15).

During this renewed building spurt, three exiles arrived from Babylon with
an offering of silver and gold. Directed by God, the prophet Zechariah crafted
a crown from these materials, and taking the high priest Joshua with him, acted
out a prophecy in the house where the visitors were staying:

The word of the Lord also came to me saying, "Take an offering from
the exiles, . . . make an ornate crown, and set it on the head of Joshua the son

of Jehozadek, the high priest. Then say to him, 'Thus says the Lord of hosts, "Behold, a man whose name is *Branch* [*semah*], for He will branch out from where He is; and He will build the temple of the Lord. Yes, it is He who will build the temple of the Lord, and He who will bear the honor and sit and rule on His throne. Thus, He will be a priest on His throne, and the counsel of peace will be between the two offices." ' " (Zech 6:9-13, NASB).

According to other OT passages the expression, "Branch" (*semah*), is a technical term for the Messiah (a branch from the house of David).[14] By declaring the *crowned* Levitical high priest to be "the Branch," Zechariah also foretold the double offices of kingship and priesthood the Messiah would take under God's direction.

Twice the prediction underscores the fact that the Messiah will "build the temple of the Lord." Since the Messiah's priestly rule was yet future, the prophecy obviously transcended the local temple construction that was in the process of being completed by Zerubbabel (Zech 4:9). During His reign as king-priest, the Messiah would build another and more important Temple: the church! He alone could accomplish this aspect of the plan of salvation.[15]

Furthermore, the Messiah would both "sit and rule on His throne" and would be "a *priest* on His throne" (vs. 13). This is a remarkable announcement—that the messianic Branch of the Judaic house of David would assume the functions of the priesthood of the house of Levi by God's direction! The NT itself comments on this point: "It is evident that our Lord was descended from Judah, and in connection with that tribe Moses said nothing about priests." "Now *if he were on earth, he would not be a priest at all,* since there are priests who offer gifts according to the law" (Heb 7:14; 8:4). Thus, this enacted prediction implicitly pointed toward a further revelation that the Messiah's reign as a king-priest *would take place in heaven and not on the earth*!

The last part of vs. 13—"Thus, He will be a priest on His throne, and the counsel of peace will be between the two offices" (NASB)—is understood by scholars in two different ways. Literally, the last phrase reads, "And the counsel of peace shall be between the two of them." Thus, the American Revised Version (ARV) renders the phrase, "And the counsel of peace shall be *between Them both.*" The question is whether the prophet is referring to two offices/roles (kingship/priesthood) or to two *Persons* (the Messiah/Yahweh)?

In the nation of Israel, the offices of king and priest were kept separate by God's arrangement. Priesthood belonged to the Aaronic house of the Levites, whereas kingship belonged to the Davidic house of the tribe of Judah.[16] Since Zechariah's prophecy plainly indicates that the Messiah would unite the roles of kingship and priesthood, many scholars opt for the interpretation that the Messiah would simply unite these two offices in a harmonious manner in His personal reign (as reflected in the NASB version cited above).

However, the echoes of Psalm 110:1, 4 (that the Messiah will sit on Yahweh's throne as a king-priest) are so strong that others, we think more correctly, take the literal expression, "the two of them," to refer to Yahweh and the Messiah co-ruling in the kingdom of grace to carry out the plan of salvation. Hence, the ARV rendering is to be preferred: "And the counsel of peace shall be between Them both."[17]

The Priestly Messiah's Temple (Dan 9:24).

Although brief, the three prophecies reviewed above clearly announced the future, priestly ministry of the Messiah. Priests, however, do not function apart from temples or other sacred places. But since the Mosaic ritual laws prevented a Messiah of non-Aaronic origin from serving in the Jerusalem temple (cf. Heb 7:13, 14; 8:4), where would He minister? Does any prophecy foretell of the Messiah's ministry in a heavenly temple/sanctuary? We believe the prophecy of Daniel 9:24-27 points in that direction.

In this famous prophecy the angel Gabriel announced the *time* for the Messiah's long-awaited appearance.[18] The prophecy centers largely upon His sacrificial death that would "put an end to sin," would "atone for iniquity," and would "bring in everlasting righteousness" (vss. 24, 26). But the final event in the Messiah's three and one-half year ministry on earth would be "to anoint *a most holy place [qōdeš qodāšîm]."*

The expression, *qōdeš qodāšîm,* literally, "holy of holies" and its variants (the holy of holies, holies of holies) occur 43 times in the OT.[19] Apart from this single reference in Daniel, every instance of this expression found elsewhere in the Scriptures (with the possible exception of 1 Chr 23:13)[20] is applied to some aspect of the sanctuary tabernacle/temple and its rites.

Since the phrase quite often carries an adjectival force, it is commonly rendered "most holy." For example, the golden altar is described as being "most holy to the Lord" (Exod 30:10). On occasion the phrase can be rendered (with the definite article) as a substantive: "the Most Holy [Place]," that is, the Second Apartment of the sanctuary (Exod 26:33, 34). The sanctuary tent, its several pieces of furniture, altars, and utensils were all regarded as "most holy [qōdeš qodāšîm]" (Exod 30:26-30), as were also the incense, sin and guilt offerings (Exod 30:36; Lev 6:14-17 cf. 6:25; 7:1; 10:12), and any "devoted thing" (Lev 27:28). The evidence is abundant that *qōdeš qodāšîm* is sanctuary terminology.

Although past Jewish and Christian expositors have identified the Daniel 9:24 phrasing (literally, "to anoint holy of holies") with the anointing of the Messiah, the overwhelming use of the expression in the OT suggests that it refers to a sanctuary/temple and should be translated in the manner indicated by the translators of the RSV: "to anoint a most holy place."

But where would such a hallowed place be found? And what would its anointing signify? Moses anointed the tabernacle-sanctuary in a ceremony which inaugurated the Levitical priestly ministry (Exod 40:9-15). Although no record is left of a formal anointing of the later temples, we may safely assume that such was the case. The only sanctuary-temple that could have been "anointed" by the Holy Spirit at Christ's inauguration as King-Priest would have been the heavenly one attested to in the NT (Hebrews/Revelation). "Now the point in what we are saying is this: *we have such a high priest,* one who is seated at the right hand of the throne of the Majesty in heaven, *a minister in the sanctuary and the true tent which is set up not by man but by the Lord*" (Heb 8:1, 2).[21]

Some have suggested the anointing of the *qōdeš qodāšîm* in Daniel 9:24 indicates that only "the Most Holy Place"—the Second Apartment of the earthly sanctuary—is functional in heaven. In other words, the "holy place" (first apartment) of the Israelite sanctuary is thought to represent the Mosaic era, while the Most Holy Place (Second Apartment) represents Christ's ministry in heaven during the Christian Era. In this manner, Christ has only one phase of ministry, namely, intercession in "the Most Holy Place."

However, such reasoning does violence to the Daniel text and Israelite understanding, as well as to the typology undergirding the sanctuary system. The usual way to designate the Second Apartment was to turn the adjectival expression into a substantive by adding the definite article to the second word in the expression to form a Hebrew construct, with the resultant translation, "the Most Holy [Place]" (i.e., Exod 26:33, 34; 2 Chr 5:7). Without the definite article the expression seems to carry only an adjectival thrust, meaning that some object or place is *very sacred,* that is "most holy." Since the expression in Daniel 9:24 appears *without* the definite article, the force of the expression is that *a very sacred* [place]—a *Most Holy* [place] would be anointed for the Messiah's priestly service. The intent is simply that the heavenly sanctuary—a very sacred place—was to be inaugurated in the sense that a new phase in the divine plan of salvation was to begin with Christ's priesthood.

The Israelite mind would have regarded the two-apartment sanctuary as the *single* house of God, His dwelling (cf. Exod 25:8), and could not have imagined a separation of the apartments. The *priestly ministration* in each apartment was inextricably locked into each other. Furthermore, the suggested, different fulfillments of the two apartments turn the sanctuary typology on its head. The daily ministry in the first apartment was as symbolic of certain aspects of Christ's priestly ministry as was the yearly priestly ministry in the second. The notion that Christ has only a "Most Holy Place" ministration in heaven in the Christian Era leaves out all fulfillments of the priestly type associated with the first apartment.

We may safely conclude, therefore, that the prophecy of Daniel 9:24 foretold the anointing or inauguration of the heavenly temple in a new sense. Now would begin the priestly, mediatorial ministry of Christ based on the merits of His actual, sinless life and atoning death. The divine plan of salvation would now move from the realm of *promise* to the realm of *fact* (cf. Heb 9:15; Rom 3:23-26).

Summary

Exalted Victor and glorified Redeemer, Christ presently reigns as king-priest from His Father's universal throne.

Both OT prophecies and NT statements affirm the truth that Christ serves as humanity's high priest before God in heaven. Moreover, we may assert as an unchallenged, scriptural truth that Christ's priestly ministry is as essential to the plan of salvation as was (and is) His vicarious death.[22] Without Christ's priestly mediation, Calvary would have been in vain. While the cross is a perfect atonement for sin, it requires *both* the sacrificial death *and* the priestly application of the merits of that sinless Offering to achieve the full objectives of the plan of salvation as Heaven designed it.

Calvary fully paid the debt of the world's sin (1 John 2:2). Christ died "once for all time" (*ephapax*, literal reading, Heb 7:27) and will never die again. But the objective atonement accomplished by the Godhead at the cross *saved none automatically* (Rom 3:24-26; 5:18, 19). Divine grace extended to the repentant sinner on the basis of the cross must be individually accepted, and its merits must be accounted to the believer individually through the priestly intercession of Jesus Christ. His priesthood is as central to the salvation process as is His death which activates and requires it. In the following chapters we will explore the scope and significance of our Lord's present activity in the heavenly sanctuary which began at the time of the festival of Pentecost (A.D. 31).

———————◆———————

Endnotes

1 *"Hupsoō,"* AG 858.

2 For helpful remarks on the exaltation and glorification of Christ, see Walter F. Specht, "Christ's Session, Enthronement, and Mediatorial and Intercessory Ministry," SA[1], 326-361; SA[2], 145-175.

3 SDABC 7:772.

4 "The sanctuary in heaven is the very center of Christ's work in behalf of men. It concerns every soul living upon the earth" (Ellen G. White, GC 488).

5 Matt 22:44 (= Mark 12:36; Luke 20:42, 43); Matt 26:64 (= Mark 14:62; Luke 22:69); Acts 2:33, 34; 5:31; 7:55, 56; Rom 8:34; Eph 1:20; Col. 3:1; Heb 1:3, 13; 8:1; 10:12; 12:2; 1 Pet 3:22.

6 See Matt 22:41-45 (= Mark 12:35-37; Luke 20:41-44).

7 From the very first promise (Gen 3:15) God's people began to look forward to the coming of a Redeemer to save humanity from its sinful condition. Sacrificial ritual and divine prophecy increasingly filled in the features of the Messiah and His ministry. From the OT perspective, which the NT writers adopt, the long-hoped-for appearing of the Messiah would mean that "the ends of the ages have come" (1 Cor 10:11, NASB), or "the end of the times" (1 Pet 1:20). Thus, the NT writers regard the present age or time, that is, the Christian Era, as "these last days" (Heb 1:2). However, they see this present era of the Messiah's reign from heaven as also having "last days" or a "last time" (cf. 1 Pet 1:5; 2 Pet 3:3; 2 Tim 3:1; Jude 18). Jesus likewise speaks of "the close of the age" (Matt 13:39, 40, 49; 28:20).

8 See Heb 5:10; 7:1, 10, 11, 15, 17 and the reasoning that runs through Heb 7 as the priesthoods of Levi and Melchizedek are compared.

9 Much fruitless speculation has been generated in attempts to identify Melchizedek. He was simply a God-fearing ruler who lived in Abraham's time and whose royal priesthood and unrecorded genealogy made him an ideal messianic type. Responding to some who argued that the Amorite king was a bodily manifestation of Christ, Ellen White wrote, "It was Christ that spoke through Melchizedek, the priest of the most high God. Melchizedek was not Christ, but he was the voice of God in the world, the representative of the Father" (RH, Feb. 18, 1890, cited in SDABC 1:1093).

10 "Taxis," AG 811.

11 In its hiphil form, the verb *sdq* can carry the nuances, "declare righteous, justify;" "justify, vindicate the cause of, save;" "make righteous, turn to rightousness" among other meanings. See *"sdq,"* BDB 842, 843.

12 In its hiphil form, the verb *pg'* carries the nuances, "make entreaty," or "interpose," or "interpose in behalf of someone." See *"pg',"* BDB 803.

13 Says J. Alec Motyer, "Isaiah 53:11 is one of the fullest statements of atonement theology ever penned. (i) The Servant knows the needs to be met and what must

be done. (ii) As 'that righteous one, my servant' he is both fully acceptable to the God our sins have offended and has been appointed by him to his task. (iii) As righteous, he is free from every contagion of our sin. (iv) He identified himself personally with our sin and need. (v) The emphatic pronoun 'he' underlines his personal commitment to this role. (vi) He accomplishes the task fully. Negatively, in the bearing of iniquity; positively, in the provision of righteousness" (*The Prophecy of Isaiah* [Downers Grove, IL: InterVarsity Press, 1993], 442).

14 Jer 23:5; 33:15; Zech 3:8. Cf. Isa. 11:1 (*nēṣer*) for a parallel term. The personage represented by the "Branch" in Zech 6:12 is regarded as the Messiah by Jewish sources (Aramaic Targum, Jerusalem Talmud, and the Midrash). See Kenneth L. Barker, *Zechariah,* ExpBC 7:640.

15 Cf. Matt 16:18, "I [Christ] will build my church;" 2 Cor 6:16, "We [Christians] are the temple of the living God;" 1 Pet 2:4, 5, "Like living stones be yourselves built into a spiritual house."

16 During the Hasmonean rule (143-63 B.C.), the roles of political leadership and priesthood merged.

17 Commenting on Zech 6:19-15, Ellen G. White writes, "As a priest, Christ is now set down with the Father in His throne. . . . Upon the throne with the eternal, self-existent One, is He who 'hath borne our griefs, and carried our sorrows,' . . . His intercession is that of a pierced and broken body, of a spotless life. The wounded hands, the pierced side, the marred feet, plead for fallen man, whose redemption was purchased at such infinite cost. 'And the counsel of peace shall be between Them both.' The love of the Father, no less than the Son, is the foundation of salvation for the lost race . . ." (GC 416).

18 We will examine this prophecy in more detail later on.

19 My count.

20 1 Chr 23:13 can be translated to read, "Aaron was set apart to sanctify him as most holy . . ." (NASB). However, other translations read, "Aaron was set apart to consecrate the most holy things . . ." (RSV). This is the only passage in which the expression may possibly apply to a person, but there is no unanimous agreement among the translators.

21 See discussion in SDABC 4:852; William H. Shea, "The Prophecy of Daniel 9:24-27," DARCOM 3:82, 83.

22 "The intercession of Christ in man's behalf in the sanctuary above is as essential to the plan of salvation as was His death upon the cross. By His death He began that work which after His resurrection He ascended to complete in heaven. We must by faith enter within the veil, 'whither the Forerunner is for us entered.' . . . Jesus has opened the way to the Father's throne, and through His mediation the sincere desire of all who come to Him in faith may be presented before God" (Ellen G. White, GC 489).

2

Sanctuaries of Salvation

Christians sometimes wonder why Christ's ministry on earth was so short! The two millennia that have stretched away since His resurrection and ascension seem to have rendered Heaven silent. Has God forgotten the world He once "so loved . . . that he gave his only Son" to redeem (John 3:16)? By no means! It is the biblical teaching about the priesthood of Jesus Christ that draws aside the curtain, permitting us to visualize by faith the multiple activities of our High Priest in behalf of humanity. God has not abandoned the plan of salvation so carefully laid in eternity past.[1] The Saviour's priestly mediation is an essential part of that plan.

As observed earlier, Jesus Christ now serves in heaven as "a minister in the sanctuary and the *true [alēthinos] tent [skēnē]* which is set up not by man but by the Lord" (Heb 8:2).

In this passage the apostle provides a pointer. The Greek word *alēthinos* denotes something that is "genuine" or "real."[2] The word in this instance is used "in contrast not to what is false, but to what is symbolical."[3] If the heavenly sanctuary (set up by the Lord) is the genuine and real sanctuary, then its earthly counterpart, the Israelite sanctuary tabernacle/temple (set up by man) is the "symbolic" sanctuary. Thus, it is evident that a definite, vertical relationship exists between the earthly symbol and the heavenly reality. A thorough grasp of the former will provide understanding of the latter and will enable us to comprehend better the nature and scope of Christ's priestly activities since His ascension. The typical rituals of the ancient worship on earth "open the heavens," as it were, for the modern Christian.[4]

The Vertical Dimension

The biblical records do not present Moses as the originator of the tabernacle and its services. Five times reference is made to a plan divinely revealed to him on Mount Sinai.[5] "And let them make me a sanctuary," God instructed him, "that I may dwell in their midst. According to all that I show you concerning the *pattern [tabnît]* of the tabernacle, and of all its furniture, so you shall make it." "And see that you make them after the *pattern [tabnît]* for them, which is being shown you on the mountain" (Exod 25:8, 9, 40).

The Hebrew word *tabnît* (pattern) is a feminine noun derived from the verb *bānāh,* "to build." It occurs 23 times in the Hebrew Bible. The term can carry the nuance of a three-dimensional model, shape, or form[6] or of a "plan," a set of written specifications (1 Chr 28:11-19). Thus, Moses in vision[7] received not only verbal instructions which he recorded (Exod 25-31), but from the usage of *tabnît,* we may reasonably infer that he was also shown some kind of three-dimensional model of the structure he was to build.[8]

The significance of the term *tabnît* (pattern), however, is not dependent on whether Moses was shown a model or simply architectural specifications, or both. The question rather is whether the term signifies only an idea in the mind of God or points to a higher reality with objective existence—namely, a heavenly sanctuary, a heavenly dwelling place of the Deity.

Archaeological researches in this century have shed light on Near Eastern thought patterns concerning heavenly and earthly relationships. "Behind Ex 25," says Leonhard Goppelt, "stands the ancient oriental idea of a mythical analogical relation between the two worlds, the heavenly and the earthly, the macrocosm and the microcosm, so that lands, rivers, cities, and especially temples have their originals."[9] Frank Cross, Jr. states, "Probably the conception of the *tabnith,* the 'model' (Exod 25:9), also goes back ultimately to the idea that the earthly sanctuary is the counterpart of the heavenly dwelling of a deity."[10]

Israel's Understanding

When God commanded Moses to erect a sanctuary for Him, Israel apparently recognized that the structure would symbolize God's *heavenly dwelling* as well. This is evidenced by the cherubim figures hovering over the Ark of the Covenant and also worked into the fabric of the tabernacle's linen ceiling and inner veil. These represented the angelic hosts surrounding God's throne in the heavenly courts.[11]

Furthermore, the people were instructed to pray, as they assembled before the tabernacle with their first-fruits offering, *"Look down from thy holy habitation, from heaven,* and bless thy people Israel and the ground which thou hast given us . . ."* (Deut 26:15).

The exchange between God and Solomon concerning the permanent sanctuary-temple, underscored once again the Israelite understanding of the two dwelling places of God. While the Temple was under construction, God said to Solomon, "Concerning *this house* which you are building, if you will walk in my statutes . . . *I will dwell among the children of Israel"*(1 Kgs 6:12, 13). Later, as the glory of the Lord flooded the temple on the day of its dedication, Solomon commented, "The Lord . . . has said that he would dwell in thick darkness. I have built thee *an exalted house, a place for thee to dwell in for ever"* (1 Kgs 8:12, 13).

But in his dedicatory prayer the king exclaimed, "But will God indeed dwell on the earth? Behold, heaven and the highest heaven cannot contain thee; how much less this house which I have built!" (vs. 27). And then, in the body of his prayer, Solomon pleaded, "Hearken thou to the supplication of thy servant and of thy people Israel, *when they pray toward this place;* yea, hear thou *in heaven thy dwelling place;* and when thou hearest, forgive" (vs. 30). The king repeated the essence of this petition seven times more.[12]

This understanding of dual dwelling places for the Deity caused no confusion. Israel recognized the heavenly sanctuary as God's primary abode. "The Lord looked down from his *sanctuary [qōdeš]* on high, from heaven he viewed the earth" (Ps 102:19, NIV). "The Lord is in his holy *temple [hêkal]*, the Lord's throne is *in heaven"* (Ps 11:4). "Let the Lord God be a witness against you, the Lord from his holy *temple [hêkal].* For behold, the Lord . . . *will come down* and tread upon the high places of the earth" (Mic 1:2, 3). "The Lord is in his holy *temple [hêkal]*; let all the earth keep silence before him" (Hab 2:20)[13] The OT evidence fully supports the view that Israel was well aware of a vertical link between God's heavenly abode and His earthly dwelling in their tabernacle/temple sanctuaries.

Confirmation by Hebrews

Three passages in the Epistle to the Hebrews compare and contrast the earthly and heavenly sanctuaries (Heb 8:2-5; 9:11, 12, 23, 24). The statements are linked together by explicit expressions to the effect that *the heavenly sanctuary* was "not" set up "by man" (8:2), or "made with [human] hands" (9:11, 24).[14] Conversely, the *earthly sanctuary* is acknowledged as being of human construction under the direction of Moses (8:5). Two of these passages (8:2-5; 9:23, 24) clearly define the relationship between the two sanctuaries.

Hebrews 8:2-5. "We have such a high priest . . . a minister in the *sanctuary* and the *true tent* which is set up not by man but by the Lord. . . . Now if he [Christ] were on earth, he would not be a priest at all, since there are priests who offer gifts according to the law. They serve a *copy [hupodeigma]* and *shadow [skia] of the heavenly sanctuary.*"

Hebrews 9:23, 24. "Thus it was necessary for the *copies [hupodeigma] of the heavenly things* to be purified with these rites [animal sacrifices], but the heavenly things themselves with better sacrifices than these. For Christ has entered, not into a sanctuary made with hands, *a copy [antitupos]*[15] of the *true one [alēthinos]*, but into heaven itself, now to appear in the presence of God on our behalf."

In these passages the vertical linkage between God's earthly and heavenly dwellings is affirmed. The earthly sanctuary is viewed in connection with the heavenly in a relationship of *copy* to *original*, of *shadow* to *substance*. In support of this association the apostle cites the instructions given to Moses: "See that you make everything according to the *pattern* which was shown you on the mountain" (Heb 8:5; cf. Exod 25:40, *tabnît*). He thereby indicates that the *tabnît*-model/specifications shown to Moses in vision did indeed reflect a higher reality: the heavenly dwelling place of God.[16]

Perhaps, it is not necessary to observe that a "copy" or a "shadow," while not as important as the "original" and the "substance" of something, still has an important role in explaining to both ancient and modern believers the dimensions of the plan of salvation. However, defining the earthly sanctuary and its ritual ministrations as a "shadow" (*skia*) meant more than that the rites dimly portrayed divine truths to the Israelites. The rituals also functioned as typological prophecy. They inspired hope in that they *foreshadowed* better things to come.[17]

Two NT passages observe this feature of the earthly sanctuary service. "For since the law [ritual regulations] has but a *shadow [skia] of the good things to come* instead of the true form of these realities . . . " (Heb 10:1). "These [ritual regulations] are only a *shadow [skia] of what is to* come; but the substance belongs to Christ" (Col 2:17). For the spiritually illumined, the sacrificial services encouraged a forward look, providing in the typical rites the promises of the coming Messiah—His atoning death and priestly ministry.

Confirmation by Revelation

Although the Greek word *naos* (temple) can refer to the inner shrine of a sacred building, it is a common word used in the NT Gospels for the Jerusalem temple. The term also appears 15 times in the book of Revelation, and, for the most part, refers to the temple dwelling of God in heaven.[18] In his vision John saw angels exit from the temple (Rev 14:15, 17; 15:6), and heard a great voice from its interior directing them (16:1), and on another occasion proclaiming, "It is done!" (16:17).

One reference definitely ties the heavenly temple-sanctuary to the earthly tabernacle/temple sanctuary: "After this I [John] looked and *in heaven [en tō ouranō]* the temple, that is, *the tabernacle of Testimony,* was opened" (Rev 15:5, NIV). "The tabernacle of Testimony" was one of the OT designations for the earthly sanctuary, because it enshrined within its walls the tables of the Ten Commandments—the testimony (Num 1:50). John would have recognized by this very expressive name for the heavenly temple an immediate linkage to the earthly tabernacle/temple sanctuary.

Within the heavenly temple John also observed certain familiar objects: "Before the throne, seven lamps were blazing" (Rev 4:5, NIV); these are probably to be understood as analogous to the seven-branched lampstand (*menôrāh*) of the earthly sanctuary. In two other scenes John sees "the golden altar [of incense] before the throne" (Rev 8:3; 9:13). At yet another point in the vision, he states, "God's temple in heaven was opened, and the ark of his covenant was seen within his temple" (Rev 11:19). Finally, the prophecy intimates that the "courtyard" of the heavenly sanctuary is the earth (cf. Rev 11:1, 2).

With the data now before us, we may summarize the biblical evidence regarding the vertical link between the earthly and heavenly sanctuaries: (1) Moses made the original earthly sanctuary according to a model and specifications given to him in vision. (2) Israel understood that the sanctuary in their midst was a counterpart of the heavenly dwelling place of God, the heavenly sanctuary-temple. (3) The Epistle to the Hebrews affirms that the earthly sanctuary was indeed a copy and shadow of the heavenly sanctuary-temple. (4) The apostle John testifies that he saw the heavenly sanctuary-temple and some of its components in vision.

Thus, the evidence for the reality of a heavenly sanctuary-temple is abundant. In this heavenly sanctuary-temple Jesus Christ, our King-Priest, performs His ministry in behalf of all those who seek after God.[19]

The Nature of the Heavenly Sanctuary-Temple

At this point a word of clarification is in order. While desiring to understand Christ's priestly ministry in the heavenly sanctuary, we must not expect to find an exact one-to-one correspondence between the earthly and heavenly sanctuaries. For example, according to the Scriptures humanity was created "in the image of God" (Gen 1:26, 27), but obviously man is not exactly like God, although he reflects his Creator in some aspects. In like manner the earthly sanctuaries of Israel only faintly reflect the glories of the celestial abode of Deity,[20] and Christ's ministry deals with the moral and spiritual aspects of salvation and not with the sprinkling of physical blood.

When we speak about heaven and the heavenly sanctuary, we are talking about celestial things that are far beyond human comprehension. Hence, in order for God to communicate to us, He must do so by representing those heavenly realities in human terms and symbols familiar to us. The heavenly sanctuary-temple and its activities are, therefore, represented to the prophets (and thereby to us) in the forms of the earthly sanctuary and its symbols.

For example, Jesus is depicted as a slain lamb (although now alive) with seven horns and seven eyes (Rev 6:6). The Holy Spirit in His multiple operations is represented by "seven lamps of fire . . . burning before the throne" (Rev 4:5, NKJV; cf. 1:4, 5). The intercession of the Saviour is represented by an angel at a golden altar of incense, mingling incense with the prayers of God's people as they pray to Him (Rev 8:3, 4).

There is *a true reality* behind the symbols shown to the prophets, however. Jesus is real, and so is His intercession. The Holy Spirit is real. The sanctuary-temple of God is real too, even though it is shown in heaven in symbol as the "tabernacle of the Testimony" (Rev 15:5, NIV).[21]

The plan of salvation is, in a sense, a "statement" of abstract truths. The earthly sanctuaries of Israel were constructed and provided with certain furnishings and rituals to portray in a visible, concrete manner the various facets and aspects of that plan. They provide a *pictorial representation* of salvation realities. In the larger panorama of this picture the altar of burnt offering depicted the great atoning, substitutionary death of our Lord. The two-phase priestly ministration in the sanctuary apartments traced the future phases of Christ's priestly ministry in behalf of penitent sinners.

It is not the physical nature of either sanctuary that is important. Both are real in their respective spheres (earth or heaven). As far as the biblical doctrine of the sanctuary is concerned, it is what the structures represent or teach about the great moral controversy between Christ and Satan and about the plan of salvation that matters. The dwelling places of the Deity propose to teach us spiritual truths, and we must not miss those truths by undue attention to the medium, either earthly or heavenly.

A Problem in Translation and Interpretation

In recent years a few modern English translations (following a certain line of interpretation) have rendered Hebrews 9:12—a passage dealing with the onset of Christ's priestly ministry—as follows: "He did not enter by means of the blood of goats and calves; but *he entered the Most Holy Place [ta hagia]* once for all by his own blood, having obtained eternal redemption" (NIV; cf. TEV). But other scholars have rendered the same passage in this manner: "The blood of his sacrifice is his own blood, not the blood of goats and calves; and thus he has entered *the sanctuary [ta hagia]* once and for all and secured an eternal deliverance" (NEB; cf. JB). As can be seen by the different renderings, the Greek expression *ta hagia* is translated "the Most Holy Place" by some and "the sanctuary" by others. The first understand that Christ entered a specific apartment (the Most Holy Place) upon His ascension; the second understand that He simply entered "the sanctuary" in heaven without specifying any apartment. Why the variance in translation? How should the expression *ta hagia* be understood?

The Greek phrase *ta hagia* is derived from the adjective *hagios,* meaning "holy." The expression occurs ten times in the Epistle to the Hebrews and is generally conceded to appear in nine of the passages in the form of a *neuter, plural noun* (literally, "the holies," or "the holy [places]"). In Hebrews 9:1 the term is written as a neuter, singular noun (*to hagion*) and is regularly translated "sanctuary" (literally, "the holy," or "the holy [place]").[22] At issue is the proper rendering of the plural forms from Hebrews 9:8 and onward.

The use of the plural form (*ta hagia*) as a designation for the entire earthly sanctuary is abundant in the Greek Septuagint (the LXX, a translation of the Hebrew Bible made in the third and second centuries B.C.). Both the singular (*to hagion*) and the plural (*ta hagia*) are employed to designate the sanctuary, although the plural form is used more than twice as many times as the singular.[23]

For example, in the instructions given Israel shortly after the erecting of the tabernacle, God said, "You shall keep my sabbaths and reverence my *sanctuary [ta hagia]:* I am the Lord (Lev 26:2, LXX). Nine hundred years later God used the same designation for Solomon's temple just before its destruction by Babylonian arms: "Moreover this they have done to me: they have defiled my *sanctuary [ta hagia]* on the same day and profaned my sabbaths" (Ezek 23:38, LXX).

Since the writer of the Epistle to the Hebrews consistently draws his citations of the OT from the Septuagint, it is reasonable to assume that he is following that version's fairly common practice of employing *ta hagia* as a descriptive term for the entire sanctuary. Consequently, *ta hagia* should be regarded as a general term and should be translated as "sanctuary" except in Hebrews 9:2, 3 where the two apartments (holy, Most Holy) are explicitly specified.[24] And the NEB rendering is to be preferred: "[Christ at His ascension] has entered the sanctuary [*ta hagia*] once and for all and secured an eternal deliverance" (Heb 9:12).

But if *ta hagia,* apart from Hebrews 9:2, 3, should be rendered with the neutral term "sanctuary," why do some scholars insist on translating the expression with the phrase, "Most Holy Place"? The answer is two-fold: Their translation is influenced by (1) their exegesis and interpretation of Hebrews 9:1-10, particularly, vs. 8, and (2) the epistle's allusions to the Day of Atonement service, a rite linked to the high priest's ministration in the Second Apartment of the earthly sanctuary once a year. We will examine these two points briefly.

Hebrews 9:1-10. This passage contains a linguistic peculiarity which contributes to the confusion in determining the meaning of vs. 8, the key verse in the passage. The problem is this: *Each* of the two apartments of the earthly sanctuary described in this passage is designated a "tabernacle" or "tent" (*skēnē*). Thus, the apartment containing the golden lampstand and the table with its bread is referred to as "the *first* tent/tabernacle" (*hē protē skēnē,* Heb 9:2, 6). The Second Apartment containing the ark of the covenant is likewise referred to as a "tent/tabernacle" (*skēnē,* Heb 9:3 , 7).[25] On the other hand "tabernacle" or "tent" was a very common designation in the OT for the sanctuary Moses constructed at Sinai (cf. Exod 40:38, LXX, *skēnē*).

Furthermore, the writer of Hebrews refers to the heavenly sanctuary as "the true *tent*" (*skēnē,* Heb 8:2) and as "the greater and more perfect *tent*" (*skēnē,* Heb 9:11), implying that the earthly sanctuary was the "first" tent—symbolic, and less than perfect.

So, the direction the translation of Hebrews 9:8 will take has been determined by how the translator renders the phrase "the *first* tent *[skēnē]*" in Hebrews 9:8. Does "the first tent" in this verse refer to *the first apartment* of the earthly sanctuary? That is, is the apostle *comparing two apartments*—the first apartment of the sanctuary on earth with the Second Apartment or Most Holy Place in heaven? Or, does "the first tent" refer to "the first [original] tent" or tabernacle constructed by Moses? That is, is the apostle *comparing two sanctuaries* (the first, earthly; the second, heavenly)? We believe the latter to be the case.

Having announced that the *first covenant* (made at Sinai) had the services of a "sanctuary" (Heb 9:1), and after having described its two apartments, their furnishings, and the two priestly ministrations corresponding to these apartments (Heb 9:2-7), the apostle concludes his brief presentation in this manner (translating literally):

"This [a reference to the foregoing] the Holy Spirit indicating [that] the way of [= into] *ta hagia* has not yet been revealed while *the first tent* still has a standing" (vs. 8).

This summary statement is immediately followed by a brief critique of the earthly sanctuary system: "(All this is symbolic, pointing to the present time.) The offerings and sacrifices there prescribed cannot give the worshipper inward perfection. It is only a matter of food and drink and various rites of cleansing—outward ordinances in force until the time of reformation" (Heb 9:9, 10, NEB). The apostle's observations obviously include the rites conducted in connection with both apartments, not just one. Thus the critique in vss. 9, 10 supports the view that the "first tent" of vs. 8 is the inspired writer's designation for the entire two-apartment sanctuary constructed by Moses, the rites of which were only typical and could not in fact cleanse the believer of moral sin and guilt.

All scholars agree that *ta hagia*[26] in vs. 8 refers to *the heavenly reality.* Those who believe that the expression "first tent" in vs. 8 refers to *the first apartment* of the earthly sanctuary, infer then that *ta hagia* must refer to "the Most Holy Place" in heaven (see NIV). Consequently, in the NIV the rest of the references to *ta hagia* (except in Heb 9:24) are translated "the Most Holy Place."

On the other hand, if the expression "the first tent" refers back to the whole description of the earthly sanctuary (Heb 9:1-7), that is, to the tent/tabernacle constructed by Moses, then the natural translation of *ta hagia* in vs. 8 is "the sanctuary." And the sense of the passage is as rendered by the NEB: "By this the Holy Spirit signifies that so long as the earlier tent [the Mosaic tent] still stands, the way into the sanctuary [the heavenly] remains unrevealed." Thereafter, the NEB consistently translates the remaining *ta hagia* expressions with "the sanctuary."

Which translation is correct? It is the *context* of Hebrews 8, 9 that determines and resolves the question. At this point, starting with Hebrews 8, the apostle introduces a discussion on *the two covenants* (the first: made at Sinai; the second: the new covenant foretold by Jeremiah, and already alluded to in Hebrews 7:22). A key verse in the presentation, Hebrews 9:1, indicates that each covenant has its respective sanctuary: the earthly sanctuary belonged to the first covenant; the heavenly sanctuary belongs to the second or new covenant. Thus, in his discussion the apostle compares *the entire* sanctuary of the first covenant with *the entire* sanctuary of the second or new covenant. This can be seen in the literary arrangement of his argument:

A   The *heavenly* sanctuary (Jesus, High Priest of), 8:1-5
  B   The *new covenant* (Jesus, Mediator of), 8:6-12
  B' The *old covenant* (obsolete, ready to vanish), 8:13–9:1
A' The *earthly* sanctuary (temporary until the time of reformation),
      9:1-10

We conclude then that the context of Hebrews 8, 9 plainly indicates that the "first tent" expression in vs. 8 refers to the original Mosaic tabernacle and that *ta hagia* in the same verse would be translated "the sanctuary," the way it is often translated in the Septuagint. Hebrews 9:8 is simply stating that the typical sanctuary legitimately operated on earth. As long as it had "a standing," the new way into the heavenly sanctuary by virtue of Christ's atoning death was not revealed.

But with the advent of Christ "the time of reformation" has come. And the apostle concludes on a joyous note: "*But now Christ has come, high priest* of good things already in being. The tent of his priesthood is a greater and more perfect one, not made by men's hands, that is, not belonging to this created world; the blood of his sacrifice is his own blood, not the blood of goats and calves; and *thus he has entered the sanctuary once and for all and secured an eternal deliverance*" (Heb 9:11, 12, NEB).

Day of Atonement Allusions

Some think the Epistle to the Hebrews teaches that Calvary fulfilled the Day of Atonement type. Others argue that the antitypical day of atonement began with Christ's ascension to heaven because He ascended to the Most Holy Place (the allegation we have reviewed).

In reply, we must bear in mind that *all* animal offerings, whether daily or yearly, public or private, pointed the believer to Calvary, just as every priest (high priest or common) typified the coming priesthood of Christ. In this sense, Calvary did indeed fulfill the sacrificial aspects of the Day of Atonement, but it did not exhaust the theological ramifications of the rite.

There is no question that Day of Atonement imagery is alluded to in these chapters. But the essential question to ask is, Why? Is the apostle explaining the theological meaning of the yearly ritual? If so, why does he not comment on its central ceremony: the banishment of the scapegoat? Or, does he actually pursue an altogether different purpose: to argue the inadequacy of animal blood to atone and purge moral sin? We believe the latter to be his intent.

Actually, allusions are made to *both* the daily sacrifices (Heb 7:27; 10:11, 12) and the Day of Atonement sacrifices, as well as to all the typical blood rites under the general blood rubric (Heb 9:22). Three passages are generally thought to be "unambiguous" references to the Day of Atonement rites (Heb 9:6, 7, 25, 26; 10:1-4).[27] These are linked together by the repetition of the Greek word for "year" (*eniautos*), since the rites of that day were performed yearly. The high priest is noted in two of the statements also.

1. Hebrews 9:6, 7. "Under this arrangement, the priests are always entering the first tent [the first apartment] in the discharge of their duties; but the second [tent-apartment] is entered only *once a year [hapax tou eniautou]*, and by *the high priest* alone, and even then he must take with him the blood which he offers on his own behalf and for the people's sins of ignorance" (NEB).

2. Hebrews 9:25, 26. "Nor is he [Christ] there [in the heavenly sanctuary, 8:1, 2] to offer himself again and again, as the *high priest* enters the sanctuary *year by year [kat' eniauton]* with blood not his own. . . . But as it is, *he has appeared once and for all at the climax of history to abolish sin by the sacrifice of himself*" (NEB).

3. Hebrews 10:1-4. "For the law contains but a shadow, and no true image, of the good things which were to come; it provides for the same sacrifices *year after year [kat' eniauton]*, and with these it can never bring the worshipers to perfection for all time. If it could, these sacrifices would surely have ceased to be offered, because the worshipers, cleansed once for all, would no longer have any sense of sin. But instead, in these sacrifices *year after year [kat' eniauton]* sins are brought to mind, *because sins can never be removed by the blood of bulls and goats*" (NEB).

These passages themselves explain why the apostle alludes to the Day of Atonement rite, the *climaxing* yearly ritual of the Israelite sacrificial system. First, the shedding of the blood of animal sacrifices was *repetitious*. "Year after year" the same sacrifices had to be repeated. There could be no finality.

Second, the reason for the repetition—even for the Day of Atonement sacrifices—was "because sins can never be removed by the blood of bulls and goats." No shedding of animal blood could ever atone for moral sin. *Only* the "better" sacrifice, the better blood of Jesus Christ, could purge human sin and guilt (Heb 9:23). Again, we must underscore the point: not even the blood of the Day of Atonement sacrifice—the apex of the rites—could atone for human sin. *Only* "the blood of Christ, who through the eternal Spirit offered himself without blemish to God, [could] purify [the] . . . conscience from dead works to serve the living God" (Heb 9:14). It is the "better"sacrifice/blood of Christ that is being *contrasted* with the insufficiency of animal blood to purge sin.[28]

Jesus Christ met the sin issue head-on, so to speak, by atoning for the sins of the world *once for all time*. His sacrifice is the only effective sacrifice ever offered. "He has appeared once for all at the end of the age to put away sin by the sacrifice of himself. . . . so Christ, [has] . . . been offered once to bear the sins of many" (Heb 9:26-28). "But when Christ had offered for all time *a single sacrifice for sins,* he sat down at the right hand of God" (Heb 10:12). Thus, it is abundantly evident from the allusions themselves that the writer is endeavoring to show the utterly ineffectual nature of the sacrificial system *in itself*—even with its climactic rite of the Day of Atonement—to atone and to expiate human sin.

4. Hebrews 6:19, 20. In addition to these generally accepted allusions to the Day of Atonement is the passage in Hebrews 6:19, 20. "That hope we hold. It is like an anchor for our lives, an anchor safe and sure. It enters in *through the veil [eis to esōteron tou katapetasmatos], where Jesus has entered on our behalf as forerunner,* having become a high priest for ever in the succession of Melchizedek" (NEB).[29]

Scholars, who argue that in Hebrews 6:19, 20 the apostle is referring to the *second* veil that closed off the Most Holy Place from view, link this passage with Leviticus 16:2 where a similar expression is used for the same veil (*pārōket*). Other OT usages of the *pārōket* veil as the inner veil may also be cited.[30] But the correct identity of the veil in Hebrews is clouded when the Greek Septuagint version is consulted for its usage of *katapetasma* (veil), the Greek term that is used in Hebrews 6:19.

The Jewish translators of the Septuagint applied *katapetasma* not only to the veil of the Most Holy Place, but also to the veil at the entrance of the first apartment, and to the veil hanging at the entrance of the court![31] The fact that the apostle in Hebrews takes all his citations of the OT from the Septuagint means that he might very well have applied *katapetasma* to the "first" or entrance veil of the sanctuary in Hebrews 6:19, 20. Later, he does indeed refer to the veil before the Most Holy Place of the earthly sanctuary as "the *second curtain*" (*to deuteron katapetasma,* Heb 9:3), implying that he understood the sanctuary to have had a "first" "curtain" or *proton katapetasma.* For these reasons, other scholars have concluded that in Hebrews 6, the apostle is simply referring in a general manner to Christ's entrance into the heavenly sanctuary, the dwelling place of God, and that the phrase "within the veil," in this context contains no Day of Atonement allusion.[32]

Did Christ upon His ascension enter into the heavenly sanctuary, the dwelling place of God (general terms), or did He enter into the Most Holy Place of the heavenly sanctuary (specific terms)? The ambiguity of the context of Hebrews 6:19, 20 and the ambiguity of the usage of *katapetasma* (veil) in the Greek Septuagint which the apostle draws upon, leaves the question open. Scholars line up on both sides, probably a majority opting for the Most Holy Place.

But we need not be overly concerned by this scholarly confusion. If we should concede for the sake of argument that the apostle intended for his readers to understand his statement about Christ's entrance into the heavenly sanctuary at His ascension as an allusion to the high priest's entrance into the Most Holy Place on the Day of Atonement, we must ask the question, Why? As we have previously noted, the apostle's interest is not in unpacking and explaining the theological meanings of the Day of Atonement rite. Rather, he argues to show the inadequacy of animal blood, even Day of Atonement blood, to purge sin. Only the better sacrifice/blood of Jesus Christ could truly atone for sin. So, what do the Day of Atonement rites have to do with Jesus Christ's entrance into heaven? It is evident that the apostle is trying in his epistle to show (if we may lay the matter of veils aside for the moment) that through Christ's victory on Calvary the way directly to God (by virtue of the Saviour's merits) is open! *No barrier remains!* The tearing of the inner veil in the Temple at the time of Christ's death on the cross signaled the same truth the apostle is making in Hebrews: in a fundamental way the issue of sin no longer obstructs the repentant sinner's access to God (cf. Eph 2:18).

In a sense, the veils over the entrance to the two apartments of the sanctuary (and especially, the inner veil) illustrated the barrier that lay between the sinner and the Deity because of sin. Physically, the people could not come closer to God than the court, the common priests no farther within than the first apartment (Heb 9:6). Only once a year was the inner veil drawn aside, and then only by the high priest who entered the Most Holy Place with animal blood and incense (Heb 9:7). But now, the atoning blood of Christ has removed in reality for all time the sin barrier. Now, the penitent sinner can come boldly to the throne of grace by a new and living way: *through the actual merits of the true High Priest* (Heb 10:19-22; 4:14-16) who now appears, not just once a year, but *always* (Heb 7:24, 25) in the presence of God "on our behalf" (Heb 9:24).[33]

The Epistle's application of Day of Atonement imagery to underscore the believer's open access to God is not intended—nor does it—to displace the theological import of the Day of Atonement ritual with its special scapegoat rite foreshadowing the final judgment.

Thus, whether the imagery of Christ's entrance into heaven to appear

before God in our behalf is couched in general terms or Most Holy Place terms
is no issue, nor are the allusions to Day of Atonement sacrifices for sin. The
intent of the apostle is clear: Repentant sinners now have a new and vital way
to approach God—no longer by animal blood and sin-weakened priests, but
by Jesus Christ, the true and real high priest, who by virtue of His efficacious,
atoning sacrifice is able to save all who come to God by Him (cf. Heb 7:25).
By such a message the apostle sought to arouse the discouraged Hebrew
Christians to look up and to fasten their faith on Jesus Christ, their better priest,
ministering the merits of His better blood for them in the very presence of God,
in the better sanctuary of a better covenant.[34]

Conclusion

Both the OT and the NT affirm the priesthood of the Messiah. The OT
predicted it and intimated He would minister in heaven (Dan 9:24). The NT
affirms that He is, indeed, a king-priest in the heavenly sanctuary of which the
Israelite sanctuary was a "copy" (Heb 8:1-5). Since the earthly sanctuary is a
copy and shadow of the heavenly sanctuary where Jesus Christ is presently
ministering, a study of its services can enable us to know more precisely the
nature of His priestly ministry. This typical institution has much to teach us.

But how shall we correctly interpret the shadow-types of the sanctuary?
What valid principles of interpretation can we employ that will truly give us
insight into the nature and scope of Christ's priestly service? We turn now to
explore the scriptural principles essential for a sound interpretation of the
earthly types.

---------◆---------

Endnotes

1 A number of passages refer to the various aspects of the plan as determined before
earth's creation: 1 Cor 2:7, 8; Rom 16:25; Eph 3:8-12; 2 Tim 1:9, 10; 1 Pet
1:18-20; Titus 1:2; Eph 1:3-12; Matt 25:34, 41; 13:35. "The Godhead was stirred
with pity for the race, and the Father, the Son, and the Holy Spirit gave
Themselves to the working out of the plan of redemption" (Ellen G. White, CH
222). "The plan for our redemption was not an afterthought, a plan formulated
after the fall of Adam. . . . From the beginning, God and Christ knew of the
apostasy of Satan, and of the fall of man through the deceptive power of the

apostate. God did not ordain that sin should exist, but He foresaw its existence, and made provision to meet the terrible emergency" (Id., DA 22).

2 *"Alēthinos,"* AG 36.

3 Marcus Dods, *The Epistle to the Hebrews.* EGT 4:321.

4 "Important truths concerning the heavenly sanctuary and the great work there carried forward for man's redemption were taught by the earthly sanctuary and its services" (Ellen G. White, GC 414).

5 Exod 25:9, 40; 26:30; 27:8; Num 8:4.

6 Josh 22:10, 28, 29; Ps 106:20; Ezek 8:3, 10.

7 The verb "to see" (*rā'āh*) appears in all five passages, implying that Moses saw a model or set of plans (see n. 5). The verb is conjugated in either the hiphil or hophal forms, which gives a causative sense, so that the phrases could be rendered, "According to all that I cause you to see" and "which you were caused to see on the mountain" (Exod 25:9, 40). This suggests that Moses received in a state of vision the instructions to build the sanctuary.

8 "He [God] presented before Moses a miniature model of the heavenly sanctuary, and commanded him to make all things according to the pattern showed him in the mount" (Ellen G. White, SP 4:5).

9 Leonhard Goppelt, "Tupos as the Heavenly Original According to Exod 25:40," *TDNT* 8:56.

10 Frank M. Cross, Jr., "The Priestly Tabernacle," *The Biblical Archaeologist Reader* (Missoula, MT: Scholars Press, 1975), 1:220. For an extended discussion of *tabnît,* see Richard M. Davidson, "Typology in the Book of Hebrews," DAR-COM 4:156-169. Although some modern scholars reject the idea that the *tabnît*-model reflects a heavenly reality, there is a wide consensus that it does.

11 Exod 25:18; 26:1, 31.

12 See 1 Kgs 8:32, 34, 36, 39, 43, 45, 49.

13 See *"qōdeš,"* BDB 871, 2a. For a more extended discussion regarding Israelite understanding of a heavenly sanctuary/temple, see Niels-Erik Andreasen, "The Heavenly Sanctuary in the Old Testament," SA[1], 67-86; SA[2], 63-79.

14 Herbert Kiesler, "An Exegesis of Selected Passages," DARCOM 4:67.

15 Since *tupos* (type) can mean both "original" and "copy," *antitupos* carries that same ambiguity too. See "antitupos," AG 75. In Heb 9:24 the real, genuine sanctuary in heaven is viewed as the original or *tupos;* hence, the earthly sanctuary is regarded as an antitype or copy pointing to the heavenly reality. See Leon Morris, *Hebrews,* ExpBC 12:91.

16 The apostle's statements are not to be construed to mean that the heavenly sanctuary consists of a tent or is similar to some Phoenician temple. The language simply means that the earthly sanctuary/tabernacle/temple pointed to a heavenly reality—a reality far beyond man's ability to grasp. Of necessity, the directions to build were given in architectural terms familiar to Israel.

17 *"Skia,"* AG 763.

18 *Naos* (temple) appears in Revelation to be used in different senses: (1) Rev 3:12, possibly as a metaphor of the heavenly church/assembly. Cf. Heb 12:23; (2) Rev 11:1, 2, here the emphasis seems to be upon the theological significance of the temple; (3) Rev 11:19; 14:15, 17; 15:5-8; 16:1, 17 as a heavenly reality where God dwells; (4) Rev 21:22, to denote that the plan of salvation has been accomplished and no need remains for Christ's priestly intercession. Now, worship is face to face; cf. Rev 7:15.

19 See Ellen G. White, GC 415.

20 Ibid., 414.

21 "The document [Hebrews] thus sets out a series of bases for Christian confidence—*real* deity, *real* humanity, a *real* priest, a *real* covenant, a *real* sacrifice, *real* purification, *real* access, and in keeping with these, a *real* sanctuary and ministry" (William Johnsson, "The Heavenly Sanctuary—Figurative or Real?" DARCOM 4:50).

22 Heb 8:2; 9:1-3, 8, 12, 24, 25; 10:19; 13:11.

23 See Alwyn P. Salom, "*Ta Hagia* in the Epistle to the Hebrews," DARCOM 4:219-227.

24 In Heb 9:2 the first apartment of the tabernacle is explicitly called "Holies" (*hagia,* neuter plural) or "Holy [Places]"; likewise in vs. 3 the Second Apartment is designated "Holies of Holies" (*hagia hagiōn*) or "Most Holy [Places]." Since the articles of furniture that occupied these rooms are mentioned, it is clear that these *plural* expressions are being used to designate only one apartment each. This in no way negates what has been said above, as the Septuagint also at times employs the plural forms for the individual apartments. For example, *first* apartment, 1 Kgs 8:8, *ta hagia; Second* Apartment, 2 Chr 4:22; 5:7, *ta hagia tōn hagiōn.* See "Hagios," AG 9, 10.

25 This peculiarity of designating *an apartment* of the sanctuary by the *same* term that was applied to *the whole sanctuary* is already present in Lev 16:16, 17, 20 in which the expression, "tent of meeting," is applied to the first apartment, although it was being used at the same time to designate the entire tabernacle (cf. Exod 40:34, RSV). In a similar manner, Solomon's temple is designated a "house" (*bayit,* 1 Kgs 6:14) as is both the first apartment ("house," *bayit,* 1 Kgs 6:17) and the Second Apartment ("house," *bayit,* 2 Chr 3:8, 10, KJV).

26 The actual inflection of the phrase is *tōn hagiōn* in vs. 8. We simply use the nominative plural (*ta hagia*) by way of convenience and ease of understanding for the reader in our discussion of its use in Hebrews.

27 It is argued by some that the phrase, "the blood of goats and bulls" (Heb 9:13), definitely proves this chapter to be a Day of Atonement passage. But the inclusion of the sprinkling of holy water made from the ashes of a sacrificed red heifer in the same verse (a rite not mentioned as performed on the Day of Atonement) indicates the writer is following another line of argument. Bulls and goats were offered on other occasions besides the Day of Atonement (see Num

28, 29). Hence, their widespread use and association gave rise to a general expression which denoted all animal sacrifices. See Pss 50:9-13; 66:15). " 'The blood of goats and bulls' is a general term covering not only the sacrifices of the Day of Atonement but other sacrifices as well (we may compare the ironical question of Ps 50:13 . . .)" (F. F. Bruce, *Epistle to the Hebrews,* NICNT 201, 202).

28 "Why then does the Day of Atonement enter the argument? . . . The argumentation of 8:1–10:18 is shaped to bring out the superiority of the blood of Christ. Its force is that, whatever value the OT sacrifices might have had, they could not in themselves provide final putting away of sins: 'For it is impossible that the blood of bulls and goats should take away sins' (10:4). So the argument is that the OT services, *even at their high point,* were inadequate . . . . no finality in purging sins" (William G. Johnsson, "Day of Atonement Allusions," DAR-COM 4:118, author's emphasis. See full article, 105-120).

29 Whereas the NEB does not interpret the Greek phrase *eis tou esōteron katapetas-matos,* other translations do. For example, "A hope that enters into the inner shrine behind the curtain, where Jesus has gone as a forerunner on our behalf" (RSV); "It enters the inner sanctuary behind the curtain, where Jesus, who went before us, has entered on our behalf" (NIV). The expressions, "inner shrine behind the curtain" and "inner sanctuary behind the curtain" are interpreta-tions—not translations—of the simple phrase "within the veil." They are intended to convey the idea that Christ entered the Most Holy Place of the heavenly sanctuary upon His ascension.

30 Johnsson, "Day of Atonement Allusions," DARCOM 4:109, 110.

31 *Katapetasma* is used in the LXX to describe the veil of the court five times, the first veil six times, and the second or inner veil 23 times. See George E. Rice, "Hebrews 6:19—Analysis of Some Assumptions Concerning Katapetasma," DARCOM 4:229-234.

32 Ibid., 234.

33 The Levitical system did not in a moral sense obstruct the sinner's approach to God. The priests served as intermediaries, even as Jesus does. The weakness of the system lay in the fact that it was only a shadow-type, and intended to be only a shadow-type. As such, it was unable to deal permanently with the sin problem. Its function was to point the repentant sinner forward to the actual Redeemer to come who alone would be able to purge sin ("to put an end to sin, and to atone for iniquity, to bring in everlasting righteousness," Dan 9:24). See Alberto R. Treiyer, "Antithetical or Correspondence Typology?" DARCOM 4:187-198.

34 To understand the purpose for which Hebrews was written, see "Daniel & Revelation Committee Report," DARCOM 4:1-3; William G. Johnsson, "He-brews: An Overview," DARCOM 4:13-33.

3

Principles of Interpretation

The major problem for the exposition of the Israelite sanctuary system is the sparseness of explanatory data. The OT writers make no attempt to spell out the symbolism, apparently assuming it was understood. Fortunately, we do have certain OT passages and emphases (as well as NT statements) to help us grasp the essential meaning and significance of Israel's worship. The OT sacrificial system and its terminology form a backdrop to the writings of the NT. The Epistle to the Hebrews especially furnishes important information, so that we stand in no real doubt about the sanctuary's basic teachings.

New Testament Terminology

In his letter to the Hebrews the apostle employs several terms to describe the earthly sanctuary's function and relationships (*parabolē, antitupos,* and *skia*). These words shed light on the nature of Israel's fundamental religious institution and how we should interpret its meaning for Christians.

Parabolē (Heb 9:9)

Parabolē carries the nuances of "type," "figure," "symbol," or "illustration."[1] The Mosaic tabernacle/tent is compared with the heavenly sanctuary thus: "By this the Holy Spirit signifies that so long as the earlier tent [the Mosaic tent] still stands, the way into the [heavenly] sanctuary remains unrevealed. All this is *symbolic* [*parabolē*], pointing to the present time"

[NEB]; or, as the RSV renders the last clause, "which is symbolic [*parabolē*] for the present age."

Our English word "parable" derives from the Greek term. God designed the sanctuary system to function as a great, ritual parable to illustrate the truths of the plan of salvation, as we shall eventually see. Therefore in order to interpret the sanctuary symbolism correctly, it is important to understand the nature of parables.

Literally, a parable refers to that which is "placed beside something." We place a parable—perhaps a story—beside an abstract truth in order to illustrate that truth, to clarify and thereby to fasten it in the mind more effectively. The parables Jesus told usually emphasized one major point. Unlike an allegory, the details of a parable are not generally intended to have any significance. They simply round out the story and serve to contribute to the major emphasis being made. Furthermore, the parable must itself be understood by the truth it is designed to illustrate.[2]

The sacrificial rituals and festivals of the earthly sanctuary form a complex parable designed to illustrate the several truths that make up the plan of salvation. But we must let Scripture point out these truths so that we do not get mired down and lost in speculations over the minute details which have no real significance in spiritual terms, but serve only to round out the ritual "story."

Antitupos (Heb 9:24)

Like *parabolē,* the term *antitupos* is employed only once by the Bible writer to describe the earthly sanctuary. Our English word "antitype" derives from it. The essential meaning is "corresponding to." It may be translated with the nuances of "copy," "antitype," or "representation."[3]

The apostle uses the term when he compares the two sanctuaries. "For Christ has entered, not into a sanctuary made with hands, a copy [*antitupa,* literally, 'antitypes'] of the true one [the heavenly sanctuary]" (Heb 9:24).[4]

For our purpose it is not necessary to explore the reasons why the earthly sanctuary is here designated an "antitype" of the heavenly reality and not the other way around (see n. 4). It is sufficient only to observe that the term serves notice on *the typological nature of the earthly sanctuary.* A biblical type is a divinely-designed prefiguration that may be based on historical persons, such as Adam (Rom 5); events, such as the Israelite exodus (1 Cor 10); or institutions, such as the earthly sanctuary (Heb 8) which point forward to a fulfillment in later times.[5]

Types are, therefore, like prophecies. Instead of being embodied in words, the sanctuary types were prophecies embodied in rituals, foretelling and pointing ahead to a future, antitypical fulfillment.

Skia (Heb 8:5; 10:1)

The apostle also designates the earthly sanctuary a "shadow" (*skia*) of the heavenly sanctuary (Heb 8:5). But it is more than a projection of dimly perceived truths from the solid "substance" of the heavenly reality. The term can also carry the nuance of "foreshadowing" as in Hebrews 10:1. "The law has . . . a *shadow [skia] of the good things to come.*" In this instance, "the law" refers to those divine instructions governing the ritual worship of the sanctuary and its festivals.

These three terms clearly indicate that the earthly sanctuary was preeminently designed to be a teaching device, teaching truth by symbol and type and leading Israel like "a kind of *tutor*" (Gal 3:24, NEB). But what truth or truths was the sanctuary designed to teach?

Salvation: The Subject of the Sanctuary

Early in the Epistle to the Hebrews, the apostle warns his Jewish Christian readers against following the example of their unbelieving ancestors who came out of Egyptian slavery (the Exodus), but died before reaching the land of Canaan (Heb 3:7-19). His continuing comments give us a clear insight into what the sanctuary teaching-device was all about.

"Therefore, since the promise of entering his rest still stands, let us [Hebrew Christians] be careful that none of you be found to have fallen short of it. For we [Hebrew Christians] also have had *the gospel preached [euaggelizō] to us,* just as *they [the Hebrews in the Exodus] did;* but the message they heard was of no value to them, because those who heard did not combine it with faith" (Heb 4:1, 2, NIV).

This is an important assertion. The *gospel*—the good news of salvation from sin through a divine Redeemer (or, in broader terms, God's plan of salvation)—was taught to Israel during the Exodus from Egypt. How, or by what means was it taught? The apostle does not say, but it is implied throughout the epistle. There was only one institution from which Israel could have learned the gospel during their wanderings: the tabernacle-sanctuary with its priestly ministrations.

The religion of the Old and New Testaments is the same. The only difference between the *biblical* religion of patriarch, Israelite, and Christian is that before Christ's advent the faith was taught by symbol and type, but after His coming it has been taught by the realities of His saving actions. The same "gospel"—the same plan of redemption—is portrayed throughout Scripture from Genesis to Revelation, and for that reason its closing presentation in the endtime bears the designation, "the *everlasting* gospel" (Rev 14:6, KJV).

Thus, it is evident from this statement in Hebrews that *the overall subject of the Israelite sanctuary ritual is the gospel/plan of salvation.* The substitutionary sacrifices of animals and the mediation of their blood by a priesthood portrayed basic aspects of God's plan to save sinners. These two general truths are stressed in the book of Hebrews. The author compares (1) the blood of animal sacrifices with the better blood of Christ's sacrifice on the cross (Heb 9:11-14), and (2) the Levitical priesthood with Christ's better priesthood (Heb 8:1, 2).

This view of the subject matter of the earthly sanctuary is also confirmed by Colossians 2:17. Having listed certain aspects of the ritual system, the apostle says of them, "These are no more than a *shadow [skia]* of what was to come; *the solid reality is Christ's*" (NEB). Jesus Christ, and all He stands for within the plan of salvation, is the substance—the solid reality which projects the shadow-types of the earthly sanctuary. And these in turn find their antitypical fulfillment in the reality of His death and priesthood.

Significance for Interpretation

Since the sanctuary parable illustrates the gospel/plan of salvation, its symbols and types must be studied in the light of those Bible passages dealing with the various aspects of that plan.[6] Every scripture touching on this broad subject has its part in unfolding the meaning of the types. Thus, the sanctuary symbolism will illustrate and illumine the gospel plan, and in turn will also be clarified by the truths of the gospel plan presented elsewhere in the Bible. There is a two-way exchange here. Sanctuary typology helps us understand salvation truth, and salvation truth helps us to understand the meaning and significance of sanctuary typology. If we allow both to function as God designed, we will find that the typology of the Israelite sanctuary system does not teach anything that is not taught or alluded to elsewhere in Scripture regarding the plan of salvation, and it will often clarify it.

Could a person find salvation in Christ without a knowledge of the Hebrew sanctuary? Of course. Why then study these ancient types? We answer by asking another question. Could an individual make a living with only a high school education? Yes. Why then should we encourage him/her to attend college or vocational school? Simply because further education can greatly enrich and enhance our lives and happiness. Likewise, the study of God's salvation truths cast in the form of parable and type can greatly enrich our understanding and appreciation for the plan of salvation and the great God who proposed it at infinite cost to Himself.

A reflective study of the Israelite sanctuary system will lead the Christian to a more intelligent faith and will focus his/her attention upon the living Christ in heaven. In the heavenly sanctuary we recognize the command center for the plan of salvation. It is there that our Lord ministers the merits of His sinless life and atoning death to repentant sinners, guides in the affairs of His church, and carries out His eternal purpose in the world. There, as an anchor for our souls, is Jesus Christ, our high priest, who is able to save to the uttermost all who come to God. He lives "to make intercession" in our behalf (Heb 7:25).

Major Categories of Antitypical Fulfillment

When we say that a biblical *type* is a divinely-designed prefiguration, we usually think of it as meeting a single antitypical fulfillment. For example, the apostle Paul states that "Adam . . . was a *type [tupos]* of the one who was to come [the Messiah]" (Rom 5:14). Just as there is only one "first" Adam, there is only one "second" Adam, Jesus Christ, appearing as the antitypical fulfillment of the type (cf. 1 Cor 15:45-47).

However, the Israelite sanctuary is a *complex* ritual parable; therefore, its typology is also complex. This fact is not always recognized, and failure to do so sometimes results in misleading interpretations. The NT clearly demonstrates that the typical institution of the Israelite sanctuary has *several* antitypical fulfillments. It is not that a single type has more than one meaning. Rather, *the institution* of the sanctuary is understood by the NT writers to have *more than one emphasis.* Under the Spirit's inspiration the NT writers call our attention to two major categories of antitypical fulfillments: union/reunion and atonement.

Union/reunion. Shortly after God and Israel solemnized the Sinai covenant (Exod 24:1-11), the Lord commanded Moses, "Let them make me a sanctuary, that *I may dwell in their midst*" (Exod 25:8). The Israelites saw this promise fulfilled in a visible manner when the pillar of cloud "covered the tent of meeting, and the glory of the Lord filled the tabernacle" on the day of its dedication (Exod 40:34). Thereafter, "the cloud of the Lord was upon the tabernacle by day, and fire was in it by night, in the sight of all the house of Israel" (Exod 40:38).

The movement of the book of Exodus, like a grand orchestral symphony, comes to its great finale with God dwelling in visible union with His people,

His redeemed people. Toward this end the emigration from Egypt had moved. The Lord Himself states this as a *reason* for the divine mission to rescue Israel from slavery: "I will dwell among the people of Israel, and will be their God. And they shall know that I am the Lord their God, who brought them forth out of the land of Egypt *that I might dwell among them;* I am the Lord their God" (Exod 29:45, 46).

The significance of the divine purpose is heightened when we recall that the sin of Adam and Eve had fractured the relationship between God and humanity. The assertion of independence from God's authority had resulted in banishment from Eden, estrangement from God, and the dissolving of the original, intimate relationship with Him.

Now, the Lord promises to dwell among Israel and to restore the bond of union: "*I will make my abode among you,* and my soul shall not abhor you. And I will walk among you, and will be your God, and you shall be my people" (Lev 26:11, 12).

First, a miraculous deliverance from slavery. Then, the establishment of an intimate fellowship between God and His redeemed ones. *The visible sanctuary centered Israel's attention on God's endeavors to effect a reconciliation with the human family.*

1. Incarnation. The first *antitypical* fulfillment of the sanctuary institution, within the category of "union/reunion" noted in the NT, pertains to the incarnation of God the Son. The apostle John seems to borrow the very language of the Exodus account to describe the awesome event: "The Word [God the Son] became flesh and *dwelt* [*skēnoō,* 'to pitch a tent,' 'to tabernacle'] among us" (John 1:14). For more than thirty-three years Christ tabernacled with the human family, His divine nature veiled by His humanity.

2. Believer. Another antitypical fulfillment of the "union/reunion" emphasis of the sanctuary institution is the believing Christian who is now in a *bond of union* with God. The apostle Paul writes, "Do you not know that *your body is a temple of the Holy Spirit* within you, which you have from God?" (1 Cor 6:19). This inspired understanding may have grown out of Jesus' own reference to "the temple of his body" (John 2:21), or may refer directly to His promise to indwell the believer (John 14:17; cf. Rom 8:11; 2 Tim 1:14). Thus, the believer is seen as a temple-sanctuary with the divine presence being the Holy Spirit prompting and guiding the life.

3. Church. The NT writers regularly employ sanctuary imagery when writing about the church. They see the Christian church, in general terms, as one of the distinct, antitypical fulfillments of the Israelite sanctuary. God's words in Leviticus 26:11, 12 and similar statements become the basis for the

NT's inspired application: "I will establish my *Tabernacle [miškān] among you* and will not spurn you. *I will walk to and fro among you; I will become your God and you shall become my people*" (NEB).

On this basis the apostle Paul asserts, "What agreement has the temple of God with idols? *For we* [the Christian church] *are the temple of the living God; as God said, 'I will live in them and move among them, and I will be their God, and they shall be my people'* " (2 Cor 6:16). In his first letter to the Corinthian believers, he had written in a similar vein: "Do you not know that *you are God's temple and that God's Spirit dwells in you*? . . . For God's temple is holy, *and that temple you are*" (1 Cor 3:16, 17; cf. Eph 2:20, 21).

The language of the apostle Peter is even closer than Paul's to the sanctuary type: "Come to him, to that living stone, rejected by men but in God's sight chosen and precious; and like living stones be yourselves built into a spiritual house, to be a holy priesthood, to offer spiritual sacrifices acceptable to God through Jesus Christ" (1 Pet 2:4, 5).

4. Eternal reunion. The ultimate antitypical fulfillment of the sanctuary institution in terms of "union/reunion" will be realized in the new earth. Here the objective of the plan of salvation—full and open fellowship between God and His people—will finally be achieved. Again, this antitypical application is described in sanctuary language: "Then I, John, saw the holy city, New Jerusalem, coming down out of heaven from God, . . . And I heard a loud voice from heaven saying, 'Behold, the *tabernacle [skēnē]* of God is with men, and He will dwell [*skēnoō*, "pitch tent"] with them, and they shall be His people. God Himself will be with them and be their God'" (Rev 21:2, 3, NKJV).

From this brief review of the NT data we see four antitypical fulfillments of the Israelite sanctuary institution. It is important to note that *these applications are quite general.* All lie within the single category of "union/reunion," emphasizing the divine purpose to bring about a reuniting of God with the human family. First, God seeks reunion with His people Israel by placing His tabernacle/temple sanctuary in their midst.[7] The incarnation itself provided a unique fulfillment of the divine intent to be "God with us." Through the indwelling of the Holy Spirit, in both the individual and the corporate church, we see two other antitypical fulfillments of the ancient sanctuary. Finally, the earthly types and partial fulfillments fade away and are replaced by the grand reality of face-to-face fellowship between the Deity and His earthly family in the world to come (Rev 22:4).

Atonement. The second major category of *antitypical fulfillment* of the Israelite sanctuary institution focuses on the sin problem—the rebellion that shattered the harmonious union that once existed between the Creator and all the intelligent creation. Sin originated in heaven among the angelic hosts, a part of which—under the leadership of Satan (formerly known as Lucifer, Isa 14:12)—rebelled against the authority and will of the Creator and were expelled from heaven (1 John 3:4, 8; Rev 12:4, 7-9). Through Satan's deceptions Adam likewise chose to disobey his Creator and to assert his own independence (Gen 3:1-6). And thus, "sin came into the world through one man and death through sin" (Rom 5:12).

The plan of salvation, devised in eternity, now went into effect.[8] Adam and Eve, along with Satan, heard the promise of a coming Redeemer who would conquer their mutual enemy. The Lord said to Satan, in their hearing, "I will put enmity between you and the woman, and between your seed and her seed; he [the Saviour who would come] shall bruise your head [a fatal blow, cf. Rom 16:20], and you shall bruise his heel [Calvary; cf. Luke 22:53]" (Gen 3:15).

With the promise came the institution of the sacrificial system, a system designed to teach them the gospel: salvation through faith in that Redeemer who would make expiation and reconciliation for human sin by His substitutionary death. The Bible does not record the first sacrifices, but begins with comparing the accepted sacrifice of Abel's lamb with the unaccepted, bloodless offering presented by Cain (Gen 4:4, 5). Already, in the dawn of the new sin-situation, the dictum of Hebrews 9:22 began to sound: "Without the shedding of blood there is no forgiveness of sins."

By means of the animal type, Abel and the later patriarchs were taught to look forward by faith to the advent of "the Lamb of God, who [would take] away the sin of the world!" (John 1:29). And they were accepted by God and forgiven on the basis of their faith or trust in His promise to do so. "By faith Abel offered to God a more acceptable sacrifice than Cain, through which he received approval as righteous, God bearing witness by accepting his gifts [that is, Abel's sacrificial offerings]" (Heb 11:4).

1. Patriarchal altars. Patriarchal religion centered around the altar of sacrifice. When Noah left the ark, his first act was to build an altar to the Lord and to offer "of every clean animal and of every clean bird," a burnt offering to the Lord who had brought him and his family safely through the Flood (Gen 8:20).

The chief sacrifice of the patriarchal age was the "burnt offering" ('olāh). Later, the patriarchal burnt offering became the foundational sacrifice of the Israelite sanctuary: the morning and evening sacrifice, the daily, public sacrifice (Exod 29:38-42). The patriarchal sacrifice also gave its name to the large, bronze altar in the court of the sanctuary (cf. Exod 38:1). In the altar with its burnt offering and in the patriarchal leader of the family or clan (an embryonic priest), we can already discern what will become the chief features of the Israelite sanctuary: sacrifice and mediation.

2. Israelite sanctuary system. The national religion of Israel was a flowering out, an elaboration of the ancient religion of the patriarchs. It was a natural development (by divine design) of the earlier sacrificial system. The time had arrived for God's people to be given further insights into the nature of the Deity, the sin problem, and the means by which God would effect reconciliation with man, thereby restoring the former harmonious union between the Creator and His intelligent creation.

New light does not nullify old light. The essentials of *sacrifice* and *mediation* seen in the patriarchal age in the form of victim and father-priest are now enlarged upon in a new context: the tabernacle/temple sanctuary—the dwelling place of God with His people (Exod 25:8; 29:45).

a. Sacrificial blood. For the first time in Scripture, the typological meaning of *sacrificial blood* is explained. God informed Moses, "The life of the flesh is in the blood; and I have given it to you for making atonement for your lives on the altar; for, as life, it is the blood that makes atonement. . . . For the life of every creature—its blood is its life" (Lev 17:11-14, NRSV; cf. Gen 9:4).

The blood of the animal was indeed its life. Thus, sacrificially shed blood meant *a life given,* that is, *a life laid down in behalf of the person presenting the offering to God.* Since the priest mediated the shed blood in behalf of the offerer, it is clear that God intended by these acts to foreshadow the substitutionary, atoning death of the coming Redeemer. Every sacrifice, whether offered in the public rites or as a private offering, regardless of its particular emphasis (sin offering, burnt offering, thank offering, etc.) foreshadowed the promised Redeemer's substitutionary death.[9]

b. Certified priesthood. With the establishment of a central sanctuary came also the institution of an official priesthood. The common Hebrew word for priest is *kōhēn.* There is uncertainty as to the original meaning of the word, but many scholars believe it derives from the verb *kûn,* meaning "to stand." Thus, they infer the root idea of *priest* to be "one who stands before God as His servant, or minister."[10]

The priesthood is a fully developed institution in Israel. Whereas patriarchal religion seems to have focused on the sacrifice, in the Israelite cultus emphasis is placed on the priesthood and its manipulation of the blood of the sacrifices and the offering of incense. Why this enlarged emphasis? What insight into the plan of redemption was God desiring to clarify to Israel?

Another aspect of the process of reconciliation is being accentuated in the office of the priesthood, namely, *the need for mediation between God and man.* In the sanctuary system the chasm that separates God and man is symbolically bridged by the priesthood, composed of persons certified by God to mediate between Him and the people. Since the high priest could perform any of the functions of the common priests, the priesthood was regarded as subsumed in him.

3. Priesthood of Jesus Christ. From the viewpoint of atonement for sin, the typical sacrificial systems of the patriarchs and Israel meet their complete *antitypical fulfillment in the reality of Christ's death and subsequent priestly ministry in the heavenly sanctuary.* The sin problem, treated ceremonially in the earthly sanctuary, is now being resolved by the Saviour's atoning death and on-going priesthood. Inasmuch as the atoning priesthood of Jesus Christ is the subject of our study, we will not elaborate on the antitype here.

In summary, it should be noted again that the antitypical fulfillments of the Hebrew sanctuary institution may be classified under either of two general categories: union/reunion or atonement. Both have valid and distinct antitypical fulfillments, but should not be mixed in the process of interpretation.

Misleading Interpretations

A failure to grasp the divine purpose for the earthly sanctuary and its correct antitypical significance for Christians has led to many confused interpretations. For example, a recent commentary chooses to ignore the biblical testimony regarding an objective sanctuary in heaven. Rather, it argues that "the true tent . . . set up by the Lord" (Heb 8:2) is really just the individual Christian. The priestly ministry of Christ takes place within the believer.

The author asserts, "The outer court corresponds to the body; the Holy Place, to the soul; and the Most Holy Place, to the spirit. Even the furniture of the tabernacle corresponds to elements in us. For instance, the furniture of the Holy Place was the lampstand, the table of bread, and the altar of incense. If the Holy Place is the soul of man, these pieces would suggest the mind (lampstand), the emotions (bread as a symbol of social intercourse) and the will (altar of incense, which reflects the choices God approves)."[11]

The same author summarizes his interpretation in this manner: "All of this strongly suggests that what Moses saw on the mountain was the human person as we are meant to be, the dwelling place of God—the Holy of Holies." "Jesus, *as high priest of the good things that are already here* [italics his], has found a way to repossess the human spirit and cleanse it with the 'better sacrifice' of himself (9:23), and to dwell within forever by means of the eternal Spirit (9:14)."[12]

As observed earlier, one true, antitypical fulfillment of the earthly sanctuary is the believer indwelt by the Holy Spirit (1 Cor 6:19, 20). But the
confused interpretation cited above results from implicitly denying Christ's
antitypical priesthood in the heavenly sanctuary before the Father (Heb 8:1,
2; 9:24). The author cited above collapses Christ's heavenly priestly ministry,
restricting it solely to His work within the individual.

Unfortunately, a similar confusion of the two major categories of antitypical fulfillments of the Hebrew sanctuary typology arose early in Seventh-day
Adventist circles and continues presently in some quarters. Elder William
Spicer, later to become president of the General Conference, records an
interview he had with Dr. John Harvey Kellogg in 1902 (only 39 years after
the completed organizing of the denomination in 1863).

> "Where is God?" I [Spicer] was asked [by Kellogg]. I would naturally
> say, He is in heaven; there the Bible pictures the throne of God, all the
> heavenly beings at His command as messengers between heaven and earth.
> But I was told that God was in the grass and plants and in the trees. . . .
> "Where is heaven?" I was asked. I had my idea of the center of the
> universe, with heaven and the throne of God in the midst, but disclaimed any
> attempt to fix the center of the universe astronomically. But I was urged to
> understand that heaven is where God is, and God is everywhere—in the grass,
> in the trees, in all creation. There was no place in this scheme of things for
> angels going between heaven and earth, for heaven was here and everywhere.
> *The cleansing of the sanctuary that we taught about was not something in a*
> *faraway heaven.* "The sin is here . . . [Dr. Kellogg said, pointing to his heart],
> and here *is the sanctuary to be cleansed.*"[13]

Here again, the antitypical priesthood of Jesus Christ in the heavenly
sanctuary is mistakenly coalesced and truncated by confusing it with the
believer as a temple indwelt by the Holy Spirit. The focus shifts the attention
from Christ in His heavenly role to the believer on earth and his/her concerns.

Other interpreters have gone to more fanciful lengths by imposing psy-
chological categories onto the individual believer: the court stands for the
body, the holy place represents the conscious mind, and the Most Holy Place
symbolizes the subconscious mind. From this model a whole scenario of
end-time events has been imagined!

Still others argue that the sanctuary is intended to teach the incarnation of
God the Son—with the holy place portraying His humanity, and the Most Holy
Place, His deity. Yet another assumption is that the sanctuary represents in its
antitype the several stages of Christian experience: the court stands for

justification; the holy place, sanctification; and the Most Holy Place, perfection. Other fanciful ideas have emerged as sincere persons have attempted to "personalize" antitypical fulfillments of the sanctuary types.

This concern to find more personal antitypical fulfillments of the Hebrew sanctuary typology may appear on the surface to be innocent. Certainly, it has led to fanciful conjectures. But ultimately, it may rob the Christian of a true and correct understanding of the priesthood of Jesus Christ. While there is a relationship between Christ's heavenly priesthood and the individual as a temple of the Holy Spirit, the Bible does not erase the differences. Christ has a distinct, atoning, priestly ministry in the heavenly realm according to the Scriptures. This should warn us away from endeavors (however pious) to spiritualize His heavenly ministration into a subjective, personal experience.

Such misleading interpretations of sanctuary symbolism have one thing in common: They are speculative in nature. *No direct* biblical statements can be cited for their support. It is easy to read into symbols a wide range of ideas, but we must not let our imaginations push us into the realm of fancy. Although the Bible does compare the Christian to a temple, the Scriptures do so in the most general manner. They never apply a specific meaning for the court, the apartments and furniture, or the rituals to a personalized, individual experience.

Understanding the typical sanctuary as a parable designed to teach the fundamental truths of the plan of salvation as it centers in the person and work of Christ will keep us close to a "Thus says the Lord." Our only safety is to stay close to the Scriptural explanations of this important, complex parable of saving truth.[14]

Doctrine of Christ's Priesthood: A Construct

Very few teachings of the Bible can be summarized in a verse or two. The doctrine of the seventh-day Sabbath is stated fairly comprehensively in the fourth precept of the Ten Commandments (Exod 20:8-11). But for most doctrines, a series of passages is required to round out a full presentation of all aspects of the teaching.

Basis for a Construct

Is it proper to employ such a hermeneutical principle to arrive at a full understanding of a given truth? Yes, because of the unity of the Scriptures. Since "all scripture is inspired of God" (2 Tim 3:16), that is, by God the Holy Spirit (cf. 1 Pet 1:11; 2 Pet 1:21), He is essentially the Author of the

Scriptures. The various Bible writers were His penmen. Consequently, it is a valid—and a required procedure—to assemble and compare what the different Bible writers have to say on the same subject. We may rightly assume that the Holy Spirit would never contradict Himself.

Jesus demonstrated the correctness of this approach to Bible study ("comparing spiritual things with spiritual," 1 Cor 2:13, RSV, margin) when He revealed by a series of passages from the OT its complete teaching about the Messiah. " 'Was it not necessary that the Christ should suffer these things and enter into his glory?' And beginning with *Moses and all the prophets,* he interpreted to them *in all the scriptures* the things concerning himself." "These are my words which I spoke to you, while I was still with you, that everything written about me in *the law of Moses* and *the prophets* and *the psalms* must be fulfilled" (Luke 24:26, 27, 44).

The doctrine of the atoning priesthood of Jesus Christ in the heavenly sanctuary is likewise a construct. The doctrine is drawn and systematized from a variety of biblical materials. These include the following:

1. The Israelite sanctuary types.

2. The prophecies of Daniel and Revelation that touch on Christ's priestly ministry.

3. Christ's parables, particularly those that have a bearing on the final judgment.

4. Didactic teachings in either Testament which relate to the gospel/plan of salvation. Since the earthly sanctuary is a complex parable and a typical prefiguration of the gospel/plan of salvation, all passages of the Bible dealing with this subject are essential to a full and balanced understanding.

From such biblical data the doctrine of Christ's priesthood is fleshed out. The two major ministrations of the Levitical priests, corresponding to the two apartments (holy place and Most Holy Place), point to the two sequential phases of His ministry and provide insight into the nature of His activities in each ministration. The great apocalyptic prophecies of Daniel and Revelation, among other things, provide a time frame for His ministrations. The parables as well as other portions of the Scriptures pertaining to the gospel/plan of salvation, are illumined by the sanctuary typology and in turn shed explanatory light on the types.

Typology and Doctrine

In recent years it has been argued that the Epistle to the Hebrews denies the existence of any continuity between the Levitical ministrations in the OT sanctuary and the ministrations of Jesus Christ in the NT heavenly sanctuary.

Consequently, it is asserted that it is improper to use Levitical typology to establish doctrine; and in addition, it is not legitimate to argue from the type to the antitype.

For example, such an argument would say that although the priests in the earthly sanctuary had a two-phase sequential ministration (the daily and yearly services), it does not follow that Christ in the heavenly sanctuary has a two-phase, sequential ministration to match.

It is true that the apostle contrasts the priesthood of Jesus with the Levitical priesthood, but Jesus' "better" sacrifice and priesthood does not mean "in opposition to," but simply indicates something "superior," something "more definitive" than the Levitical system.[15] A fair reading of the epistle demonstrates the falseness of the above claims. Note the following facts:

1. The apostle clearly affirms the continuity of the two sanctuaries in his comparison of the earthly sanctuary as "a copy *[hupodeigma]* and *shadow [skia]* of the heavenly sanctuary" (Heb 8:5). Thus, the relationship of the earthly to the heavenly is one of "copy" to "original," of "shadow" to its "substance." Such terminology plainly indicates a continuity of basic contours. The apostle naturally emphasizes the contrasts, because the *type* is only a pictorial representation, whereas the *antitype* is the true reality. Furthermore, where basic differences are noted, the apostle is at pains to cite OT passages which anticipated those changes.[16] There is no conscious attempt to collapse the continuity between the two sanctuaries and priesthoods.

2. Is it proper to establish a Bible doctrine from typology? The apostle does in the Epistle to the Hebrews! Note his argument in the following important passage:

"Thus it was *necessary* for the *copies* [the earthly sanctuary] of the heavenly things [the heavenly sanctuary] to be purified with these rites [animal sacrifices], but the heavenly things themselves [the heavenly sanctuary] with better sacrifices [Calvary]" (Heb 9:23).

This is purely a typological argument, one that is not based on any didactic statement in Scripture. The reasoning is plain: Since the earthly sanctuary *had to be cleansed by blood,* so the heavenly sanctuary *has to be cleansed by blood.* Whereas the former had to be cleansed by animal blood, the latter has to be cleansed by Christ's blood. Whatever may be implied by the cleansing of the heavenly sanctuary, it is regarded as an antitypical fact, *because it is taught in the earthly type.*[17]

3. The same passage also demonstrates that the apostle endorsed the propriety of reasoning from the type to the antitype. Since *the earthly type* required cleansing, the *heavenly antitype* also requires cleansing. The same

kind of reasoning is presented in Hebrews 8:3. "For every high priest is appointed to offer gifts and sacrifices; hence *it is necessary* for this priest [Jesus Christ] also to have something to offer." Again, the argument moves from type to antitype. Just as the high priests offered gifts/sacrifices in the type, so must Jesus Christ, our high priest, have something to offer in the antitype. The former offer the merits of animal blood; the latter, the merits of His own blood. In both these instances the apostle's focus on the type led him to understand what would occur in the antitypical fulfillment.[18] Since the type demonstrates that the Levitical priesthood discharged in sequence two distinctly different ministrations, we are on sound scriptural ground to believe that Christ also ministers in two distinct, sequential ministrations.

It is evident, then, from even this brief survey of the Epistle to the Hebrews—that "the earthly sanctuary, with its apartments and services modeled after the heavenly original, may be regarded as instructive in clarifying the essential features of our Lord's priestly ministry in the heavenly sanctuary."[19]

The apostle not only endorses the use of sanctuary typology to establish the doctrine of Christ's priesthood and ministry, but he also sees the Holy Spirit using the entire sanctuary parable as a teaching mechanism in itself. After describing the Israelite sanctuary and alluding to its two divisions of ministration, he boldly asserts, "By *this the Holy Spirit signifies* that so long as the earlier tent [the Mosaic tabernacle/temple sanctuary] still stands [literally, 'has a standing'], the way into the sanctuary [the heavenly sanctuary] remains unrevealed" (Heb 9:8, NEB). Until Christ became man's high priest subsequent to His incarnation and death, the Holy Spirit taught humanity the gospel by directing their attention to the types of the sacrificial system. *The Holy Spirit intended repentant sinners to understand from the typical sanctuary the doctrine of salvation.* There was no other way to approach God than through this system with its shadow types of the promised Redeemer (cf. John 4:22). That was the message the Holy Spirit taught Israel and her neighbors through the sanctuary's typology.

Clarifying the Concept of Atonement

Lying at the heart of Christ's priestly ministry is the biblical teaching of atonement. His is an atoning priesthood. Since there is confusion in some quarters over this term, we introduce the problem briefly in this chapter on principles of interpretation. We will continue to address the subject in succeeding pages. But a few definitions may be helpful for the reader to grasp.

For most Christians the word "atonement" narrows down to the act of sacrifice, the shedding of blood. Thus, for them, the term centers only in the cross, that is, in Christ's death, and has no other meaning. But the Bible itself views the atonement from a much wider perspective. The English term, "atonement," simply stated, embraces the concept of *reconciliation*. The Bible views this grand theme[20] in three different, but related ways:

Atonement by Sacrifice

The sacrificial death of Jesus Christ, in a legal sense, met the penalty for all human sin. In that sense, His death reconciled the world to God. "While we were enemies we *were reconciled [katallassō] to God*" (Rom 5:10, cf. vs. 18). "All this is from God, who through Christ reconciled [*katallassō*] us to himself" (2 Cor 5:18). "Whom [Christ Jesus] God put forward as an expiation by his blood" (Rom 3:25).[21]

Christ's death on the cross may be properly described as a "complete atonement." It lacked nothing. His death fully exhausted the demands of divine justice. He Himself described this aspect of His saving work as "finished" (John 19:30). He will never die again. "He has appeared *once for all [hapax,* once for all time] at the end of the age to put away sin by the sacrifice of himself" (Heb 9:26). Without question Calvary accomplished a full expiation for sin—a true and complete atonement—and is the foundational stone for reconciliation between God and man in Heaven's devised plan of salvation.[22]

Atonement by Mediation

We must not misunderstand the strong statements about the significance of Christ's death just cited above. Sometimes the death of Christ is referred to theologically as "the objective atonement" to describe what the Godhead did *for* and *apart from* sinful humanity. "God put [Christ Jesus] forward as an expiation by his blood, *to be received by faith*" (Rom 3:25).

According to the Scriptures the reconciling death of Jesus *did not automatically save the world,* as is sometimes taught. Such a conclusion not only endorses an erroneous universalism, but it negates the very necessity for Christ's priesthood. No need would exist for priestly mediation if salvation for the world occurred at the instant of His death. *But the biblical truth is that no one can be saved apart from the priestly ministry of Christ.* He mediates the merits of His death only to the repentant sinner who comes seeking salvation from God and who receives *by faith* His pardon and acceptance.[23]

Consequently, *applications* of Christ's once-for-all-time sacrifice are also described as "atonement" in the Scriptures. For example, in the sanctuary typology, the repentant sinner came to the sanctuary confessing his sin and presenting his sin offering. After the animal was slain, the priest received the blood and placed some of it upon the horns of the altar of burnt offering and burned the fat also on the same altar. In explaining the priestly manipulation of the blood, God said, "The *priest* shall make *atonement [kipper] for him* for the sin which he has committed, *and he shall be forgiven*" (Lev 4:35).

Here, depicted pictorially in the types, is *atonement by Christ's mediation.* Through the *applied* blood of the sacrifice the penitent's sin was covered, or more accurately, expiated/wiped away.[24] *Not until* the blood of the sacrifice was mediated (placed on the horns of the altar) did the penitent stand reconciled to God.

In like manner, every sinner who comes to God appealing to the merits of Christ is *at that point*—and not before—personally brought into a state of reconciliation with God by Christ's mediation in the penitent's behalf. Christ's mediation of His merits is not a repeat of His finished work on the cross, but is an application of its benefits, an absolute requirement if a repentant sinner is to be reconciled to God.[25] Thus, one aspect of Christ's activity in heaven is to bring about personal atonement or reconciliation of repentant sinners with God.

Atonement by Judgment

The "Day of Atonement" (Lev 16—literally, "the day of atonements," *kippurim,* Lev 23:27)—foreshadowed in the sanctuary typology the final disposition of the sin problem. When this ritual was over, the sanctuary, people, and camp were ceremonially clean. As we shall see, the "Day of Atonement" symbolized the final judgment. In the final judgment we see the ultimate effect of Calvary, resulting in the total resolution of the sin problem. The final judgment will ring down the curtain on human history and will destroy Satan and all the effects of sin. Atonement by the final judgment—the last phase of Christ's priestly ministry—will fully vindicate the Godhead and affirm the redeemed and will reconcile the universe into one harmonious whole (cf. Eph 1:10).

By way of summarizing, we may say that the scriptural teaching about atonement (reconciliation) is extensive. Atonement by Christ's sacrifice is complete and finished; divine justice is fully satisfied. But atonement by Christ's priestly mediation is ongoing and continues to reconcile repentant sinners to God. Atonement by final judgment—the last phase of Christ's priestly ministration—will complete the process of reconciliation and will result in a universe of loyal, intelligent beings, fully satisfied, and living in loving obedience to their Creator. Atonement by judgment is the last act in the divine process to restore peace and tranquility to the vast created universe of intelligent beings.

The Bible's wider view of the atonement enables us to understand better the role of Christ's priestly ministry in the plan of salvation. It will also guard us from accepting misleading and false theories regarding God's plan of salvation and His true gospel (cf. Gal 1:7-9).

The Atoning Priesthood of Jesus Christ

Perhaps, at this point what was said earlier about the title of our study ("The Atoning Priesthood of Jesus Christ") should be repeated, since it impacts on the interpretation of our subject. While Christ's sacrificial death and His subsequent high priestly ministry are commonly viewed as two distinct actions on His part, in a very real sense they form a whole. According to the insights derived from the sanctuary types, Christ's death and priesthood form an *indivisible* unit. Separated from His priesthood, Christ's sacrificial death would have no saving power. Separated from His sacrificial death, Christ's priesthood would have no meaning. It is the sacrificial, substitutionary death of Jesus Christ *united with* His priestly ministry before the Father in heaven that makes human salvation possible. We can no more divide the death of Jesus and His priesthood, than we can divide the Trinity. And that is why a study of the atoning priesthood of Jesus Christ must embrace His death on Calvary.

———————— ◆ ————————

Endnotes

1 "*Parabolē*," AG 617.

2 For example, the issue of morality is not the point in the parable of "The Hidden Treasure," Matt 13:44. Rather, Jesus is emphasizing the accidental finding and the value of truth. This is the object of the parable, and not the moral failure of the tenant farmer to report his find to its rightful owner.

3 See "Antitupos," AG 75.

4 "The word *typos* 'type' is ambiguous and may mean the original or a copy. Thus *antitypos,* 'corresponding to the *typos,*' is also ambiguous. It may mean the fulfillment of what is foreshadowed in the type, as in 1 Peter 3:20, 21, where the Flood is no more than a foreshadowing and baptism the *antitypos,* the significant thing. Here it seems the other way around. The *antitypos* is the copy, the shadow,

of the real thing that is in heaven. The earthly antitype points us to the heavenly reality, 'the true one' " (Leon Morris, *Hebrews,* ExpBC 12:91. Used by permission of Zondervan Publishing House).

5 For a useful article on biblical typology, see Richard M. Davidson, "Typology in the Book of Hebrews," DARCOM 4:121-186.

6 "The significance of the Jewish economy is not yet fully comprehended. Truths vast and profound are shadowed forth in its rites and symbols. *The gospel is the key that unlocks its mysteries. Through a knowledge of the plan of redemption,* its truths are opened to the understanding." Ellen G. White, COL 133, emphasis added. "The types of the Jewish economy *are made plain by the gospel"* (Id., Ed 124, emphasis added). "The sanctuary in heaven . . . *opens to view the plan of redemption,* bringing us down to the very close of time and revealing the triumphant issue of the contest between righteousness and sin" (Id., GC 488, emphasis added).

7 It was God's intent for the temple-sanctuary to become the worship center for the world, "a house of prayer for all peoples" (Isa 56:6, 7).

8 See ch. 2, n. 1.

9 "Every dying victim was a type of Christ, which lesson was impressed on mind and heart in the most solemn, sacred ceremony, and explained definitely by the priests. Sacrifices were explicitly planned by God Himself to teach this great momentous truth, that through the blood of Christ alone there is forgiveness of sins." Ellen G. White, 1SM 107.

10 R. Abba, "Priests and Levites," *IDB* (1962), 3:877; John J. Davis, Moses and the Gods of Egypt (Grand Rapids, 1971), 270, 271; Roland de Vaux, *Ancient Israel* (New York, 1961), 346.

11 Ray C. Stedman, *Hebrews. The IVP New Testament Commentary Series,* Grant R. Osborne, ed. (Downers Grove, IL: InterVarsity Press, 1992), 96, 97, n.

12 Ibid., 97, 98.

13 W. A. Spicer, "How the Spirit of Prophecy Met a Crisis," Copy A, 19, 20, cited in Arthur L. White, *Ellen G. White: The Early Elmshaven Years* (Washington, DC: Review and Herald Publishing Assn., 1981), 5:289, 290, emphasis added.

14 "God's people are now to have their eyes fixed on the heavenly sanctuary, where the final ministration of our great High Priest in the work of the judgment is going forward—where He is interceding for His people." "Satan is striving continually to bring in fanciful suppositions in regard to the sanctuary, degrading the wonderful representations of God and the ministry of Christ for our salvation into something that suits the carnal mind. He removes its presiding power from the hearts of believers, and supplies its place with fantastic theories invented to make void the truths of the atonement, and destroy our confidence in the doctrines which we have held sacred since the third angel's message was first given. Thus he would rob us of our faith in the very message that has made us a separate people, and has given character and power to our work" (Ellen G.

White, Ev 223, 225).

15 Alberto R. Treiyer, "Antithetical or Correspondence Typology," DARCOM 4:189.

16 Richard M. Davidson, 4:177, 178.

17 Ibid., 173, 174.

18 Ibid., 174.

19 Ibid., 171.

20 "The sacrifice of Christ as an atonement for sin is the great truth around which all other truths cluster. In order to be rightly understood and appreciated, every truth in the word of God, from Genesis to Revelation, must be studied in the light that streams from the cross of Calvary. I present before you the great, grand monument of mercy and regeneration, salvation and redemption—the Son of God uplifted on the cross" (Ellen G. White, GW 315. See also Id., SDABC 6:1084, col. 2).

21 "Christ was crucified, but in wondrous power and glory He rose from the tomb. He took in His grasp the world over which Satan claimed to preside, and *restored the human race to favor with God.* And at this glorious *completion of His work,* songs of triumph echoed and re-echoed through unfallen worlds." Ellen G. White, *The Youth Instructor,* April 16, 1903, cited in SDABC 7A, 476; also in QOD 680, emphasis added. Id., "Christ made satisfaction for the guilt of the whole world . . . " (1SM 392).

22 "The death of Christ upon the cross made sure the destruction of him who has the power of death, who was the originator of sin. When Satan is destroyed, there will be none to tempt to evil; the atonement will never need to be repeated; and there will be no danger of another rebellion in the universe of God. That which alone can effectually restrain from sin in this world of darkness, will prevent sin in heaven. The significance of the death of Christ will be seen by saints and angels . . . " (Ellen G. White, SDABC 5:1132).

23 "All men were indeed reconciled to God, and it is possible to call this universal or world justification, but never in the sense of absolving every individual sinner of his sins before faith and without faith, never in the sense of abolishing the personal justification which God pronounces only the instant he kindles faith" (R.C.H. Lenski, *The Interpretation of St. Paul's Epistle to the Romans* [Columbus, OH: Wartburg Press, 1945], 374).

24 See Pierre Winandy, "The Meaning of *Kipper* in Daniel 9:24," DARCOM 3:119-127.

25 "This reconciliation has no effect in the life of any individual sinner until he receives it, until he himself is reconciled to God. That Christ has accomplished the reconciliation means that the way is open wide. 'Whoever will, may come.' But come he must if he would be there. . . . Christ has made the way open for them. Let them enter" (Leon Morris, *The Atonement—Its Meaning and Significance* [Downers Grove, IL: InterVarsity Press, 1983], 145).

4

The Great Estrangement

Under What Authority?

Every individual is subject to authority. Absolute freedom does not exist either in the natural world or in human society. The dropout thinks to escape authority by leaving home and school to join the armed services, only to find a stricter authority! Even the simple kite "must submit" to the authority of the cord which holds it, if it is to soar successfully. If you are seriously sick, submission to the authority of the best physician obtainable is a necessity.

The question then is not, "How may I escape authority?" but, rather, "Under what authority will my life be made the most meaningful—both now and eternally?" The most useful *religious* authority in the universe would be one which would foster the fullest development of my mental, physical, and spiritual powers. Such an authority would be motivated by a genuine, loving concern for me, for only in an atmosphere of acceptance, and appreciation, and understanding could I develop to my full potential.[1]

Creation

The Scriptures begin with the creation of our earth by God. "In the beginning God created the heavens and the earth" (Gen 1:1). Although the full Godhead was involved in the creation, the apostle John declares that God the Son functioned as the active Agent who spoke it into existence: "All things were made through him, and without him was not anything made that was made. . . . He was in the world, and the world was made through him, yet the world knew him not" (John 1:3, 10; cf. Ps 33:6-9).

The apostle Paul goes further to ascribe the existence of the total cosmos—populated with angels and other intelligent beings as well as humanity—to the creative powers of God the Son. "For in him [Christ] all things were created, in heaven and on earth, visible and invisible, whether thrones or dominions or principalities or authorities—all things were created through him and for him. He is before all things, and in him all things hold together" (Col 1:16, 17).

Since the Scriptures describe God's character as loving and compassionate (1 John 4:8), it follows that His authority (under which all intelligent beings were placed) is a governing authority motivated only by love. Such an authority seeks only the best interests of the creation. Under such an authority the individual's fullest potential may be realized.

But another factor is involved. If loving obedience to the divine governance is to be voluntary, intelligent beings must be created as free moral agents, endowed with the right of choice. To be programmed like robots would render fellowship with God and allegiance to Him meaningless. "Intelligent" robots would differ little from the animals governed by instincts. Jesus alluded to humanity's freedom of choice in His request: "If you love me, you will keep my commandments" (John 14:15). God desires only such service as naturally springs from an intelligent appreciation of His character.

How can it be known whether the Creator's authority is really best? In the dawn of the creation, His was the only authority known. However, a set of circumstances arose in the courts of heaven to force this question on the attention of the intelligent creation. Actually, there are but two options: (1) One could trust the Creator's word for it, (2) or one could submit to another authority in an attempt to prove the Creator wrong.

Although the following remarks anticipate our further discussion, it may be helpful at this point to make two observations: (1) Since a governing authority based on love is unselfish, it will always govern in the best interests of the governed. Laws, requirements, or restraints will always have the ultimate interest of the creation at heart, although at first they might not be perceived to be so. (2) Any other authority, by the nature of things, will be an authority motivated by selfishness. Such an authority will ultimately exploit and ruin its subjects. It might promise much, might even permit its subjects apparent freedom, but ultimately its very nature will be ruinous to the best interests of its peoples.

Heaven's Constitution

Animate, as well as inanimate, nature operates under marvelous physical laws. No true science of nature could exist if the universe were not orderly.

Plants and animals function in harmony with the laws governing their existence, as suns and galaxies move in their ordained orbits. The absence of natural law would result in chaos in the realm of nature. In a real sense, no one breaks physical laws; they break the transgressor! A wise Creator has placed His creation under natural law for their happiness and well-being.

The Creator has also placed His intelligent creation under moral law.[2] Moral law expresses the will of the Creator for these beings, because they are able to make moral choices. Moral law does not oppress. Divine love could design only just and good commands. Furthermore, obedience is no drudgery to one who loves the Lawgiver. Since "love does no wrong to a neighbor," the apostle Paul avers, "love is the fulfilling of the law" (Rom 13:10). It follows then that the intelligent beings brought into existence by a Creator whose very nature is love would have possessed loving hearts themselves and would have delighted to obey any command of God. They would have been motivated by a supreme love for their Creator.[3]

The Ten Commandments, brief, comprehensive, and authoritative (Exod 20:3-17) define the duty of human beings to the Creator and to one another. These ten precepts adapt the moral law to the conditions of humanity.[4] Jesus summarized their essential intent in two aspects of the principle of love: "You shall love the Lord your God with all your heart, and with all your soul, and with all your mind. This is the great and first commandment" (Matt 22:36-38). This briefly summed up the first four precepts. The last six precepts were summarized in a similar manner: "And the second is like it, You shall love your neighbor as yourself. On these two commandments depend all the law and the prophets" (vss. 39, 40; cf. Rom 13:8-10). We may safely infer that love's twofold principle expresses God's will to all orders of His intelligent creation and is adapted to them in precepts as it is to humanity.[5]

Although the Ten Commandments were not given in written form until God proclaimed them on Mount Sinai and wrote them on tables of stone (Exod 20; Deut 10:4), it is evident from the records of Genesis that the human family knew these precepts orally.[6]

The Decalogue (literally, "the ten words," Exod 34:28, RSV, margin) is central to the sin problem and Heaven's solution to that problem.[7]

As we shall see, the Creator's authority, government, and the imposition of His will (moral law) upon the intelligent creation became a matter of contention which led to a wrenching estrangement between the Deity and a large portion of the angels and the order of humanity. The importance of the moral law as expressed to humanity in the Ten Commandments can be seen by its position in the Israelite sanctuary:

> The most sacred city in Old Testament times was the city in which God had chosen to make His abode. The most sacred place in that city was the temple. The most sacred place in the temple was the most holy place. The most sacred object in the most holy was the ark, within which were enshrined the tables of stone upon which God had written the Ten Commandments, the law of life, the oracles of God. This law was the center around which the whole service revolved, the ground and reason for every ritual. Without the law the temple services were meaningless.[8]

The Challenger

Surprising as it may be, evil originated in heaven! "I saw Satan fall like lightning from heaven," asserted Jesus (Luke 10:18). In a prophetic "flash-back" John the Revelator "saw" in symbolic vision the first war ever fought. Challenging the authority of the Deity, Satan led out in an insurrection of angels against the government of God. "Now war arose in heaven, Michael [a heavenly name for God the Son] and his angels fighting against the dragon; and the dragon and his angels fought, but they were defeated and there was no longer any place for them in heaven. And the great dragon was thrown down, that ancient serpent, who is called the Devil and Satan, the deceiver of the whole world—he was thrown down to the earth, and his angels were thrown down with him" (Rev 12:7-9).

Satan (a Hebrew word meaning, "adversary") was a highly placed angel, the instigator of this rebellion and leader of those angels who "sinned" against God (2 Pet 2:4), who chose "not [to] keep their own position but left their proper dwelling" (Jude 6) to continue warring against their Creator. Two OT passages appear to disclose the original character, position, and motives of Satan as he served the Creator in heaven (see Ezek. 28:11-17; Isa 14:12-15). In these prophecies which deal primarily with the kings of Tyre and Babylon, the veil seems to drop away from the human kings to reveal the mastermind who controlled them and whose character and outlook they assimilated.

Satan (or Lucifer, his designation in Isaiah's prophecy, Isa 14:12, NKJV) is described thus: "You were the anointed cherub who covers; I established you; You were on the holy mountain of God; You walked back and forth in the midst of fiery stones. You were perfect in your ways from the day you were created, Till iniquity was found in you" (Ezek. 28:14, 15, NKJV). In some mysterious way this exalted, sinless angel began to cherish feelings of jealousy and envy toward the Godhead. Although a dependent, created being, he came to covet the divine authority: "I will be like the Most High" (Isa 14:14, NKJV).

The Issues

The rebellion among the angels did not spring full-strength overnight, as it were, nor did it arise without an *apparent* rationale to justify it. However, in a perfect universe which lacked nothing, it remains a mystery why a created, dependent being should aspire to the throne of the Self-existent Creator—an impossibility in the very nature of things. Nevertheless, in his attempt to do so, Lucifer raised several issues to justify his actions.

Issue: God's law (will). The simplest definition of sin is given by the apostle John: "Everyone who sins breaks the law; in fact, sin is lawlessness" (1 John 3:4, NIV). But sinning involves more than the breaking of ethical rules, or even the moral principle of love itself. The Bible equates God's law with His *will.* "I delight to do thy *will,* O my God; thy *law* is within my heart" (Ps 40:8; cf. Rom 2:17, 18). Sin, therefore, is viewed as a deliberate rebellion against the *Person* of the Creator. Sinners flaunt and spurn the very character of God and despise His love. "Against thee, thee only, have I sinned, and done that which is evil in thy sight," cried a brokenhearted David (Ps 51:4).

It is also evident that the Creator's personal will—as expressed through the principles and precepts of His moral law—is not arbitrary or harsh (cf. 1 John 5:3). He is a God of love, and His expressed will is always for the benefit and happiness of His creatures. When a mother forbids her child to touch a hot clothes-iron, her love has placed limits upon him by her expressed will. Is her "law" arbitrary? Is it not dictated by a loving concern for her child? Is his personal liberty being restricted? Will he truly be happier under the tyranny of his own perverse will which urges him to touch the hot metal? It is clear then that when God expresses His will through moral law to either heavenly or earthly beings, He does so in loving concern for their happiness. If a command appears to restrict, it is only because love would keep us from injurious consequences.

When the Scriptures say that "the devil [Satan] *has sinned* from the beginning" (1 John 3:8), we may rightly infer that Lucifer challenged the necessity for holy beings like the angels to be subject to God's commands. He would have considered the law of God as a restriction to angelic liberty. The apostle's statement indicates that Lucifer eventually rejected divine authority, threw off the yoke of submission to God's government, and openly chose to violate the commands of His expressed will.[9]

Issue: God's character. Behind the expressed will of God in the moral law is the character of the Lawgiver. By calling God's law into question, Lucifer called the Creator's character into question. If the moral law as expressed to angels was unnecessary and restrictive to personal liberty (as Lucifer apparently claimed), then God must have ulterior motives in placing His intelligent creation under such a law. And, if so, it might be reasonably argued that His motives were bad. Perhaps, the Godhead gained a sense of power by arbitrarily subjecting the creation to blind obedience. The Scriptures imply that such must have been the reasoning of Lucifer.

Jesus' description of the archrebel is germane to this issue. "He was a murderer from the beginning, and has nothing to do with the truth, because there is no truth in him. When he lies, he speaks according to his own nature, for he is a liar and the father of lies" (John 8:44). In effect, Christ describes Lucifer as the first murderer and liar. But whom did he kill or lie about in heaven before his expulsion? He killed no one literally, but the apostle John points the finger at "hatred" as the root of murder (1 John 3:15).

Jesus alludes to the strange feelings that eventually came to be cherished in the mind of this brilliant angel.[10] With murderous hate burning in his heart against the Deity, Lucifer went about heaven misrepresenting God to the other angels. Only by subtle lying about the divine character and government could he ever have succeeded in persuading a third of the angels (cf. Rev 12:4, 9)—against their better judgment—to cast their lot with him.

Issue: autonomy of the creature. The fundamental issue raised by Lucifer against the divine government concerned the proper relationship between the Creator and the intelligent, created being. Since God is the source and sustainer of life ("For with thee is the fountain of life," Ps 36:9), it follows that all created beings are dependent upon the Creator for their very existence. The desire and attempt to be independent of God is the primary sin of the creature and is at the heart of the rebellion—to challenge the divine government and to throw off the yoke of obedience.

Lucifer—the first sinner—sought to be free from God's authority. Isaiah's prophecy reflects this: "You said in your heart, '*I will ascend* to heaven; above the stars of God *I will set* my throne on high; *I will sit* on the mount of assembly in the far north; *I will ascend* above the heights of the clouds, *I will make* myself like the Most High' " (Isa 14:13, 14). Five times Lucifer boasts what *I* (he) will do. Self became the center of his being, expelling the natural attitude of self-sacrificing love which the Creator implanted within him at his creation. Lucifer desired to be his own god. This is the issue of autonomy: the rebelling creature says, "I don't need you, God; I am fully capable of running my own life."

Issue: The divine exercise of justice and mercy. This problem, evidently raised by Lucifer, is hinted at in the Scriptures which describe Satan as "the *accuser of our brethren* . . . who accuses them day and night before our God" (Rev 12:10; cf. Zech 3:1-5). The issue is, How can the Creator be both just and merciful? If obedience to God's expressed will is so vital to the happiness of the intelligent creation, then He can only exercise justice against those who violate it. He cannot show mercy to the sinner. Justice and mercy are mutually exclusive attitudes. Hence, since the Fall of man, Satan charges God with unfairness whenever He shows mercy to repentant sinners who come seeking forgiveness and acceptance. Satan accuses them before God for their numerous sins. He denies the rightness of God's action to extend forgiving grace to sinners.

It can be seen at once that any issue pertaining to the exercise of the divine attributes of justice and mercy will immediately call into question the validity of the plan of salvation. At the time of Lucifer's rebellion, of course, the plan was unknown to the intelligent creation. It was a "secret," locked within the heart of God from eternity (cf. Rom 16:25, 26). This particular issue enables us to perceive how real a problem sin and rebellion pose to the Godhead. Divine love and compassion for the intelligences of His creating have not changed or abated. But how can a holy God extend mercy to the rebellious sinner—penitent though he/she may be—and yet be just and true to His own nature?

These four issues Lucifer raised in the great rebellion which took place in heaven about the time of the creation of earth. The revolt led to his expulsion from heaven along with other angels who sided with him (Rev 12:7-9). Heaven's highest angel had directly challenged the Deity. God's moral law and government were rejected, His character and motives questioned and besmirched. The so-called right of the creature to be free from the Creator's control was asserted. Furthermore, the exercise of justice and mercy on the part of a just God was challenged as incompatible with His essential holiness. Here the great controversy between God and Satan had begun. These issues would develop further in the arena of later human history.

The Fall

The Creator provided the first man and woman with a beautiful garden for their home (Gen 2:8), laying but one simple restriction upon them: "You may freely eat of every tree of the garden; but of the tree of the knowledge of good and evil you shall not eat, for in the day that you eat of it you shall die" (Gen 2:16, 17). Like the angels, Adam and Eve were created free moral agents. The test provided them an option to obey God because they loved Him, or to disobey by asserting their own wills in opposition to His.

Although the prohibition was light, Satan's employment of it to deceive Eve enabled him to raise in her mind the same issues that had led to his own revolt in heaven (see Gen 3:1-6). Using a serpent—lying on a branch of the forbidden tree as a medium—Satan engaged the unsuspecting Eve in conversation by misstating God's words: "Did God say, 'You shall not eat of any tree of the garden'?" (Gen 3:1).

Eve corrected Satan by noting that the prohibition pertained only to a single tree, and they were not even to touch it, lest they die (vss. 2, 3). In response, Satan, speaking through the serpent, makes two remarks—intended to fasten like a burr in her mind. He says no more, leaving the innuendo to do its baleful work. "You *will not die.* For God knows that when you eat of it your eyes will be opened, and *you will be like God,* knowing good and evil" (vss. 4, 5).

Satan knew that Adam and Eve would never throw off their allegiance to the Creator unless their concept of His character changed. They already knew God more intimately than they knew him, and they had no natural desire to disobey Him. Hence, Satan's temptation was carefully phrased to create doubt and mistrust. Satan could reasonably assume that the couple had already wondered why God had imposed a restriction on this particular tree, and he took advantage of that wonder.

The tempter has now suggested a plausible reason for the prohibition which would lead Eve to think thoughts like this: "God has withheld this tree from us because He knows if we eat its fruit, we will be like Him. But He doesn't want us to be like Him, to know all things as He does. He apparently wants to restrict us and keep us ignorant, so He can more easily order and direct our lives. It seems evident that God has some hidden motives in withholding the fruit of this tree."

Such a line of reasoning, once entertained, would lead Eve to distrust God's motives and ultimately His character. In those brief moments Eve accepted Satan's doubt and quickly forgot what she had previously thought about her Creator. Once on the downward path, the next steps came easily and quickly. If God's motives were not to be trusted, then His word—the prohibition and threat of death—were probably not true either. With these two points now firmly embedded in her thinking, her final act was to assert her own autonomy: to exercise her will and disobey God's command. Eve clutched the fruit and ate. And "when the woman saw that the tree was good for food, and that it was a delight to the eyes, and that the tree was to be desired to make one wise, she took of its fruit and ate; and she also gave some to her husband, and he ate" (vs. 6).

Eve was "deceived" by Satan into reasoning as she did, but according to the apostle Paul, Adam openly chose to violate the will of his Creator after Eve's act (1 Tim 2:14). He evidently accepted Eve's view of the matter. As head of the race, Adam is held accountable in Scripture for implicating the race in sin.

When we compare the issues in the fall of Lucifer with the issues raised in the fall of man, we see a marked similarity. Both sinning angels and sinning man question (1) the divine character, (2) the divine commands, and as a result (3) they assert their creaturely independence above the expressed will of God.[11]

It is evident from these accounts that the greatness of a wrong act does not constitute the primary essence of sin. Sin—at its heart—is the assertion of creaturely independence from God. The sinner refuses to be submissive to the divine authority, whether the rebellion be on a cosmic scale or within a single heart. Sin is the same for angel or man: a determined stubbornness to submit to no god but self. Modern humanism reflects sinful man's primary problem.

Consequences of the Fall

The Scriptures provide no theory on how it was possible for the Fall of our first parents to affect their descendants. Nevertheless, it clearly describes the resultant depravity and corruption that immediately affected the race because of Adam's action. The classical passage on this linkage is the apostle Paul's extended statement in Romans 5:12-19. His opening sentence reads, "Therefore as *sin came into the world through one man and death through sin,* and so death spread [*dierchomai,* go through] to all men *because* (*eph' hō*) all men sinned" (Rom 5:12).

The apostle speaks about the *universality* of both sin and death as the result of Adam's sin and break with God. We must not misconstrue the term "spread" to mean that sin slowly moved from person to person until all eventually were infected. Paul is simply saying that *death* is universal because *sin* in the human family is universal, the race having been corrupted by Adam's sin.

Augustine (fifth century) and others focused on the prepositional phrase, *eph' hō* in this verse, translating it to read "in whom"—meaning, "in Adam." The phrase was interpreted to mean that the whole human race was in the loins of Adam and thereby each potential human personally sinned when he sinned.[12] However, the prepositional phrase is simply doing duty as a conjunction meaning "because," "inasmuch as," "for this reason that," etc.[13] and is so used elsewhere in the NT.[14]

This kind of exegesis, promulgated by the church of Rome and surprisingly by some Protestants as well, truly strains the passage.[15] The apostle is not writing about the sins of unborn, nonexistent humans who made up Adam's genetic potential for a posterity! Rather, Paul is speaking about the effect of the sin of one person, Adam, who as the father of the potential race, sinned in Eden. Paul's repeated statements in the passage are too clear to be misunderstood. We list them:

a. "Sin came into the world *through one man* and death through sin" (vs. 12).

b. "Because of *one man's trespass,* death reigned *through that one man*" (vs. 17).

c. *"One man's trespass led to condemnation for all men"* (vs. 18).

d. "For as by one man's disobedience many [= all] *were made [kathistēmi]*[16] sinners" (vs. 19).

The apostle's plain statements cannot be wished away: Adam's one sin "made" his descendants sinners and brought them under "condemnation." There is no way to construe these statements of vss. 18, 19 to mean that Adam's one sin really means his sin and the sins of his unborn, non-existent progeny. Paul's thrust in the passage is too plain and gives no support to such a fanciful theory. In some mysterious way (which the apostle does not explain), Adam's sin and rebellion implicated the human race yet to be born.

When Lucifer sinned against God (1 John 3:8), his personal rebellion did not make the rest of the angelic host sinners. No organic link exists between angels.[17] On the other hand Adam and Eve were created male and female, the divine purpose being that they and their descendants would reproduce and populate the earth (Gen 1:26-28). When Adam and Eve chose to sin against God, they deliberately separated from their Creator to live independently of His expressed will. They rejected the authority of a loving Creator in favor of their own, self-centered authority. The Creator never forced the pair to make such a choice; they could have chosen to resist Satan's doubt and to have remained loyal to their Creator. But their choice—either way—would naturally affect their unborn descendants for good or ill.

Sin and its outworkings is a mystery (cf. 2 Thess 2:7) we do not fully comprehend. The divine judgments that fell on the couple and their banishment from Eden, with its access to the tree of life (Gen 3:16-24), affected the future of the unborn race, although the judgments tended in some respects to counter the ill results of Adam's transgression. While Adam's future descendants did not personally sin when he sinned, it was only natural they would share in *the consequences* of Adam's separation from God.[18] When Adam fell, he pulled his future family down with him into a state of alienation and estrangement from God.[19] Depravity and death became their lot as well as Adam's.

Man's relationship with God. Adam's rebellion estranged the race from God. Humanity was separated from Heaven—"having no hope and without God in the world" (cf. Eph 2:12). As rebels against God, sinful humans are described as "enemies" (Rom 5:10). They are "by nature children of wrath" (Eph 2:3), that is, under divine judgment. Were it not for the plan of salvation, divine wrath would react against sin with destruction, "for our God is a consuming fire" (Heb 12:29). "By sin man was shut out from God. Except for the plan of redemption, eternal separation from God, the darkness of unending night, would have been his."[20]

Adam's disobedience brought about a fundamental change in humanity's attitude toward God's will. A chief characteristic of the sinner is his/her opposition to God's law. "For the mind that is set on the flesh is hostile to God; *it does not submit to God's law, indeed it cannot*" (Rom 8:7). Like our first parents, we sinners tend to justify disobedience and to blame God for our faults and troubles (cf. Gen 3:11-13).

Man's life. Subsequent to the Fall, divine judgment was executed on the sinful pair. The sentences involved not only themselves, but their posterity as well, and they were banished from Eden and the tree of life (Gen 3:16-24). Separated from the life-giving Source, Adam and Eve and their descendants lost the prospect of an unending life that had been conditional upon their obedience. The death sentence fell: "You are dust, and to dust you shall return" (vs. 19). Death, from that point on, became the inevitable fate of humankind.

Since Jesus spoke of resurrection from the common death which affects both believers and unbelievers (John 5:28, 29), this consequence of Adam's sin may be properly referred to as "the first death." This death which faces every human being is to be distinguished from "the second death" (Rev 20:14; 21:8) which phrase the Bible writer uses to describe the final destruction of the impenitent at the end of the age. No resurrection occurs from the "second death."

Man's mind. Adam's fall resulted in the depraving of his nature and that of his descendants. The "image of God" (cf. Gen 1:26) within was marred and the mental powers perverted. Every aspect of the person—intellect, emotions, will, etc., was affected by the sinful condition. Sinners are "darkened in their understanding, alienated from the life of God because of the ignorance that is in them, due to their hardness of heart" (Eph 4:18). "None is righteous, no, not one; no one understands, no one seeks for God. All have turned aside, together they have gone wrong; no one does good, not even one" (Rom 3:10-12).

Even the best acts of humanity tend to be permeated with self. As the prophets so accurately describe the human condition, "all our righteous deeds are like a polluted garment" (Isa 64:6). "The heart is deceitful above all things, and desperately corrupt; who can understand it?" (Jer 17:9).[21] Both the reasoning and the actions of unregenerated persons are warped by a self-centered spirit. Man is his own god; his will, supreme.

Man's dominion. The Creator designed that the human family would exercise dominion over the earth (Gen 1:28). But in succumbing to Satan's deception, Adam and his descendants came under Satan's "dominion of darkness" (Col 1:13). For the time being Heaven has allowed the usurper to exercise control over the earth, and Satan is referred to as "the god of this world" and "the ruler of this world" (2 Cor 4:4; John 12:31; cf. Luke 4:5-7).

The hand of the archrebel has been heavy on both mankind and the natural world. The face of nature has been blighted (cf. Gen 3:18), and "the whole creation has been groaning as in the pains of childbirth right up to the present time" (Rom 8:22, NIV).

Fallen Angels Permitted to Live?

When Lucifer sought his independence from God by challenging His law and government and character, the charges came as startling new ideas to the angel hosts. Rebellion against the Creator had never occurred before. Heaven's highest angel raised questions and sowed seeds of doubt and distrust. The insurrection was large and deep-seated. The loyal angels did not understand the significance of disobedience.

If God had blotted out the rebels, He would have destroyed the very basis of His government: voluntary, loving obedience to His authority. A display of force (with the issues unclear) would not have terminated the rebellion. Fear of the Creator would have supplanted love, and questioning and revolt would have risen again and again.

Time must be allowed for the spirit of lawlessness to develop its principles, to come to full maturation and fruition. Not until then would the intelligent universe see the true nature of transgression against the Creator with its heartbreaking results. Not until then would they concur wholeheartedly in its eradication. For this reason Heaven has permitted the continued existence of Satan and the other fallen angels.

Earth has become the laboratory to demonstrate to the universe the depths to which Satan and sin will corrupt and ruin the race. The Creator was not responsible for the sinful rebellion of Adam and Eve, nor for the fearful consequences of their choice. But He has not abandoned His creation. In this same laboratory He has provided a full revelation of His character and law through the incarnation of His Son, Jesus Christ. Through Him God has also provided at great cost a plan of salvation from sin's dominion—full and free to any son or daughter of Adam who desires to accept it (Rev 22:17).[22]

The Divine Objectives

With the fall of Adam and Eve Satan gained what appeared to be a signal victory in his controversy with the Creator. Mankind, as well as a multitude of angels, flouted God's authority. The rebellion instigated in heaven has spread. Earth is in revolt and estranged from heaven. Satan has established a beachhead on the planet, as it were, in his war against the Deity.

Without going into a detailed analysis of the plan of salvation, we may deduce from the Scriptures, at this point, four major objectives the Deity intends to accomplish through the plan's provisions:

1. To clear (vindicate) the character, law, and government of God from all charges.

2. To reaffirm and secure the loyalty of the *unfallen,* intelligent creation.

3. To effect the salvation of all sinners who will respond to the divine invitation to return and accept the Creator's gracious lordship.

4. To destroy Satan and the rebel angels, impenitent sinners, and all the effects of sin.[23]

As far as sinful humanity is concerned, sin has created four basic problems. The plan of salvation must resolve these in a satisfactory manner if man's deliverance is to take place.

1. Humanity is now in a state of rebellion, alienation, and separation from God. A Mediator is needed to reconcile this tragic estrangement (1 Tim 2:5; John 14:6).

2. The penalty of sin, eternal death, hangs over the race. Divine justice has decreed it as the only possible way in which the scourge of sin may be removed from the universe (Rom 6:23). Man desperately needs a Saviour who can meet this judgment (cf. Isa 53:4-6).[24]

3. The power of sin in the life has depraved every aspect of the human being and left the sinner powerless to deliver himself/herself ("I am carnal, . . . sin . . . dwells within me," Rom 7:14-20). Sinners need a divine re-creation (cf. 2 Cor 5:17).

4. Humanity has lost both its life and dominion. Death is a "veil that is spread over all nations" (Isa 25:7). It is an "enemy" that cannot be resisted

(1 Cor 15:26). And the dominion of this earth has been lost to Satan. A Life-giver is needed (cf. 1 John 5:11), and One who is able to dispossess the usurper (cf. John 12:31; Rev 12:10).

The plan of salvation addresses the issues raised in the rebellion of the angels and mankind. It also provides marvelous deliverance and restoration for the human race, for all who will respond to its provisions. The sanctuary parable illustrates in ritual form how the plan is being carried out through the atoning priesthood of Jesus Christ, to which subject we now return.

———— ◆ ————

Endnotes

1 Frank Holbrook, *Shadows of Hope. Breakthrough With God's Word.* Richard E. Harris, ed. (Washington, DC: Department of Education, General Conference of Seventh-day Adventists; Pacific Press Publishing Association, Mountain View, CA, 1976), 7-9, adapted.

2 "While everything in nature is governed by natural law, man alone, as an intelligent being, capable of understanding its requirements, is amenable to moral law. To man alone, the crowning work of His creation, God has given a conscience to realize the sacred claims of the divine law, and a heart capable of loving it as holy, just, and good; and of man prompt and perfect obedience is required. Yet God does not compel him to obey; he is left a free moral agent" (Ellen G. White, 1SM 216).

3 Frank Holbrook, *Shadows of Hope,* 16, 17, adapted.

4 "The law of God existed before the creation of man or else Adam could not have sinned. After the transgression of Adam the principles of the law were not changed, but were definitely arranged and expressed to meet man in his fallen condition" (Ellen G. White, 1SM 230).

5 "Everything in nature, from the mote in the sunbeam to the worlds on high, is under law. And upon obedience to these laws the order and harmony of the natural world depend. So there are great principles of righteousness to control the life of all intelligent beings, and upon conformity to these principles the well-being of the universe depends. Before this earth was called into being, God's law existed. Angels are governed by its principles, and in order for earth to be in harmony with heaven, man also must obey the divine statutes" (Ellen G. White, MB 48).

6 Cf. First Table: Gen 35:1-4; 2:1-3; Second Table: Gen 18:19; 4:8-11; 39:7-9; 19:1-10; 44:8; 12:11-13. The apostle Paul demonstrates in one inclusive state-ment that the Ten Commandments were known orally in the period from

Creation to Moses: "Sin indeed was in the world before the law was given [at Mount Sinai], but sin is not counted where there is no law. Yet death reigned from Adam to Moses, even over those whose sins were not like the transgression of Adam," (Rom 5:13, 14). The presence of sin in the era between Adam and Moses demonstrates a knowledge of the precepts of the Ten Commandments which the antediluvians chose to violate and ignore.

7 "Those only who acknowledge the binding claim of the moral law can explain the nature of the atonement" (Ellen G. White, 1SM 229).

8 M.L. Andreasen, *The Sanctuary Service.* 2nd ed., rev. (Washington, DC:Review and Herald Publishing Assn., 1947), 253.

9 "He reiterated his claim that angels needed no control, but should be left to follow their own will, which would ever guide them right. He denounced the divine statutes as a restriction to their liberty and declared that it was his purpose to secure the abolition of law; that, freed from this restraint, the host of heaven might enter upon a more exalted, more glorious state of existence" (Ellen G. White, GC 499).

10 "Evil originated with Lucifer, who rebelled against the government of God. Before his fall he was a covering cherub, distinguished by his excellence. God made him good and beautiful, as near as possible like Himself" (Ellen G. White, SDABC 4:1163).

11 "There was nothing poisonous in the fruit itself, and the sin was not merely in yielding to appetite. It was distrust of God's goodness, disbelief in His word, and rejection of His authority, that made our first parents transgressors, and that brought into the world a knowledge of evil. It was this that opened the door to every species of falsehood and error" (Ellen G. White, Ed 25).

12 "Considered one of the *cruces interpretum,* much ink has been used in an effort to interpret this simple phrase which is a mere conjunction. It never means 'in whom' (Origin, Vulgate: *in quo,* sc., *Adamo peccante*); nor as the Catholic exegesis would have it: *in lumbis Adami,* the whole race in the loins of Adam, physically or ideally in Adam as the representative" (R.C.H. Lenski, *The Interpretation of St. Paul's Epistle to the Romans* [Columbus, OH: Wartburg Press, 1945], 361).

13 H. E. Dana and Julius R. Mantey, *A Manual Grammar of the Greek New Testament* (New York: The Macmillan Company, 1927, 1955), 106; *"Epi,"* AG 287.

14 "We groan, being burdened, because [*eph' hō*] we do not want to be unclothed" (2 Cor 5:4, NASB); "That I may lay hold of that for which [*eph' hō*] also I was laid hold of by Christ Jesus" (Phil. 3:12, NASB).

15 Logically, wouldn't such a view require even Jesus to have sinned (personally) in Adam?

16 *"Kathistēmi,"* AG 391.

17 Since angels are genderless, they do not marry nor have children; hence, there is no race of angels, as such. Evidently each was a separate creation. Cf. Matt 22:29,

30; Mark 12:25; Luke 20:34, 36.

18 "The first Adam was created a pure, sinless being, without a taint of sin upon him; he was in the image of God. He could fall, and he did fall through transgressing. *Because of sin his posterity was born with inherent propensities of disobedience*" (Ellen G. White, SDABC 5:1128, emphasis added).

19 For a brief review of the various theories Christians have proposed on the relationship between Adam and the human race in terms of the Fall, see Edward Heppenstall, *The Man Who Is God* (Washington, DC: Review and Herald Publishing Assn., 1977), 106-125.

20 Ellen G. White, Ed 28.

21 "Man was originally endowed with noble powers and a well-balanced mind. He was perfect in his being, and in harmony with God. His thoughts were pure, his aims holy. But through disobedience, his powers were perverted, and selfishness took the place of love. His nature became so weakened through transgression that it was impossible for him, in his own strength, to resist the power of evil" (Ellen G. White, SC 17).

22 The Scriptures reveal no plan of salvation for the fallen angels. Only their destruction is determined (see Matt 25:41). Evidently, due to their intimate knowledge of the Creator—dwelling in His immediate presence (cf. Ps 103:19-21; Rev 5:11)—there was nothing more God could reveal of Himself to bring them to repentance and submission to Him. On the other hand man was deceived into sinning. A plan that would expiate the sins of the race and would reveal the true character of the Creator might lead many to choose voluntarily to be on the Lord's side. See Ellen G. White, GC 492-504 for a sketch of the protracted efforts by the Deity to prevent Lucifer and his associate angels from making the irrevocable decision to break with the Creator and to assert their independence.

23 "The plan of redemption had a yet broader and deeper purpose than the salvation of man. It was not for this alone that Christ came to the earth; it was not merely that the inhabitants of this little world might regard the law of God as it should be regarded; but it was to vindicate the character of God before the universe. . . . The act of Christ in dying for the salvation of man would not only make heaven accessible to men, but before all the universe it would justify God and His Son in their dealing with the rebellion of Satan. It would establish the perpetuity of the law of God and would reveal the nature and the results of sin" (Ellen G. White, PP 68, 69).

24 It is often asked, Why could not God have simply forgiven Adam and Eve their sin and given them another chance? Why is it necessary for a penalty to be paid in order to forgive them? The answer lies in the character of the holy God and the terrible nature of sin. Even human government would quickly collapse into anarchy if no punishment were forthcoming from the courts of justice in response to the criminal acts of its citizens. Just so, in the divine government. The following remarks by Ellen G. White shed light on God's response to human

rebellion: "Had God pardoned Adam's sin without an atonement, sin would have been immortalized, and would have been perpetuated with a boldness that would have been without restraint" (SDABC 1:1082). "Were there no justice, no penalty, there would be no stability to the government of God. It is the mingling of judgment and mercy that makes salvation complete. It is the blending of the two that leads us, as we view the world's Redeemer, and the law of Jehovah, to exclaim, 'Thy gentleness hath made me great' " (SDABC 5:1133).

5

The Altar and the Cross

The sanctuary parable underscores three important concerns of priestly activity in the rituals: (1) the offering of animal sacrifices, (2) the ministration of sacrificial blood and intercession at the golden altar, (3) the ministration of final judgment. Since the ritual activity began each day at the altar of burnt offering in the court, we will analyze its significance first.

The NT writers unequivocally equate the ritual sacrifices of animals in the sanctuary service with the death of Jesus Christ on Calvary. Their many references to the "blood" of Christ are allusions to the ancient practice.[1] "He has appeared once for all at the end of the age to put away sin by the *sacrifice [thusia]* of himself," declares the apostle (Heb 9:26). "Christ . . . offered for all time a single *sacrifice*" (Heb 10:12). "For every high priest is appointed to offer gifts and *sacrifices;* hence it is necessary for this priest [Jesus Christ] also to have something to offer" (Heb 8:3).

The superiority of Christ's shed blood [His life laid down for sinners] is argued over against mere ceremonial cleansing by animal blood. "For if the sprinkling of defiled persons with *the blood of goats and bulls* . . . sanctifies for the purification of the flesh [ritual cleansing], how much more shall *the blood of Christ* . . . purify your conscience from dead works to serve the living God" (Heb 9:13, 14). In light of this strong NT linkage we may safely affirm that the sacrifices offered on the altar of burnt offering were intended to foreshadow the one, great, antitypical death of Jesus Christ, the world's Saviour.[2]

The Morning and Evening Public Sacrifices

Sacrificial activity occurred only in connection with the altar of burnt offering. Constructed of acacia wood overlaid with bronze, the altar stood within the courtyard near the entrance to the two-apartment sanctuary (Exod 27:1-8). The golden altar before the veil of the Most Holy Place served only for the burning of incense (Exod 30:9).

Two categories of sacrifices were made each day: (1) the public offerings, better known as "the morning and evening sacrifices," (or, "the daily"); and (2) the private offerings of the people. Additional public offerings were made in connection with the Sabbath, new moon feasts, and the annual festivals.

The public, daily burnt offering—sacrificed morning and evening—was the sanctuary's centerpiece, as it were (Exod 29:38-42). Retained from the practice of the patriarchs, it formed the foundation of the true faith. It took priority over all other sacrifices[3] and was central to Israel's worship. Whether public or private all other sacrifices were in addition to it.[4] The "continual burnt offering" or "daily," was never allowed to go out, but burned continuously "around the clock" (Lev 6:9-13)[5] Furthermore, the sacrifice was comprehensive in that the priesthood offered it for *all* Israel.

The hours appointed for the morning and evening sacrifices (at which time the incense on the golden altar and the oil in the lamps were renewed, Exod 30:7, 8) became the national hours for prayer (cf. Luke 1:10; Acts 3:1). Jews who lived in distant lands prayed toward the sanctuary at these hours (cf. 1 Kgs 8:30; Dan 6:10). The ever-burning sacrifice represented to the spiritual Jew the constant availability of God's forgiveness and acceptance through the Redeemer prefigured in the sacrifices (cf. John 1:29) as well as the nation's consecration to God.[6] Although sickness or distance might prevent a penitent worshiper from offering his own private offering, yet through this constant sacrifice, God's grace was continuously available to him day or night.

The "daily" burnt offering was not a "limited atonement," designed for a select few. It was offered by the priesthood in behalf of all Israel. Since God intended for the sanctuary to be called "a house of prayer for all peoples" (Isa 56:7), the efficacy of this sacrifice embraced the Gentiles as well who were drawn to the true God by His Spirit and the witness of His people.

So it is with the atoning death of Christ prefigured in the daily sacrifice. His merits are available to all who will receive Him. "For God so loved *the world* that he gave his only Son, that whoever believes in him should not perish but have eternal life" (John 3:16). God "desires all men to be saved and to come to the knowledge of the truth" (1 Tim 2:4). It is not His desire "that any should perish, but that all should reach repentance" (2 Pet 3:9). Forgiveness and acceptance with God through the merits of Christ are always available— only a prayer away. The divine business of salvation is never closed at 5:00 p.m. or on holidays!

Private Sacrifices

Even a casual acquaintance with the sanctuary ritual indicates considerable overlap in the rites as the "gospel" is portrayed in a ceremonial manner. Nevertheless, the additional overlap or requirement usually addresses another dimension in the salvation process. This is especially true of the various kinds of sacrifices made privately at the altar of burnt offering.

While the daily morning and evening sacrifices directed the faith of the believer to the constant availability of divine grace, the offering of private sacrifices drove these same truths closer home. Private sacrifices involved the believer in the act of slaying the victim, and thus enabled the worshiper to appropriate in a more direct and forceful manner the grace and mercies of God. At this point we will briefly sketch the major categories of private sacrifices.

Burnt Offerings (Lev 1)

The "burnt offering" also continued as a private sacrifice (Lev 1). Being the original sacrifice of the patriarchal system, it could atone/expiate for sin (Lev 1:4). However, in the Israelite system it was commonly offered in tandem with a sin offering.[7] This suggests the emphasis was on the offerer's desire to dedicate or consecrate himself/herself to God. The burnt offering was the only sacrifice in which the entire animal (having been skinned, Lev 7:8) was offered on the altar (Lev 1:9, 13). The apostle Paul probably alludes to the burnt offering when he appeals to Christians to make a full dedication to God: "Present your bodies as a living sacrifice, holy and acceptable to God, which is your spiritual worship" (Rom 12:1).

Peace Offerings (Lev 3)

The expression, "peace offerings," designated a large class of sacrifices. These included thank offerings, freewill offerings, and offerings made in connection with a variety of vows. The priest burned only the fat on the altar (Lev 3:3-5, 16; 7:31). The breast and right thigh were given to the assisting priest (Lev 7:29-36). The blood was sprinkled on the altar (Lev 3:2).

In addition to expressing the joyful heart of the offerer, the distinctive feature of the peace offering was the communal meal that the flesh of the sacrifice provided for the offerer, his family and servants, and invited Levites. The sacrificial meal thereby emphasized fellowship with both God and man.[8] The communal meal of this class of sacrifices appears as a forerunner (together with the Passover meal) of the Christian rite of the Lord's Supper—the Communion service (1 Cor 10:16-18).

Sin Offerings, Guilt Offerings (Lev 4-6)

Sin offerings (Lev 4) and guilt offerings (Lev 5, 6) form two related categories of sacrifices. Since the sin offering discussed in Leviticus 4 provided for "sins unwittingly" committed (sins of ignorance, KJV), and since no sacrifice was provided for one who sinned "with a high hand," "[despising] the word of the Lord" (Num 15:29-31), it has been generally argued that the Israelite who deliberately sinned could not find forgiveness in the ritual system. But a closer look at Leviticus 5, 6 indicates that God did indeed forgive deliberate sinners *when* they repented of their wickedness. They too could find grace and acceptance through confession (Lev 5:5) and the sacrificing of the appropriate guilt offering.[9]

The guilt offering went a step further than the sin offering by teaching the repentant Israelite the principle of restitution: the willingness and the sincere endeavor to make amends with the person(s) previously injured or wronged by the penitent's sin (Lev 6:4, 5; Num 5:6-8). Offering the guilt sacrifice signified that restitution had been made (cf. Ezek 33:15).

Accessory Offerings (Lev 2)

A nonbloody gift was presented at the altar along with all burnt offerings and peace offerings. It consisted of a cereal (flour) offering (prepared in different ways), together with oil, frankincense, wine for a drink offering, and salt, "the salt of the covenant with your God" (Lev 2:1-7, 13; Num 15:4, 5, 11). The Hebrew term for the cereal offering, *minḥāh* (gift), suggests that it was intended to represent the offerer's thankful acknowledgment of his/her dependence on God for all temporal blessings.

Although the Israelite could approach God in prayer at any time or place, it is clear that the private sacrifices gave content and meaning to personal prayer. The sacrifices were prayers in themselves. If the repentant sinner sought forgiveness, he/she would offer a sin or guilt offering. If consecration or dedication was the desired end, a burnt offering would be sacrificed. Thank offerings and freewill offerings expressed the believer's joy, gratitude, and praise. The cereal accessory offering expressed grateful dependence on the gracious Creator.[10] And, since all varieties of the bloody sacrifices foreshadowed the Redeemer's atoning death (cf. Heb 9:22; John 1:29), the act of offering these sacrifices was like praying "in the name" of that Redeemer.[11]

The Necessity for an Atoning Death

Early on we noted the sanctuary's emphasis on sacrifice, the necessity for the shedding of blood. "Indeed, under the [ritual] law almost everything is purified with blood, and without the shedding of blood there is no forgiveness of sins" (Heb 9:22)[12] In like manner one of the prominent themes which runs through the gospel accounts is the *necessity* for Christ to die, if He is to accomplish His mission to save sinners. "And as Moses lifted up the serpent in the wilderness, so *must [dei]*[13] the Son of man be lifted up, that whoever believes in him may have eternal life" (John 3:14, 15).

"From that time Jesus began to show his disciples that he *must [dei]* go to Jerusalem and suffer many things . . . and be killed" (Matt 16:21 = Mark 8:31; Luke 9:22). Near the end of His earthly ministry an ignorant crowd challenged Christ on this point: "How can you say that the Son of man *must [dei]* be lifted up?" (John 12:34). Again, on the resurrection morning, the angels at the tomb reminded the startled women, "Remember how he told you . . . that the Son of man *must [dei]* be . . . crucified" (Luke 24:6, 7).

The most striking evidence for the necessity of Christ's death (if the divine plan of salvation were to achieve its objective) is furnished by His thrice-uttered, Gethsemane prayer: " 'My Father, if it be possible, let this cup pass from me; nevertheless, not as I will, but as thou wilt.' . . . 'My Father, if this cannot pass unless I drink it, thy will be done.' . . .'" (Matt 26:39-44).

If we ask, Why this compelling necessity for Christ's death? we are led back to the very character of the Trinity. "Without a holy God there would be no problem of atonement. It is the holiness of God's love that necessitates the atoning cross. . . ."[14] God's will, as expressed in His law, has been transgressed; His character has been besmirched; rebellion has flouted His authority and government; but beyond that His own holy nature has been challenged. "The Rock [God], his work is perfect; for all his ways are justice. A God of faithfulness and without iniquity, just and right is he" (Deut 32:4). "Holy, holy, holy is the Lord of hosts" (Isa 6:3).

God is not like some insensitive, stone sphinx. He is a living, vibrant Person. Sin is an open affront to His sinless Being. It cannot be tolerated in His presence or in His universe. God's internal holiness as well as His external authority as Sovereign must react against the sinful rebellion of His creatures. He must judge sin for what it is and eradicate it. The very security of the universe of intelligent beings rests upon the Creator's being true to His holy character.

"The way God chooses to forgive sinners and reconcile them to himself must, first and foremost, be fully consistent with his own character. It is not only that he must overthrow and disarm the devil in order to rescue his captives. It is not even only that he must satisfy his law, his honour, his justice or moral order: it is that he must satisfy himself."[15]

"How then can God express his holiness without consuming us, and his love without condoning our sins? How can God satisfy his holy love? How can he save *us* and satisfy *himself* simultaneously? We reply . . . that, in order to satisfy himself, he sacrificed—indeed substituted—himself for us."[16]

The Meaning of the Cross Illustrated

We submit that the sanctuary parable not only furnishes helpful insights, but it also provides the model for understanding the NT's didactic statements about the meaning and significance of the divine acts in the salvation process. It thereby serves as a corrective against misleading theological speculations. Since the patriarchal burnt offering and Israel's sin/guilt offerings centered specifically on the atoning and forgiving of sin, we will use them in combination as a convenient "window" through which to view the significance of the cross.[17] Actually, all the bloody sacrifices of the ancient altar were intended to teach God's people a number of interrelated truths about the death of the foreshadowed Redeemer.[18]

We briefly summarize the scene at the altar for the reader's imagination as the basis for our further remarks:

1. Convicted of sin, the penitent brings the specified sacrifice to the altar.

2. Placing his hand on the head of the animal, the penitent confesses his sin and guilt, thereby transferring the same to the animal as his substitute.

3. After the penitent slays the sacrifice, the attendant priest catches the blood and administers it according to the appropriate directions.

4. The priest thus makes atonement for the sin, and the penitent is forgiven.

A Moral Universe

By witnessing the death of an innocent animal as a sin/guilt offering (just as we Christians witness Christ's death as a predicted guilt offering ['āšām],

Isa 53:10),[19] the penitent Israelite was vividly reminded that he lived in a moral universe. He could not fail to see that in the death of the sacrifice, nor can we when we contemplate Calvary. Justice and judgment are foundational to the divine government as well as mercy and truth. "Righteousness and justice are the foundation of thy throne; steadfast love and faithfulness go before thee" (Ps 89:14).

In the governance of a holy God, sin and rebellion cannot be winked at nor ignored. The universe is secure only if the Creator is truly just. The penalty for sin must be enforced. Imagine the instability of any nation whose judicial system ceased to punish transgressors![20] The wildest anarchy and civil chaos would result. In the spiritual realm all respect and reverence for the Creator would vanish; sin and rebellion would be emboldened beyond all human imagination (cf. Eccl 8:11).

Obviously, in the moral realm the sacrificial death of an animal could not atone for moral offenses. "It is impossible that the blood of bulls and goats should take away sins" (Heb 10:4). Consequently, in the patriarchal and Mosaic eras repentant sinners were forgiven on the basis of divine grace and the penitent's faith in the promised Redeemer. The apostle Paul speaks to this point:

"God displayed [Christ Jesus] publicly as a *propitiation [hilastērion]* in His blood through faith. *This was to demonstrate His righteousness [dikaiosunē], because in the forbearance of God He passed over the sins previously committed* [in OT times]; for the demonstration, I say, of His *righteousness* at the present time, that He might be just *[dikaios]* and the justifier of the one who has faith in Jesus" (Rom 3:25, 26, NASB).

The apostle's statement is striking. Now, at the cross, the unfallen angels and the inhabitants of other worlds could see that God's forgiveness of repentant sinners during the millennia between Adam and Christ was not based on shed, sacrificial blood, but on the atoning death of the Redeemer yet to come—prefigured in the animal type. *But if Christ had not died, God would have been unjust to have forgiven them.* The atoning death of Christ was necessary to demonstrate God's uprightness and justice in forgiving all repentant sinners prior to the cross. The Epistle to the Hebrews confirms the fact that the death of Christ "[redeems] them from the transgressions under the first [Sinaitic] covenant" (Heb 9:15). Furthermore, the apostle implies that God would be unjust were He to forgive repentant sinners on any other basis than the atoning death of Christ.

Paul states that "God displayed [Christ Jesus] publicly as a *propitiation [hilastērion]* in His blood" (NASB). The noun *hilastērion,* "that which

propitiates," belongs to the *hilaskomai* word group which means "to propitiate."[21] Modern versions, influenced by certain scholarly studies, tend to
translate this word group with "to expiate" for the verb and "expiation" for
the nouns. "The two concepts are really very different. Propitiation means the
turning away of anger; expiation is rather the making amends for a wrong.
Propitiation is a personal word; one propitiates a person. Expiation is an
impersonal word; one expiates a sin or a crime."[22]

But does God need to be propitiated? Does His "wrath" need to be
averted? The "wrath of God," that is, His holy attitude toward sin and His
judgment on it, is a very prominent subject in both the Old and New Testaments. The expression does not denote a self-centered, human kind of anger,
but is intended to indicate the settled, divine opposition to evil that arises from
God's very nature, His holiness. God is the moral Governor of the universe,
as well as its Creator. While He is "merciful" and "abounding in steadfast
love," He also "will by no means clear the guilty" (Exod 34:6, 7).

Christ's death was not in any sense an appeasement of the Father's wrath
in the manner pagans appease their gods. Rather, His death was the means by
which the triune God chose to avert or to put away divine "wrath" in a manner
consistent with His holiness, and which would at the same time make possible
the salvation of repentant sinners. Without question the first "statement" the
altar and the cross declare is that we live in a moral universe governed by a
holy God.

Transfer of Accountability

The sacrificial animal represented the repentant sinner who brought it to
the altar. On this point we may assume the instruction given Moses in regard
to the private burnt offering was applicable to all animal sacrifices. "It shall
be accepted *for [le] him* to make atonement *for [le] him*" (Lev 1:4).

The penitent transferred his sin and guilt to this animal "stand-in" by
laying his hand on the head of the sacrifice and confessing his sin. "And he
shall lay his hand on the head of the sin offering . . ." (Lev 4:29). "When a
man is guilty in any of these, he shall *confess* the sin he has committed" (Lev
5:5; cf. 16:21). With this figurative transfer of sin from the sinner to the animal,
the latter now stood accountable or guilty.[23]

This ritual exchange of sin and accountability from the sinner to the
sacrifice foreshadowed the exchange that would take place at Calvary. "For
our sake he [God] made him [Christ Jesus] to be sin who knew no sin, so that
in him we might become the righteousness of God" (2 Cor 5:21).[24] We will
discuss this further a little later on.

Without Blemish

Repeatedly instruction is given that sacrificial animals must be "without blemish."[25] Blind, disabled, diseased, or mutilated animals were rejected, unacceptable. It is not difficult to see the reason for this requirement inasmuch as the bloody sacrifices foreshadowed the atoning death of a *sinless* Redeemer. The apostle Peter makes this linkage. "You know that you were ransomed from the futile ways inherited from your fathers, not with perishable things such as silver or gold, but with the precious blood of Christ, *like that of a lamb without blemish or spot*" (1 Pet 1:18, 19).

Since an animal did not belong to the moral creation, it could only symbolize the sinlessness of Christ by its external, unblemished features. But, as we have observed earlier on, the nature of sin includes an internal aspect—a self-centered bent—as well as external acts of wrong which issue from that inner carnality (Matt 15:19). The apostle Paul speaks for all sinful humanity when he refers to "sin which dwells within me" (Rom 7:17, 20).

But this was not the case with Christ. Neither an inner, natural bent to sin nor outward acts of sin marred Him in any manner. The Bible writers are emphatic: "*In [en] him* there is no sin" (1 John 3:5). "Who *knew [ginōskō]* no sin" (2 Cor 5:21). "He *committed* no sin" (1 Pet 2:22). And Christ Himself challenged His critics, "Which of you convicts me of sin?" (John 8:46). It is evident that Christ, the antitypical sacrifice, was all that the type demanded: He was "without blemish," in other words, sinless.

It is argued in some quarters that Christ came to earth with a self-centered, egotistical bent such as we have, but that He resisted its clamors. But there is not the slightest hint given in Scripture to suggest that His self-will *naturally* sought to be or to act independent of the Father. The sanctuary parable serves to correct this aberrant theology by emphasizing the *unblemished* qualities of the promised Redeemer. Only a sinless Saviour could make the atoning death that would provide salvation for the world.[26]

Death: Divine Judgment on Sin

Slaying a living animal with his own hand would have left a deep impression on the offerer. The animal was innocent; it stood passively before him. When he cut its throat, he knew that in reality it was his sin that was causing the death of the innocent creature. "And he shall lay his hand on the head of the sin offering, *and kill the sin offering* . . . " (Lev 4:29). In this enactment at the altar the penitent Israelite also acknowledged the divine judgment on sin.

Thus, in every dying, sacrificial victim—and in our Lord's own death—we see demonstrated God's judgment on sin: death. "The wages of sin is death" (Rom 6:23); "The soul that sins shall die" (Ezek 18:4). A holy God cannot take transgression lightly, for sin is a deep-seated rebellion against all that is good, noble, and true within the nature of the Deity Itself. Holiness and sinfulness cannot coexist. Sin must be eradicated if moral harmony is to reign in the universe. The principle of self-seeking is incompatible with the principle of self-sacrificing love. Consequently, the divine judgment on those who remain impenitent and determined to pursue a course of rebellion is eternal separation and death (cf. Rev 20:14, 15; 21:8).

Salvation by Substitution

We have touched on this point in the earlier discussion on the transfer of accountability. But much more needs to be said. We cite again the basic OT passage on the significance of the blood sacrifices:

"The life of the flesh is in the blood; and I have given it to you for making atonement for your lives on the altar; for, as life, it is the blood that makes atonement. . . . For the life of every creature—its blood is its life" (Lev 17:11-14, NRSV).

Since an animal's blood both carried and symbolized its life, its sacrificially shed blood signified its life laid down, that is, its life laid down in behalf of the offerer of the sacrifice. "The text, then, according to its plain and obvious import, teaches the *vicarious* nature of the rite of sacrifice. *Life was given for life,* the life of the victim for the life of the offerer."[27]

When the repentant sinner laid his hand upon the head of the sacrifice he had brought, and confessed his sin, the animal (in figure) became his sin-bearer, and the penalty for his sin was paid by the animal's subsequent death. Thus, it is clear that the death of the sin-bearing animal *substituted* for the offerer's rightful death. Through the sanctuary parable "window" we are enabled to see that the sacrificial death of Jesus Christ is a substitutionary death. He would be humanity's Sin Bearer. He would bear the penalty of our sins, atoning and expiating them by His death. This is the testimony of both the types and Scripture. We list a few important passages on this truth:

1. "For I delivered to you *as of first importance* what I also received, that Christ died *for [huper]* our sins in accordance with the scriptures" (1 Cor 15:3).

2. "He [Christ] himself *bore [anapherō]*[28] *our sins in his body* on the tree . . . " (1 Pet 2:24).

3. "For Christ also died for sins once for all, *the righteous for [huper] the unrighteous*" (1 Pet 3:18).

4. "He [Christ] has appeared once for all at the end of the age *to put away sin by the sacrifice of himself*. . . . so Christ, having been offered *to bear [anapherō] the sins of* many, will appear the second time . . . " (Heb 9:26-28).

5. "He [God] made Him [Christ] who knew no sin *to be sin on our behalf [huper]*, that we might become the righteousness of God in Him" (2 Cor 5:21, NASB).

We must not misunderstand the sacrificial language of these passages. Just as the sacrifice was "without blemish," so Christ was personally sinless—without moral spot or blemish. And just as the penitent's sin and guilt were transferred in figure to the sacrifice, so humanity's sin and guilt were imputed to Christ. He thereby bore our sin and guilt and died as our great Sin Bearer and Substitute, but He Himself was, in life and in death, spotless and without sin.

In addition to the sanctuary sacrifices, the prophecy of the Suffering Servant in Isaiah 53 also informed the NT writers about the vicarious nature of Christ's death. Eight of the 12 verses of this prophecy are cited in the NT as having met fulfillment in Jesus Christ.[29] The prophet sketches graphically the substitutionary sufferings and death of humanity's Sin Bearer:

> Surely he has borne our griefs and carried our sorrows; yet we esteemed him stricken, smitten by God, and afflicted. But he was wounded for our transgressions, he was bruised for our iniquities; upon him was the chastisement that made us whole, and with his stripes we are healed. All we like sheep have gone astray; we have turned every one to his own way; and *the Lord has laid on him the iniquity of us all*. . . . he *shall bear* their iniquities. . . . he *bore* the sin of many . . . (vss. 4-6, 11, 12).

Three NT passages especially clarify the substitutionary nature of our Sin Bearer's death. Two of these are statements by Christ Himself in regard to His crucifixion:

1. "For the Son of man also came not to be served but to serve, and to *give his life* as a ransom *for [anti]* many" (Mark 10:45; cf. 1 Tim 2:6). Here Christ refers to His death as "a *ransom [lutron]*. The *lutron* was the "price of release" for freeing a slave.[30] The Saviour describes sin as an enslavement; the price for our emancipation from it—His death. The significance of His statement is seen in the preposition *anti* which means "instead of," "in the place of."[31] Thus, Christ underscored the fact that His death would be vicarious or substitutionary in nature: His death would be in the place of ours.

2. "For this is my blood of the covenant, which is *poured out* for many for the forgiveness of sins" (Matt 26:28). In these words, spoken at the

institution of the ordinance of the Communion supper, Christ touches on the purpose of His death: to atone for human sin, an action humanity could not perform for itself.

3. "Christ redeemed us from the curse of the law, *having become a curse for [huper]* us—for it is written, 'Cursed be every one who hangs on a tree' " (Gal. 3:13). The apostle Paul's point is plain enough. As sinners, the human family is under the curse/condemnation of God's law before the bar of Heaven. But Christ voluntarily accepted the liability of our sins and bore the legal consequences in our stead. He took our judgment upon Himself.

In spite of the clear evidence for the substitutionary death by which Jesus Christ met the penalty for human sin—evidence portrayed in the sanctuary sacrifices and buttressed by NT declarations—there are Christians who consider the biblical teaching to be immoral.

One such group has adopted a view which some commentators in the past have suggested.[32] The argument links Romans 5:12 and 2 Corinthians 5:14 and states what may be termed a "corporate" view of the atonement, namely, "in Adam, we sinned," and "in Jesus, we died." The emphasis is on a corporate kind of linkage of the believer to Adam and Christ (as the second Adam). But this relationship is so construed that its exponents can say, "in Jesus, *we paid the penalty for sin.*"[33]

No student of the Bible would deny that it sets forth the first man and Jesus Christ under the terminology of "the first and second Adams" (cf. Rom 5:12-19; 1 Cor 15:22, 45-47). There are similarities between the two, but there are also dissimilarities. As we observed on the passage in Romans 5:12-19, Paul explains the universality of death as resulting "because all men sinned" (Rom 5:12). But he was not suggesting that unborn, nonexistent humans who made up Adam's genetic potential for a posterity—had personally sinned when the father of the race sinned! Rather, he asserts that Adam's disobedience "made" his potential posterity sinners, bringing them into condemnation (Rom 5:18, 19). This is because Adam broke with God, separated from God, and was judged by God—and the race that *eventually* developed from him *shared in the consequences* of that alienation.

If we cannot scripturally accept the Augustine/Roman Catholic view that unborn humanity genetically and potentially in the loins of Adam personally sinned, neither can we accept the truly nonscriptural view that "in Jesus, *we* paid the penalty for sin." Let us analyze the single text which is said to teach this view:

"For the love of Christ controls us, having concluded this, that one died for all, *therefore [ara]* all died; and He died for all, that they who live should no longer live for themselves, but for Him who died and rose again on their behalf" (2 Cor 5:14, 15, NASB).

In the first place, it is never wise to build an important theological teaching on a single text of Scripture, and especially a text which, because of its contracted nature, may be subject to more than one interpretation.

Second, what shall we say about the millions of humans who lived and died in the millennia between Adam and Christ's incarnation and death. In no physical sense could they be said to be in the loins of the second Adam when He died. For that matter, neither could such a notion hold true for the generations who have lived subsequently to the cross.

Third, the concept that in some manner, "we" sinners "paid the penalty for sin" is diametrically opposed to the plainest statements of Scripture that declare, "Christ [not 'we'] died for our sins in accordance with the scriptures" (1 Cor 15:3).

Fourth, the proposed interpretation makes the apostle contradict himself within the passage. Three times in the text the apostle declares "*One* died *for all*" ("one died for all . . . He died for all . . . Him who died . . . on their behalf"). It would be quite contrary to his consistent argument to insert the notion that "*we* paid the penalty for sin."

If, then, Christ truly "died for all," in what sense can Paul say, "therefore all died"? There are two simple keys at hand: (1) *Ara*, translated "therefore," is an *inferential* particle which carries such nuances in English as "so, then, consequently, you see, therefore," and the like.[34] So Paul is saying that from the fact that Christ died for all, we may infer something. (2) Paul sometimes uses the verb "to die" in the sense of "condemned to die." For example, speaking about the condemning function of the law, he observed, "I was once alive apart from the law, but *when the commandment came, sin revived and I died*" (Rom 7:9). Paul simply means that when he became aware of God's commandment—His will—the Spirit convicted him of his sin, *and thus condemned him to death.*

Thus, the apostle's statement in 2 Corinthians 5:14 may be understood in this manner: "For the love of Christ controls us, having concluded this, that one died for all, *therefore* [we infer] all *died* [stood condemned to die]" (NASB). The apostle seems simply to say that we may infer from the fact of Christ's substitutionary death for the race (John 3:16), that all humanity stood under condemnation as sinners and were doomed to die.[35] Since His amazing love prompted His vicarious, sacrificial death, it should constrain us to live for Him.

In concluding our review of the substitutionary nature of Christ's death we would observe that the sanctuary parable provides an important guideline for interpreting the significance of the cross. It also functions as a corrective against misleading interpretations. At the altar the repentant sinner transfers his sin and guilt *to* the sacrifice. In the typical enactment the sinner and his stand-in-substitute are discrete symbols. The sacrifice dies *in the place of* the sinner. In no way could the type be construed to mean that the repentant sinner *himself*—in some manner linked to the sacrifice—"paid the penalty for sin." Rather, the sacrifice paid the penalty *for* the sinner. Salvation by *substitution* is the message of both altar and cross.

Godhead Assumes Judgment on Sin

Reconciliation implies the previous estrangement of two parties. In the estrangement between God and man, we have the sin and rebellion of man on one side and the holiness or wrath of God reacting to sin on the other. Although no text says "Christ reconciled *God* to man," yet the truth is expressed in other terms. The plan must satisfy divine justice before it can reconcile humanity to God.

> It is a mistake to think that the barrier between God and us, which necessitated the work of reconciliation, was entirely on our side, so that we needed to be reconciled and God did not. True, we were "God's enemies," hostile to him in our hearts. But the "enmity" was on both sides. The wall or barrier between God and us was constituted both by our rebellion against him and by his wrath upon us on account of our rebellion.[36]

When the repentant sinner brought his burnt offering or sin offering to the altar to seek forgiveness, it would not have occurred to him that *he* was providing his own atonement. Although he had selected the sacrifice from his own herds, God had already said, "The life of the flesh is in the blood; and *I have given it for you* upon the altar to make atonement for your souls" (Lev 17:11). The triune God, not humanity, designed the plan of salvation and the sanctuary parable to illustrate it. Abraham spoke more prophetically than he realized when he said to Isaac, "God will provide himself the lamb for a burnt offering" (Gen 22:8).

But we distort the biblical view of the sacrifice of Jesus if we construe it to mean simply that at Calvary God the Father punished God the Son for the sins of a third party—humanity. The amazing truth is that *the triune God* provided the atoning sacrifice. The Godhead *took upon Themselves* their own judgment on sin. In the Christian religion no sinner attempts to placate or appease the Deity. Rather, the Deity submits to Their own decree. "God displayed [Christ Jesus] publicly as a *propitiation* [*hilastērion*] in His blood through faith" (Rom 3:25, NASB). The Godhead made an objective atonement for human sin and offers it to a penitent humanity.

God the Father did not force God the Son to make the atonement—to avert the divine wrath and to make expiation for humanity's sin and rebellion. The Son volunteered Himself; He freely chose to be a participant in the plan Deity devised in eternity.[37]

"[Christ Jesus], though he was in the form of God, did not count equality with God a thing to be grasped, but *emptied himself,* taking the form of a servant, being born in the likeness of men, And being found in human form *he humbled himself* and *became obedient unto death,* even death on a cross" (Phil 2:6-8).

"By this we know love, that he [Christ Jesus] *laid down his life for us*" (1 John 3:16).

"For this reason the Father loves me, because *I lay down my life,* that I may take it again. No one takes it from me, but *I lay it down of my own accord.* I have *power* [*exousia,* authority] to lay it down, and I have *power* [*exousia,* authority] to take it again; this charge I have received from my Father" (John 10:17, 18).[38]

At the cross *the Godhead* moved to bring about reconciliation between the estranged parties. "All this is from God, *who through Christ* reconciled us to himself" (2 Cor 5:18). While the emphasis of Paul's statement here is on reconciling man to God, it is the event of the cross that turns away His "wrath," satisfying divine justice, that makes reconciliation with fallen man possible.

God "was unwilling to act in love at the expense of his holiness or in holiness at the expense of his love. So we may say that he satisfied his holy love by himself dying the death and so bearing the judgment which sinners deserved. He both exacted and accepted the penalty of human sin. And he did it 'so as to be just and the one who justifies the man who has faith in Jesus' (Rom 3:26)."[39]

"In order to save us in such a way as to satisfy himself, God through Christ substituted himself for us. Divine love triumphed over divine wrath by divine self-sacrifice. The cross was an act simultaneously of punishment and amnesty, severity and grace, justice and mercy."[40]

"The biblical gospel of atonement is of God satisfying himself by substituting himself for us."[41] It is, indeed, an erroneous accusation to regard the biblical teaching of substitution as immoral. Calvary enabled the triune God to be both just and merciful, to uphold the honor of His character, law, and government, and yet to be able to reach out in mercy and forgiveness to any rebellious sinner who would accept His grace.

Divine Love

After the repentant sinner had slain the sacrificial animal, the attending priest caught the blood and placed some of it on the horns of the altar. In ministering the blood the priest made "atonement" for the penitent who left the courtyard "forgiven" (Lev 4:30, 31). Any spiritually minded Israelite knew that it was not possible for the blood of animals to take away sin (Heb 10:4). But he could rejoice in the gracious provisions God would ultimately provide in the promised Redeemer. By faith he accepted the divine forgiveness and acquittal. Like Abraham, who witnessed the ram's death in the place of Isaac, the penitent saw portrayed in the sacrificial victim the true Lamb of God who would take away the sin of the world (John 8:56; 1:29).

When we move through the centuries from animal sacrifices to the actual atoning death of the incarnate Son of God, we behold the unfathomable love of the triune God. No animal sacrifice could stir the heart as can Calvary! "In this is love, not that we loved God, but that He loved us and sent His Son to be the propitiation for our sins. Beloved, if God so loved us, we also ought to love one another" (1 John 4:10, 11, NASB).

Ever since the days of Peter Abelard, the French philosopher-theologian (1079-1142) who developed what is commonly designated "the moral influence" theory of the atonement, there have been Christians who have sought to divert attention from the penal/justice aspect of Christ's death. The amazing revelation of the divine love at Calvary is rightly pointed out. However, it is argued that God has no internal need to satisfy His justice. Rather, it is held that the design and purpose of the death of Jesus is solely to change the sinner's attitude and to lead him to repentance.

But if the horror of Calvary had no other meaning than to express the Creator's love, was there not some other less traumatic manner in which to demonstrate it and to move the sinner? We submit that it is the holiness or the justice of God displayed at Calvary—the triune God taking upon *Himself His* own judgment on sin—that makes His love so compelling and convincing.

> The death of Jesus on the cross cannot be seen as a demonstration of love in itself, but only if he gave his life in order to rescue ours. His death must be seen to have had an objective, before it can have an appeal. Paul and John saw love in the cross because they understood it respectively as a death for sinners (Rom. 5:8) and as a propitiation for sins (1 Jn. 4:10). That is to say, the cross can be seen as a proof of God's love only when it is at the same time seen as a proof of his justice.[42]

Once more, the sanctuary parable is a corrective to prevent untenable speculations. The altar plainly reveals the divine judgment on sin. Furthermore, it discloses how God and "the Lamb" would take Their judgment on sin upon Themselves. Holiness and justice as well as grace and mercy pervade the ritual of the altar. The type enables us to understand better Christ's propitiating and expiating death on the cross, and the driving compassion of divine love to sacrifice itself to accomplish our salvation.

———— ◆ ————

Endnotes

1 For example, see Acts 20:28; Eph 1:7; Col 1:20; Heb 13:12, 20; 1 John 1:7; Rev 1:5; 7:14, etc.

2 John 4:42; 12:32, 33. "Some wonder why God desired so many sacrifices and appointed the offering of so many bleeding victims in the Jewish economy. Every dying victim was a type of Christ, which lesson was impressed on mind and heart in the most solemn, sacred ceremony, and explained definitely by the priests. Sacrifices were explicitly planned by God Himself to teach this great and momentous truth, that through the blood of Christ alone there is forgiveness of sins" (Ellen G. White, 1SM 107).

3 For example, the first religious action the returned Jewish exiles from Babylon took in 536 B.C. was to erect the altar of burnt offering and to start again the morning and evening, public sacrifices. More than a score of years would elapse before the Temple itself would be completed (see Ezra 3:1-3; 6:15), but the daily sacrifices continued to burn and to call the former captives to a continuous renewal with God.

4 See Num 28:10, 15, 23, 31; 29:6, 11, 16, 22, 28, 31, 34, 38.

5 "The daily burnt offerings were burned on the altar, but over a slow fire so that one sacrifice would last until the next was put on (Lev 6:9). The evening sacrifice lasted until morning, and the morning sacrifice until evening" (SDABC 1:713).

6 "Every morning and evening a lamb of a year old was burned upon the altar, with the appropriate meat offering, thus symbolizing the daily consecration of the nation to Jehovah, and their constant dependence upon the atoning blood of Christ" (Ellen G. White, PP 352).

7 For example, Lev 12:8; 14:31; 15:15, 30, etc.

8 Lev 7:15-18; 19:5-8; Deut 27:7; 12:17, 18.

9 "It is frequently assumed that only inadvertent, unconscious, or unwitting sins could be atoned for with animal sacrifices in the Israelite cultus and that

conscious, deliberate, intentional sins could not be atoned for. The text usually associated with this view is Num 15:30, 31, 'But the person who does anything with a high hand, whether he is native or sojourner, reviles the Lord, and that person shall be cut off from his people. Because he has despised the word of the Lord, and has broken his commandment, that person shall be utterly cut off; his iniquity shall be upon him.' The *high-handed* sinner is one who 'reviles Yahweh' and defiantly maintains an unrepentant attitude. However, sacrificial atonement is not barred to the premeditated or intentional sinner who repents. When the intentional/deliberate sinner's attitude 'changes to one of repentance, the whole situation is altered.' The *high-handed* nature of the sinner refers to his chosen state of defiance and unrepentance, 'but not to the deliberate sinner who has mitigated his offense by his repentance' " (Gerhard F. Hasel, "Studies in Biblical Atonement I," SA[1], 104; SA[2], 101, 102).

"The usual sins we fall into are covered by the sin offering and the guilt offering. For instance, lying, stealing, cheating, and false swearing are surely intentional; yet they are specifically covered by the guilt offering (6:2-3). . . . The sense of the verb *šāgāg* [translated as sinning 'unintentionally,' or 'unwittingly,' or in 'ignorance'] will be adequately caught if in all the verses concerned here in Leviticus 4-5, the phrase 'sins unintentionally' is rendered by 'goes astray in sin' or 'does wrong' or the like" (R. Laird Harris, *Leviticus,* ExpBC 2:547, 548. Used by permission of Zondervan Publishing House).

10 For a practical discussion of the various sacrifices, see M. L. Andreasen, *The Sanctuary Service.* 2nd ed., rev. (Washington, DC: Review and Herald Publishing Assn., 1947), 88-169. For a detailed charting of all the sacrifices and their accessories, see "Outline of Sanctuary Service," SDABC 1:698-710.

11 John 14:13, 14; 16:23-27. Over the centuries most Israelites lost the meaning of the sanctuary parable, and the religion degenerated into a system of salvation by works. But there were persons in the patriarchal-Israelite tradition who understood the parabolic nature of the sacrificial system. Abraham was certainly one who saw the plan of salvation illustrated when God provided a ram to take the place of Isaac on the altar he had built on Mt. Moriah. "And Abraham went and took the ram, and offered it up as a burnt offering instead of his son" (Gen. 22:13). In the ram, Abraham discerned the coming Saviour. Jesus, evidently referring to that moving scene, declared to the Jews of His day, "Your father Abraham rejoiced to see My day; and he saw it, and was glad" (John 8:56, NASB).

12 "Gather up the strongest affirmative statements regarding the atonement made by Christ for the sins of the world. Show the necessity for this atonement and tell men and women that they may be saved if they will repent and return to their loyalty to God's law. Gather all the affirmatives and proofs that make the gospel the glad tidings of salvation to all who receive and believe on Christ as a personal Saviour" (Ellen G. White, Ev 187).

13 The Greek term carries the nuances, "it is necessary, one must, or has to." It denotes compulsion. See "Dei," AG 171.

14 P. T. Forsyth, *Work of Christ,* p. 80, cited in John R. W. Stott, *The Cross of Christ* (Downers Grove, IL: InterVarsity Press, 1986), 132.

15 Stott, *The Cross of Christ,* 129.

16 Ibid., 132, author's emphasis.

17 This approach is not intended to discount the fact that the cross also illumines the meaning of the sacrifices. Its justification is that the NT writers speak of Christ's death in terms of the typical sacrifices. Hence, the type may at times serve to restrain freewheeling theological speculations.

18 Ellen G. White, 1SM 107.

19 "Wenham notes . . . that the distinctive testimony of the guilt offering is satisfaction. Thus, in the present verse [Isa 53:10] the death of the Servant satisfied both the needs of sinful people before God and the 'needs'/requirements of God in relation to his broken law and offended holiness" (J. Alec Motyer, *The Prophecy of Isaiah,* 439).

20 "Through disobedience Adam fell. The law of God had been broken. The divine government had been dishonored, and justice demanded that the penalty of transgression be paid" (Ellen G. White, 1SM 308). "Justice demands that sin be not merely pardoned, but the death penalty must be executed. God, in the gift of His only-begotten Son, met both these requirements. By dying in man's stead, Christ exhausted the penalty and provided a pardon" (Id., 1SM 340). "At the cross justice was satisfied" (Id., 1SM 349).

21 "Hilaskomai," AG 376. For a helpful discussion of the *hilaskomai* word group, see Leon Morris, *The Atonement* (Leicester, England: InterVarsity Press, 1983), 151-176. Their use in terms of the cross atonement occur in the NT as follows: *Hilaskomai* (verb), Heb 2:17; *hilasmos* (noun), 1 John 2:2; 4:10; *hilastērion* (noun), Rom 3:25; Heb 9:5 (term is used for the mercyseat of the ark).

22 Morris, *The Atonement,* 151.

23 "The hand of the offerer was to be placed on the animal's head in symbolic acknowledgment of the substitution of the animal for the worshiper [Lev 1:4]. This is specified in the burnt offering and also in the fellowship [peace] offering (3:2, 8, 13) and the sin offering (4:4, 15, 24, 29, 33). The ritual seems to be self-explanatory but is interpreted clearly in connection with the Day of Atonement (16:21). When hands are laid on the animal and sins are confessed, the sins are in symbol transferred to the animal" (R. Laird Harris, "Leviticus," ExpBC 2:537. Used by permission of Zondervan Publishing House).

24 "Christ was treated as we deserve, that we might be treated as He deserves. He was condemned for our sins, in which He had no share, that we might be justified by His righteousness, in which we had no share. He suffered the death which was ours, that we might receive the life which was His. 'With His stripes we are healed' " (Ellen G. White, DA 25).

25 Lev 1:3; 3:1; 4:3, 23, 28, 32; 6:6, etc. The only exception allowed was an animal which had "a part too long or too short." It would be accepted for a freewill offering (Lev 22:23).

26 "Be careful, exceedingly careful as to how you dwell upon the human nature of Christ. *Do not set Him before the people as a man with the propensities of sin.* He is the second Adam. The first Adam was created a pure, sinless being, without a taint of sin upon him; he was in the image of God. He could fall, and he did fall through transgressing. Because of sin his posterity was born with inherent propensities of disobedience. *But* Jesus Christ was the only begotten Son of God. He took upon Himself human nature, and was tempted in all points as human nature is tempted. He could have sinned; He could have fallen, *but not for one moment was there in Him an evil propensity*" (Ellen G. White, SDABC 5:1128, emphasis added). "Christ did not possess the same sinful, corrupt, fallen disloyalty we possess, *for then He could not be a perfect offering.*" (Id., 3SM 131, emphasis added).

27 T. J. Crawford, *Doctrine of Holy Scriptures,* 237, 241 (author's emphasis) cited in Stott, *The Cross of Christ,* 138.

28 A technical term of the sacrificial system to which Peter's language alludes. See "*Anapherō,*" AG 62.

29 According to Johh R. W. Stott, *The Cross of Christ,* 145.

30 "*Lutron,*" AG 483.

31 "*Anti,*" AG 72, 73.

32 "Many interpreters take the aorist rigorously, and render: because all sinned, i.e., in the sin of Adam [Rom 5:12]. . . . This is supported by an appeal to 2 Cor v. 14 . . . : the death of one was the death of all; so here, the sin of one was the sin of all" (James Denney, St. Paul's Epistle to the Romans. The EGT 2:627).

33 Russell Holt, "By the Book," *Signs of the Times,* November 1993, 20 (emphasis added).

34 "*Ara,*" AG 103.

35 Other explanations, in harmony with the rest of Scripture, have been suggested for this terse expression. See SDABC 6:866, 867; Murray J. Harris, *2 Corinthians,* ExpBC 10:351, 352.

36 Stott, *The Cross of Christ,* 197, 198.

37 "The Godhead was stirred with pity for the race, and the Father, the Son, and the Holy Spirit gave Themselves to the working out of the plan of redemption. In order fully to carry out this plan, it was decided that Christ, the only-begotten Son of God, should give Himself an offering for sin. What line can measure the depth of this love? God would make it impossible for man to say that He could have done more. With Christ He gave all the resources of heaven, that nothing might be wanting in the plan for man's uplifting. Here is love—the contemplation of which should fill the soul with inexpressible gratitude! Oh, what love, what matchless love! The contemplation of this love will cleanse the soul from

all selfishness. It will lead the disciple to deny self, take up the cross, and follow
the Redeemer" (Ellen G. White, CH 222, 223).

38 " 'Authority' means that he was not the helpless victim of his enemies' violence,
but that he had both the right and the power to become the instrument of
reconciliation between man and God and between Jew and Gentile" (Merrill C.
Tenney, *The Gospel of John*, ExpBC 9:110. Used by permission of Zondervan
Publishing House).

39 Stott, *The Cross of Christ*, 152.

40 Ibid., 159.

41 Ibid., 159, 160.

42 Ibid., 220.

6

Bridging the Chasm

In the religion of Israel the shedding of sacrificial blood symbolized a life given, a life laid down in behalf of the offerer. The blood "spoke" of propitiation—averting the divine wrath; of expiation—making amends; and of gracious forgiveness. But another aspect in the process of reconciliation is accentuated by the office of the priesthood: *the necessity for mediation between God and man.*

The concept of a mediating priest is only lightly foreshadowed in the father or leading patriarch in pre-Mosaic times who offered sacrifices and prayers in behalf of the family/tribe. But in the Israelite nation the priesthood is a fully developed institution. The entire sanctuary service is grounded in its mediatory function. Whereas the patriarchal worship centered on the sacrifice, in Isreal there is a subtle shift to a focus on the ministry of an official priesthood. For example, in Israel the sacrifices had no validity in themselves. Not until the attending priest had administered the blood in the appropriate manner, did the sacrifice meet the soul needs of the repentant sinner.[1] *Priestly ministration was an absolute necessity.* This fact in the type points to the necessity for Christ's priestly ministry under the New Covenant arrangement.

But why this added emphasis? Was sin not atoned for in the sacrifice? Why the function of a priest? What insight into the plan of salvation was God desiring to clarify both for Israel and for us in the Christian Era?

Seriousness of Sin's Intrusion

The common Hebrew word for priest is *kōhēn*. Many scholars believe the term derives from the verb *kûn*, "to stand." Thus the root idea of "priest" is taken to mean "one who stands before God as His servant, or minister."[2] The theocentric nature of the priesthood is indeed stressed in the Scriptures. The priests are "to serve *me* [God] as priests," "for *my* priesthood," literally, "to me" and "for me," respectively (Exod 28:1, 3, 4). The priesthood was appointed by God and ministered for God. The terminology and concept suggests that priests were appointed both to represent God to the people, and the people to God.

The institution of a priesthood (like the attribute of God's holiness) stresses the seriousness of sin, the sharp cleavage it has made between the Creator and the creature. How could a sinful humanity reach the holy God who "dwells in unapproachable light, whom no man has ever seen or can see" (1 Tim 6:16)? And conversely, How could a holy God communicate with such without destroying them? (cf. Deut 4:24; Heb 12:29).

The physical arrangements of the sanctuary itself continuously witnessed to the enormous estrangement sin had caused. Although the tabernacle/temple sanctuary stood within the nation, surrounded by the tents or homes of the people, yet even the most spiritual Israelite dared not enter either of its apartments, lest he incur immediate death. How then could a viable union between God and humanity ever be restored?

Christ's Mediatorial Role

Since God the Father created all things through the agency of Christ in His preexistent state as God the Son,[3] we may correctly assume that the latter has served as the channel of communication between heaven and earth from the beginning.[4] Jacob received the earliest hint of such a "channel" in his dream at Bethel. "He dreamed that there was a ladder set up on the earth, and the top of it reached to heaven; and behold, the angels of God were ascending and descending on it!" (Gen 28:12). Jesus alluded to Jacob's dream and identified Himself as the ladder. "Truly, truly, I say to you, you will see heaven opened, and the angels of God ascending and descending upon the Son of man." (John 1:51).[5] By virtue of God the Son, and the saving acts *He would perform,* angels were allowed to communicate and minister to earth's inhabitants prior to His first advent (cf. Heb 1:14).

Christ exercises His mediatorial function through His office as our high priest.[6] Two important requirements were essential for this position: (1) His incarnation, and (2) His sacrificial death.

Incarnation

Although incomprehensible to the human mind, the incarnation of God the Son is the foundation stone in the plan of salvation. The whole edifice of redemption rests upon it. "Great indeed, we confess, is the mystery of our religion: He [God the Son] was manifested in the flesh" (1 Tim 3:16). The incarnation qualified Christ for priesthood in two important ways.

First, the incarnation provided Heaven *a channel* through which a true representation of the character of the Deity could be revealed to humanity. "The *Word* [God the Son] became flesh and dwelt among us, full of grace and truth; we have beheld his glory, glory as of the only Son from the Father." "No one has ever seen God; the only Son, who is in the bosom of the Father, *he has made him known*" (John 1:14, 18). So successful was Christ in this aspect of His earthly ministry, He could say to His disciples, "He who has seen me has seen the Father" (John 14:9). As "the Word," Christ makes God's thoughts and messages audible and understandable to the human family. This is part of His task: to speak for Deity, to reveal God.

Second, the incarnation enabled God the Son to become *humanity's representative.* "Every high priest *chosen from among men* is appointed *to act on behalf of men* in relation to God, to offer gifts and sacrifices for sins" (Heb 5:1). Christ could not have functioned in a priestly role unless He had assumed our humanity. It was essential for His priestly mediation that He take our nature. "Since therefore the children share in flesh and blood, he himself likewise partook of the same nature, . . . Therefore he had to be made like his brethren in every respect, *so that he might become a merciful and faithful high priest in the service of God,* to make expiation for the sins of the people" (Heb 2:14-17).

Sacrificial Death

In the typical service the high priest not only represented God to the people and the people to God, but he functioned essentially to bring reconciliation between the two estranged parties. He did this by administering the sacrificial blood to remove the barrier erected by sin. A priest could not function in his central role if he did not have sacrificial blood to minister. The same is true of Jesus Christ in His role as humanity's high priest. "For every high priest is appointed to offer gifts and sacrifices; hence *it is necessary* for this priest [Christ Jesus] also to have something to offer" (Heb 8:3; cf. 5:1). That "something," of course, is the merit of His atoning death on Calvary.

The incarnation not only qualified God the Son to be a priestly representative for man as well as for the Deity, but it enabled Him to lay down His life as "a single," all-sufficient "sacrifice for sins" (Heb 10:12). "We see Jesus, who for a little while was made lower than the angels, . . . *so that by the grace of God he might taste death for every one*" (Heb 2:9). "Though he was in the form of God, [He] did not count equality with God a thing to be grasped, but emptied himself, taking the form of a servant, being born in the likeness of men. And being found in human form he humbled himself and *became obedient unto death, even death on a cross*" (Phil 2:6-8).

It was both His incarnation and sacrificial death on Calvary that qualified Jesus Christ to "become a merciful and faithful high priest in things pertaining to God, to make propitiation for the sins of the people" (Heb 2:17, NASB). When Christ entered the heavenly sanctuary to begin His priestly office, subsequent to His ascension, He ministered the merits of "his own blood" (Heb 9:12) "in the presence of God on our behalf" (Heb 9:24).

While God the Son, as Creator, has always been the channel of communication between heaven and earth, it was His incarnation and atoning death that enabled Him to act as God's priestly mediator in the fullest sense of those terms: "For there is one God, and there is *one mediator [mesitēs]* between God and men, *the man* Christ Jesus, who *gave himself as a ransom* for all" (1 Tim 2:5, 6). In this passage the apostle links Christ's role as mediator with both His humanity and His death, the qualifying prerequisites.

"To mediate," as a simple dictionary definition might read, is "to interpose between parties as the equal friend of each, especially to effect a reconciliation." God and humanity are the two parties in the moral controversy ongoing presently in the universe. Only Jesus Christ, who is truly Divine and truly human, can mediate effectively between the Deity on the one hand and creaturely humanity on the other as an "equal friend" of both.[7]

The question may be raised, If Jesus Christ did not enter into priestly office *until* His ascension (after having qualified by His incarnation and death), how did God deal with sinners before that time?

As we will observe again, *sacrifice and priestly application of that sacrifice always go together. They are never separated in Scripture.* No sacrifice in the sanctuary system stood alone and atoned for sin by itself. It had significance *only* when the priest ministered the blood. Thus, the priesthood of Jesus Christ could not precede His incarnation and death. Rather, it must follow His death, because it is the merits of His sinless life and atoning death that He applies to repentant sinners who come to God.

Prior to Christ's death and priesthood, sinners sought God through the sacrificial system of the sanctuary (cf. Heb 9:8, NEB). Although animal blood could not in reality take away human sin and guilt (Heb 10:4), God "in his divine forbearance . . . passed over" this fact (Rom 3:25), and forgave repentant sinners on the basis of their faith in the saving acts of the Messiah yet to come. Christ's actual death and actual priestly application of the merits of His atonement to repentant sinners were both prefigured in the typical sanctuary and provided the redemption which the believers of previous ages received by faith and held by promise (cf. Heb 9:15).

Priesthood: Type and Antitype

In the sanctuary system the chasm which sin caused between God and humanity is symbolically bridged by the priesthood composed of persons certified by God to mediate between Him and His people. Through the various ministries of the priesthood, Israel could approach the holy God in penitence, praise, and worship, confidently expecting full acceptance from God.

Typical Priesthoods

Actually, in the letter to the Hebrews the apostle discusses two priesthoods: that of Melchizedek, a king-priest who lived in Abraham's time, and that of the Levitical (or Aaronic) priesthood of Israel. Both are treated as types foreshadowing the priesthood of Jesus Christ.[8] "Christ did not exalt himself to be made a high priest, but was appointed by him who said to him, . . . 'Thou art a priest for ever, after the order of Melchizedek' " (Heb 5:5, 6). "Now the point in what we are saying is this: we have such a high priest, one who is seated at the right hand of the throne of the Majesty in heaven, a minister in the sanctuary and the true tent which is set up not by man but by the Lord" (Heb 8:1, 2).

Thus, the functioning of the priesthood of Jesus Christ is the true—and only—bridge across the gulf that separates sinful man from a holy God. Jesus Himself underscored this fact when He said to His disciples, "I am the way, and the truth, and the life; *no one comes to the Father, but by me*" (John 14:6). The Epistle to the Hebrews links Christ as *the only way* to the Father with His intercessory priesthood, "He [Jesus Christ] is able for all time to save those who draw near to God *through him [di' autou],* since he always lives *to make intercession* for them" (Heb 7:25).

Heavenly and Earthly Spheres United

In a figurative sense the Israelite high priest belonged to both the heavenly and earthly spheres. If the priestly concept be subsumed under the category of

the high priest,[9] this fact may be seen reflected in his clothing. The so-called
"inner garments," worn by all priests—tunic, breeches, girdle, and head-
gear—were of materials and workmanship similar to the hangings of the court.
The "outer garments" worn only by the high priest—blue robe, ephod,
breastpiece, and turban with the inscribed golden plate—were made of material and workmanship similar to the inner curtains and inner veil of the
tabernacle.

These two kinds of clothing may have been designed to emphasize the
mediatorial role of the high priest (and his associates) who provided a living
link between the Deity residing within the tabernacle and the people who
assembled to worship outside at the entrance to the court. It would not be
difficult to perceive that the high priest actually belonged to two different
realms—the heavenly dwelling place of God (as symbolized by the tabernacle)
and the earthly dwelling place of mankind (as symbolized by the court).

The NT writers never doubt the unique nature and role of Jesus Christ on
this point. The apostle Paul declares, "For in him [the human Jesus Christ] the
whole fulness of deity dwells bodily" (Col 2:9). Only Jesus Christ, the
God-man, who belongs to both "worlds"—heaven and earth—could satisfac-
torily discharge the priestly mediatorial task the plan of salvation demands.

Qualifications

As with the sacrificial animal, so with the priest. Both were required to be
without physical blemish. "No man of the descendants of Aaron the priest who
has a blemish shall come near to offer the Lord's offerings by fire; since he
has a blemish, he shall not come near to offer the bread of his God. . . . he shall
not come near the veil or approach the altar" (Lev 21:21-23). Physical
wholeness in the type denoted the moral holiness of the antitype and pointed
to the moral excellence and sinless perfection of Jesus Christ.

"For it was fitting that we should have such a high priest, holy, blameless,
unstained, separated from sinners, exalted above the heavens" (Heb 7:26). In
His sinlessness Christ can stand before a holy God to intercede for sinners
without fear of rejection or dismissal. But although He is "separated from
sinners" in His holiness, "He is not ashamed" to call repentant sinners His
"brethren" (Heb 2:11).

It was assumed in the Levitical system that because of his own sinful
weaknesses, a high priest would "deal gently with the ignorant and wayward"
(Heb 5:2)—in other words, would be approachable by even the most fallen.
Although Jesus Christ, unlike Israel's high priests, was sinless, yet His
incarnation placed Him in the society of humanity where He experienced our

lot. His trials and temptations prepared Him to render a compassionate, understanding priesthood.

"For it was fitting that he [God], . . . in bringing many sons to glory, should make the pioneer of their salvation perfect [*teleioō,* complete] through suffering." "For because he himself has suffered and been tempted, he is able to help those who are tempted" (Heb 2:10, 18).

"Although he was a Son, he learned obedience through what he suffered; and being made *perfect* [*teleioō,* complete] he became the source of eternal salvation to all who obey him, being designated by God a high priest after the order of Melchizedek" (Heb 5:8-10).

In these passages the apostle is *not* implying that Jesus was morally imperfect. He lived in fact "without sinning" (Heb 4:15). Rather, he is speaking of Christ's trials and temptations as maturing or completing His human experience so as to make Him (for us) a more approachable High Priest.

In a third passage he makes this point specific: "Since therefore we have a great high priest who has passed through the heavens, Jesus the Son of God, let us hold fast to the religion we profess. For ours is not a high priest unable to sympathize with our weaknesses, but one who, because of his likeness to us, has been tested every way, only without sin. Let us therefore boldly approach the throne of our gracious God, where we may receive mercy and in his grace find timely help" (Heb 4:14-16, NEB).

It is significant that with the advent of the antitype, Jesus, there is a shift from a somewhat impersonal ritual to a dynamic experience with a real Person! The Christian faith centers on a living Christ, who, fully understanding us by means of His own experience, invites us to come to God through Him!

Atonement by Mediation

We have already observed that sacrifices had no validity in themselves until a priest administered the blood in the required manner. The repentant sinner needed the priest to represent him to God by applying the sacrificial blood (its merits, so to speak) in his behalf. Not until this procedure was completed was he forgiven.

The sanctuary complex was considered the dwelling place of God (Exod 25:8); consequently, it may be understood as representing God Himself. When the priest placed some of the blood of a sin offering on the horns of the altar in the court, or, in some cases, on the horns of the golden altar along with sprinkling some before the inner veil, he was, in effect, mediating before God the merits of the slain sacrifice in behalf of the repentant sinner who had only moments before confessed his sins on the head of the sacrifice. In this manner, the priest offered "sacrifices for sins" (Heb 5:1), and made "propitiation [*hilaskomai;* and expiation] for the sins of the people" (Heb 2:17, NASB). And God, in His graciousness, accepted the sacrificial substitute and forgave the penitent his sins.[10]

This mediatorial ministry of the priest—this *application* of sacrificial blood to the altars and before the veil of the sanctuary (= God)—was viewed by Israel as one aspect of making atonement for sin. It was atonement by mediation. "Then the priest shall take some of the blood of the sin offering with his finger and put it on the horns of the altar of burnt offering, and . . . shall burn [the fat] . . . on the altar, . . . and the priest *shall make atonement [kipper] for him* for the sin which he has committed, *and he shall be forgiven*" (Lev 4:35).

The English term *atonement* carries the idea of a reconciliation between two estranged parties. Just as the atoning death of Christ (in a legal, objective sense) reconciled *the world* to God (2 Cor 5:18), just so the mediation, or application, of the merits of His sinless life and substitutionary death on behalf of the penitent believer makes reconciliation with God a *personal reality*. But, as in the type, so in the antitype reality: No personal forgiveness and reconciliation occurs until the priestly Christ applies His merits before God on behalf of the repentant sinner, and the latter receives—by an intelligent faith—God's promised pardon and salvation.

Transfer of Sin/Responsibility

The blood of a sin offering—upon which the sins of an individual (or, the congregation) had been confessed—appears to have had a *double* function in the typical rites. (1) It secured forgiveness for the repentant sinner/congregation. (2) It transferred the confessed sins and responsibility to the sanctuary. Thus, atonement by priestly mediation in the typical sanctuary foreshadowed more than the simple forgiveness or pardon for sins. Part of the priestly process touched on another aspect of the plan of salvation, namely, the ultimate eradication of sin.

The sanctuary rituals portrayed this latter truth in two major steps: First, the removal of sin and guilt *from* the repentant sinner (or, congregation) *to* the sanctuary itself. Second, the removal *from* the sanctuary of the accountability of confessed sins deposited there, and the disposal of the sin problem in its entirety. The ultimate removal of the sin problem is the central focus of the yearly service on the Day of Atonement, a subject we will explore in the next chapter.

In our present remarks we will confine ourselves to the biblical data dealing with the first step: the transfer of sin and guilt from the repentant sinner/congregation to the sanctuary. This was accomplished by either of two different procedures—*a repeated ritual statement,* as it were, to assure contrite sinners of Heaven's willingness to deliver humanity from the reign of sin and its instigator, Satan. The procedures involved: (1) the priestly manipulation of the blood of the sin offering, and (2) the priestly eating of its flesh.

Manipulation of the blood. The priests administered sacrificial blood according to specific directions. After the offerer had laid his hand upon the head of the sacrifice, had confessed his sin upon it, and had slain the animal, the attending priest caught the blood in a bason.

He now handled the blood in one of two ways. If the sin offering had been sacrificed for an erring priest or for the sin of the entire congregation, he entered the sanctuary and sprinkled the blood seven times before the inner veil and placed some of it on the horns of the golden altar of incense (Lev 4:3-7, 16-18). But in the cases of rulers and common persons, the priest did not enter the sanctuary. Instead, he placed some of the blood upon the horns of the altar in the court with his finger (Lev 4:25, 30, 34). The blood of a guilt offering was "thrown on the altar [of burnt offering] round about" by the priest (Lev 7:2). In these different ways the blood of the substituting sacrifice was brought by the priest to the sanctuary and applied to its altars or sprinkled before the inner veil.

Eating the flesh of the sin/guilt offering. When the priest applied the blood of a sin/guilt offering to the altar in the court, he also ate a portion of the sacrifice. "The priest who offers it for sin shall eat it; in a holy place it shall be eaten, in the court of the tent of meeting. . . . Every male among the priests may eat of it; it is most holy" (Lev 6:26-29; cf. Lev 7:1, 6, 7).

The rule of thumb was, If the blood of the sin offering was sprinkled before the inner veil and applied to the horns of the golden altar, then *its carcass was burned* outside the camp (apart from the fat which was always burned on the altar). But if the blood was only applied to the altar in the court, then a portion of *the animal's flesh was eaten by the priest* (cf. Lev 6:30). Thus, *the blood of every sin offering* was applied to the sanctuary—either to the altar of burnt offering or to the golden altar within and before the inner veil. The eating of the flesh of the sacrifice occurred only when the blood was not administered within the holy place of the sanctuary. As we shall see, the priestly eating of the flesh will explain the significance of the priestly manipulation of the blood.

The significance of the priestly eating of the flesh of the sin offering is provided in a terrifying experience which occurred on the day the tabernacle-sanctuary service began. Among the several offerings Aaron presented before the Lord was a goat for a sin offering (Lev 9:3, 15). At a later hour, Aaron's two sons, Nadab and Abihu, who had been drinking, decided to use common fire in their censers to burn incense in the sanctuary. As they approached the entrance, they were instantly slain by an outburst of fire from the Lord. This sudden divine disapproval produced dismay and confusion, disrupting the ritual. In the aftermath certain procedures of the ceremony for that day were improperly carried out.

Later, as Moses reviewed the events of the day, he discovered that the goat for the sin offering had been burned, but its blood had not been sprinkled before the inner veil and also placed on the horns of the golden altar. Since the blood had not been administered within the sanctuary (proper procedure for this public sin offering for the congregation), the priests should have at least eaten the flesh of the sacrifice. Moses' inquiry clearly explains the meaning of this latter rite:

"Why have you not eaten the sin offering in the place of the sanctuary, since it is a thing most holy and *has been given to you that you may bear the iniquity of the congregation,*[11] *to make atonement for them* before the Lord? Behold, its blood was not brought into the inner part of the sanctuary. You certainly ought to have eaten it in the sanctuary, as I commanded" (Lev 10:17, 18).

If the priests *bore* (in figure) "the iniquity of the congregation" by eating the flesh of the sin offering, then it is evident that the sins confessed over the head of the sin offering goat had been ritually transferred from the congregation to the goat, and in turn to the priests—the personnel of the sanctuary.

It follows then, that sin and accountability were likewise transferred from the sinner to the sin offering and in turn to the sanctuary by the parallel blood manipulation when the attending priest administered the blood of the same offering to the altar in the court (or when, in other cases he administered the blood before the inner veil and on the horns of the golden altar). Both procedures—the priestly eating of the flesh and the priestly administration of the blood of a sin offering—taught the same thing: the transfer of sin and accountability from the repentant sinner (or congregation) ultimately to the sanctuary and its priestly personnel.[12]

The striking aspect about this transfer of sin and responsibility is not simply the transfer from the sinner to his substitute, the sin offering. That, of course, portrays in the symbolism a wonderful truth about Christ our Sin Bearer. But it is the further step, the transfer from the sacrifice to the sanctuary, that reveals another aspect of the salvation process. The *sanctuary* is the dwelling place of the holy God (Exod 25:8). By this further step the symbolism implies that the sanctuary (= God) assumed for the time being the penitent's sin and guilt, while the latter left the sanctuary fully forgiven and accepted.[13]

At this point, it is necessary to ask, What is the antitypical reality, the meaning of this figurative transference of sin and accountability from sinner to substitute, and what is Christ's priestly part in the antitype?

In the realm of reality—when a sinner is drawn in contrition and repentance by the Holy Spirit to accept Jesus Christ as his Saviour and Lord, Christ—in His office of high priest—intercedes His own merits before the Father in behalf of the penitent, assuming at the same time his/her sin and accountability, though He Himself is sinless. As the sinner's Substitute and Surety,[14] His atoning death is accepted by the Father as satisfying the claims of divine justice against the sinner. Christ's perfect obedience is accepted and accounted to the penitent, and he/she stands before God freely forgiven for Christ's sake and declared justified.[15] His/her name is enrolled in the Book of Life (Luke 10:30; Phil 4:3), and pardon is entered into the respective records. The penitent is graciously accepted as God's child (John 1:12; 1 John 3:1-3).

We will continue the discussion of the transfer of sin and accountability from the sinner to the sanctuary in the next chapter. For now, it will be helpful to round off our present study with a review and summarization of the priesthood's daily ministry—both in the type and its antitypical fulfillments in Christ. Here again the reader will observe a certain amount of overlap in the ritual portrayal of Christ's priestly activity.

Daily Ministration: Type and Antitype

The priestly ministry carried on in connection with the first apartment of the sanctuary may be characterized as *a ministration of forgiveness, reconciliation, and restoration.* It was a continuous ministry. The Hebrew word that highlights the various activities of service in relation to the first apartment or holy place is *tāmîd.* The word denotes the idea of "continual," "going on without interruption," that is, "continuously." Eventually, the term came to function as a noun (the *tāmîd*), apparently standing for the entire first apartment's continuous ministry described as "the continual" or "the daily."[16] The daily service involved the high priest and his associates, the altar of burnt offering in the court, and the three furnishings in the first apartment: the golden altar, the seven-branched lampstand, and the golden table with its 12 cakes of bread.

High priest/priests. Two items of the high priest's attire especially marked his role as the representative of the people and were part of the daily rites: the two onyx stones (one on each shoulder) and the 12 precious stones of the breastpiece which rested upon his chest. The names of the tribes of Israel were engraved on the stones, six on each shoulder stone, one each on the stones in the breastpiece (Exod 28:9-12, 29). "And you shall set the two stones upon the shoulder-pieces of the ephod, as *stones of remembrance* for the sons of Israel; and Aaron shall bear their names before the Lord upon his two shoulders for remembrance" (Exod 28:12). "So Aaron shall bear the names of the sons of Israel in the breastpiece of *judgment*[17] *upon his heart,* when he goes into the holy place, to bring them to *continual [tāmîd]* remembrance before the Lord. . . . thus Aaron shall bear the judgment of the people of Israel *upon his heart* before the Lord *continually [tāmîd]*" Exod 28:29, 30).

"Stones of remembrance" meant that the stones would cause God "to remember," "to recall to mind" His people Israel (though in reality the omniscient God never forgot them). In this ritual manner the high priest made a double representation of the people to God each time he entered the sanctuary. Thus, in the priestly type, Israel had continual and immediate access to God.

Naturally, the reality of Jesus Christ's priesthood greatly exceeds the human role-play of the type. "Through him [Jesus] we both [Jew and Gentile] *have access* in one Spirit to the Father" (Eph 2:18). "So now, my friends, the blood of Jesus makes us free to enter boldly into the sanctuary by the new, living way" (Heb 10:19, 20, NEB).

It is grand news we Christians can announce. Humanity has "a great high priest" who is able "to sympathize with our weaknesses," and who appeals to us to "draw near to the throne of grace, that we may receive mercy and find grace to help in time of need" Heb 4:14-16). Our High Priest knows us "by name" (John 10:2, 3), for we are engraved, not on inanimate stones, but "on the palms of [His] hands" (Isa 49:16). Unlike earthly attorneys, our priestly Advocate does not plead our innocence, for we are in truth needy sinners. Rather, He pleads in our behalf the merits of His atoning sacrifice—the only sacrifice that can purge our sins.[18]

Bronze altar of burnt offering. The daily ritual began with the renewing of the public morning and evening offering. "Now this is what you shall offer upon the altar: two lambs a year old day by day *continually [tāmîd]*. One lamb you shall offer in the morning, and the other lamb you shall offer in the evening. . . . It shall be a *continual [tāmîd]* burnt offering throughout your generations" (Exod 29:38-42). The public burnt offering burned slowly and continuously day and night, indicating the constant availability of the merits of the sacrifice. The ever-burning sacrifice extended forgiveness and acceptance to any who sought it.

In like manner Christ's merits, wrought out by His sinless life and atoning death are always available while mercy's door is open. "God exalted him at his right hand as Leader and Savior, *to give repentance to Israel and forgiveness of sins*" (Acts 5:31). He turns no one away who sincerely comes in prayer to God seeking pardon for his/her sins. "Him who comes to me I will not cast out," He assures (John 6:37). Divine forgiveness is provided at the outset of the Christian experience and also along the way whenever there is need. "If we walk in the light, as he is in the light, we have fellowship with one another, and *the blood of Jesus* his Son *cleanses* [continues to cleanse] us from all unrighteousness" (1 John 1:7).

The golden altar of incense. The golden altar, placed before the veil hanging across the entrance to the Second Apartment (the Most Holy Place), was used primarily for the burning of incense. (The blood of certain of the sin offerings was also placed on its horns). "Aaron shall burn fragrant incense on it; every morning when he dresses the lamps he shall burn it, and when Aaron sets up the lamps in the evening, he shall burn it, a *perpetual [tāmîd]* incense before the Lord throughout your generations" (Exod 30:7, 8).[19]

The renewal of the sacrifice on the altar of burnt offering morning and evening was coordinated with a similar renewing of the incense on the golden altar and a renewing of the oil in the lamps of the seven-branched lampstand. The morning and evening renewal of these three essentials of the typical, public worship (apart from private sacrifices offered by individuals throughout the day) came to be special hours of prayer for the Israelite people (cf. Luke 1:10; Acts 3:1).

In the visions given to John on Patmos we find the meaning of the priestly ministration of incense at the golden altar. In vision John saw an angel stand at the golden altar. He held in his hand a golden censer filled with incense. His task was "to mingle" the odor of the burning incense "with the prayers of the saints." The prophet observed that "the smoke of the incense rose with the prayers of the saints . . . before God" (Rev. 8:3, 4), implying that the pleasant-smelling incense made the prayers acceptable to God. The scene ritually and symbolically portrays Christ's intercessory ministry in heaven before God. But what must Christ add to our prayers as our high priest to make them pleasing and acceptable to the Father?

Jesus supplied the answer in His last conversations with His disciples before His arrest in Gethsemane. "Whatever *you ask in my name,* I will do it" (John 14:13, 14). "If you abide in me, and my words abide in you, ask whatever you will, and it shall be done for you." "So that whatever you *ask the Father in my name,* he may give it to you" (John 15:7, 16). "Truly, truly, I say to you, if you ask anything of the Father, he will give it to you *in my name.* Hitherto you have asked nothing *in my name;* ask, and you will receive, that your joy may be full" (John 16:23, 24).

Jesus is not suggesting we need only to tack His name onto our petitions to God in order to receive gracious answers. His words go deeper than that. He is asserting that it is *by virtue of Himself* that we have access to Deity and can expect to be heard. "No one comes to the Father, *but by me*" (John 14:6). As repentant sinners we are accepted with God *because* of Christ's saving acts. His merits, like incense, render our prayers acceptable to the Father when He intercedes at the same time for us.[20]

Thus, in the priestly ministry at the altar of incense, we witness in the ritual the foreshadowing of Jesus Christ's intercession in the heavenly sanctuary. "For Christ has entered, not into a sanctuary made with hands, a copy of the true one, but into heaven itself, *now to appear in the presence of God on our behalf*" (Heb 9:24). "Consequently he is able for all time to save those who draw near to God through him, since *he always lives to make intercession for them*" (Heb 7:25).

The menorah: seven-branched lampstand. The second object in the holy place connected with the daily, public worship was the menorah or seven-branched lampstand. The lampstand with its main shaft and six branches (three on either side) was hammered from a single talent of gold. It was in form a stylized almond tree or branch (Exod 25:31-40). The oil lamps, resting atop each branch, were attended by the priests twice a day—morning and evening (Exod 30:7, 8). "[Aaron] shall keep the lamps in order upon the lampstand of pure gold before the Lord *continually [tāmîd]*" (Lev 24:4).

Modern scholarship has focused on the art form of the menorah, and concludes that vegetal art forms in both the ancient Near East culture and the OT portray "a life theme." It is argued that the menorah with its life theme and lamps of fire symbolized the invisible Deity in the Israelite sanctuary.[21]

Certain biblical passages do indeed tend to support the view that the seven-branched lampstand symbolized the presence of God or some aspect of His attributes. Three passages contribute to our understanding:

1. Zechariah 4:1-14. The menorah the prophet Zechariah saw in vision appears as an adaptation of the sanctuary menorah. The focus is on *the oil* being piped to the seven lamps from two nearby olive trees. The vision implies that the oil which enables the lamps to burn is God's Spirit (vss. 5-6). The lamps themselves are identified as the "eyes of the Lord, which range through the whole earth" (vs. 10). In this instance, then, we see the all-powerful workings of God's Spirit to accomplish His purposes and are reminded of God's omniscience (all-knowing ability) and omnipresence.

2. Jeremiah 1:11. The lampstand, shaped as a stylized almond tree or branch, without doubt carried symbolic significance. The Hebrew word for "almond" (*šāqēd*) derives from the verb *šāqad* meaning "to watch," "to keep guard over," "to wake."[22] The almond tree was literally named the "wake-tree" or "watch-tree" because it was the earliest tree to "waken" and flower in the new growing season. The Lord used a representation of the almond tree to assure the prophet Jeremiah that He was "watching over [His] word to perform it" (Jer 1:11).

If the significance of the vegetal form of the lampstand (a life theme), of the almond (wakefulness/watchfulness), and of the angel's interpretation of the oil used in the seven lamps—and of the lamps themselves—of Zechariah's visionary menorah (God's Spirit; the Lord's eyes ranging the earth) be summarized, it may be inferred that the golden lampstand in the sanctuary had a symbolic meaning and was designed for more than a simple light source for the first apartment.

In addition to the ark of the covenant (in the Most Holy Place), the golden menorah in the holy place may also have symbolized the presence of God, placing an emphasis on His activity: to signify God as the source and sustainer of life (cf. Ps 36:9), the all-knowing and all-wise, ever-present Lord—ever awake and watching over His people (cf. Ps 121:1-4).

3. Revelation 4:5. The NT provides one further insight into the meaning of the golden menorah. In the representation of the heavenly temple John saw "seven lamps of fire burning before the throne." These are identified as "the seven Spirits of God" (Rev. 4:5, NASB). The context (see Rev. 1:4, 5) indicates that the expression, "the seven Spirits of God," is simply John's mode of referring to the Holy Spirit, the third person of the Godhead, in His multiple and complete (perfect) operations.

The "seven lamps" before the throne would be analogous to the seven-branched menorah in the earthly sanctuary. Thus, this NT passage places the capstone on the meaning of the lampstand hinted at in the OT. The menorah of the sanctuary symbolized the multiple operations of the life-giving, omniscient and omnipresent Holy Spirit.

This grand truth locks into the fact that it is by virtue of Christ's mediatorial, priestly office that the Holy Spirit carries on His ministry in the earth.[23] "He [God] saved us, not because of deeds done by us in righteousness, but in virtue of his own mercy, by the washing of regeneration and renewal in *the Holy Spirit, which he poured out upon us richly through [dia] Jesus Christ our Savior*" (Titus 3:5, 6). Jesus Christ, and only Jesus Christ, is *the channel* through Whom and by Whom the Holy Spirit reaches human hearts.

According to the apostle Peter, as soon as His inauguration as King-Priest at God's right hand was completed, Jesus commissioned the Holy Spirit to come to earth in Pentecostal fullness. "Being therefore exalted at the right hand of God, and having received from the Father the promise of the Holy Spirit, he [Jesus Christ] has poured out this which you see and hear" (Acts 2:33). Jesus' first priestly request was that the Father would permit Him to send the Holy Spirit (John 14:16, 26). "When the Counselor comes, whom I shall send to you from the Father, even the Spirit of truth, who proceeds from the Father, he will bear witness to me" (John 15:26).

The Holy Spirit—mediated to us through the priestly activity of Jesus—brings about conviction, conversion, and transformation of lives. It is His activity that stimulates character growth and restores "the image of God" within human hearts (John 16:8; 3:3-8; Gal 5:22; Col 3:10). Thus, the *typical,* priestly care of the menorah's lamps so that they burned brightly day and night escalates into the *actual,* multiple operations of the Holy Spirit directed in all His operations by humanity's High Priest, Jesus Christ!

The golden table/twelve cakes of bread. The significance of this article of furniture lies in the symbolism of the substances placed upon it: bread, incense, and wine. The bread is the only item discussed in detail. "And you shall set the bread of the Presence [literally, 'bread of (the) faces'] on the table before me *always [tāmîd]*" (Exod 25:30).

The expression, "bread of the Presence" should not be construed to mean that the bread symbolized the presence of God. The Hebrew phrase means that the sacred bread was placed or presented *before* or in the presence of the Lord in the sanctuary. The NT phraseology (in the Greek text) confirms the correctness of this view by describing the bread literally as "the presentation of the loaves" or "the loaves of presentation" (Heb 9:2; Mark 2:26; cf. Matt 12:4; Luke 6:4).[24]

Several important facts can be drawn from Leviticus 24:5-9 which shed light on the symbolism of the sacred bread:

1. The bread was regarded as a *sacrifice* (vs. 9).

2. It was a continuous sacrifice (*tāmîd*), always before the Lord (vs. 8).

3. It was a *renewed* offering (vs. 8). Each Sabbath a priest replaced the old bread with fresh.

4. Israel made this bread offering to God through their priestly representative (vs. 8).

5. The 12 cakes, placed in two rows of six each, denoted the 12 tribes of Israel. They probably functioned in a manner similar to the two sets of stones in the high priest's attire: "to remind" God of Israel's physical and

spiritual needs for nourishment. This inference is supported by the expression applied to the accompanying frankincense: "a memorial portion" ('azkārāh), a term derived from zākar, "to remember" (vss. 5-7).

6. The bread offering was viewed as a perpetual obligation on Israel's part—"a covenant for ever"—and it became a portion of the priests' food allotment granted to them from all the offerings (vss. 8, 9).[25]

As we have stated, Israelite offerings were *pictorial* prayers, illustrated prayers. The offering, a concrete object, had a related spiritual dimension that the worshiper sought. If he presented a sin offering, he confessed his sin and guilt, but he sought forgiveness. In a similar manner, it may be inferred that when Israel offered (through the priesthood) the twelve cakes of bread before God, she expressed—in a pictorial manner not only thanksgiving for His bounties, but also a continuous petition for both physical and spiritual food.

Israel's continuous offering of the sacred bread would have been equivalent to the Christian petition, "Give us this day our *daily* bread" (Matt 6:11). The fact that incense was linked with the bread and burned on the golden altar might imply that the prayer was heard and rendered acceptable to God through the intercession of the mediating priest.

In light of the sermon Jesus gave the Galileans on "the living bread," we may infer that just as the sacrifices and priesthood foreshadowed Christ's sacrifice and priesthood, so also the bread foreshadowed the essential, spiritual nourishment the coming Messiah would provide, as well as humanity's great need that constituted an urgent plea to God for help. "Jesus said to them, 'I am the bread of life; he who comes to me shall not hunger, and he who believes in me shall never thirst' " (John 6:35).

In the sanctuary the table was always "spread," and the reminder was always present, "That man does not live by bread alone, but that man lives by everything that proceeds out of the mouth of the Lord" (Deut 8:3). In the Christian Era that "word of the Lord" is especially spoken to us by our heavenly High Priest. And our prayer should ever be, "Bread of heaven, Bread of heaven, Feed me till I want no more."[26]

Summary

We draw attention once more to the key word tāmîd which so strikingly describes the day-by-day ministry of the priests in the earthly sanctuary: the ever-burning sacrifice (tāmîd); the ever-burning incense (tāmîd); the ever-burning lamps (tāmîd); the ever-present bread before the Lord (tāmîd); and the ever-present priest bearing the names of the people before God (tāmîd).

All systems were "Go" for the salvation of sinners. All that was necessary for forgiveness and restoration was typically provided.

The same is true of Christ's antitypical ministry in the heavenly sanctuary. All systems are "Go" too for the salvation of a world. Through Christ's high priestly mediation of the Holy Spirit sinners are convicted, converted, restored. Christ ever impleads, as man's intercessor, the merits of His sinless life and atoning death before the Father. Through the Spirit He provides spiritual truth and understanding that believers may grow in grace and spiritual knowledge.

The priestly ministry in connection with the first apartment in both type and antitype is *primarily individual-centered.* It is concerned with reconciling the sinner to God by providing a way to satisfy divine justice and securing for the penitent both forgiveness and spiritual growth. This priestly activity is thus focused on the doctrinal areas of justification and sanctification upon which the NT elaborates in plain language without symbolic ritualism.

Moreover these subjects of the first apartment ministry in type are also the concerns of Christ's antitypical ministry in the heavenly sanctuary. Hence, we properly describe His initial high priestly service as a *ministry of forgiveness, reconciliation, and restoration.* Although our High Priest assumes another aspect of ministration typified by the rituals related to the Second Apartment of the sanctuary, He never ceases His ministry of forgiveness and restoration until human probation closes.[27] Praise God! Christ has bridged the chasm!

--------- ♦ ---------

Endnotes

1 M. L. Andreasen, *The Sanctuary Service,* 47.

2 R. Abba, "Priests and Levites," *IDB* 3:877.

3 Heb 1:1, 2; Col 1:16, 17; John 1:1-3, 10.

4 "Christ was appointed to the office of Mediator from the creation of God, set up from everlasting to be our substitute and surety" (Ellen G. White, RH, April 5, 1906). "The Father has given the world into the hands of his Son, that through his mediatorial work he may completely vindicate the holiness and the abiding claims of every precept of the divine law" (Id., *BE,* January, 1887).

5 "Since the sin of our first parents there has been no direct communication between God and man. The Father has given the world into the hands of Christ, that through His mediatorial work He may redeem man and vindicate the authority and holiness of the law of God. All the communion between heaven and the

fallen race has been through Christ" (Ellen G. White, PP 366).

6 "Christ was the foundation and life of the temple. Its services were typical of the sacrifice of the Son of God. The priesthood was established to represent the mediatorial character and work of Christ" (Ellen G. White, DA 165).

7 "To be of any use, a bridge across a chasm or river must be anchored on both sides. Christ has closed the gap between deity and humanity. He has crossed the grand canyon, so deep and wide between heaven and earth. He has bridged the chasm that separated man from God. With one foot planted in eternity, he planted the other in time. He who was the eternal Son of God became the Son of Man. And across this bridge, the man Christ Jesus, we can come into the very presence of God, knowing that we are accepted because we have a Mediator" (Ralph Earle, *1 Timothy*, ExpBC 11:358. Used by permission of Zondervan Publishing House).

8 The Epistle to the Hebrews refers to both the Melchizedek and Levitical priest-hoods. By NT times the Jews had lost sight of the *symbolic* significance of the sanctuary rituals and had embraced the system as an end in itself. Discouraged Christian Jews, at the time of the writing of the Epistle, were inclined to drift back to the Temple and the worn-out rituals of the Judaism they had previously abandoned to become Christians. The apostle sought to prevent their falling away. He argued that God, who had established the Levitical priesthood with its *typical* sanctuary, had always intended to displace it by the *real* priesthood of the Messiah in the *real* heavenly sanctuary (which the former foreshadowed, Heb 8:4, 5).

He proves his point by observing that in Ps 110:4 God foretold that the Messiah would be a "priest for ever after the order of Melchizedek" (cf. Heb 5:5, 6, 10; 6:20). Thus Christ's priesthood (after the order of Melchizedek) *displaces* the old, typical Levitical order of priesthood by the command of God Himself. He notes that the Levitical system had only been designed as a type and could not in itself purge away moral sin. "Now if perfection [actual atonement for sin] had been attainable through the Levitical priesthood . . . , what further need would there have been for another priest to arise after the order of Melchizedek, rather than one named after the order of Aaron [Levitical]? *For when there is a change in the priesthood, there is necessarily a change in the* [ritual] *law as well*" (Heb 7:11, 12). "A former commandment [the Levitical ritual law] *is set aside* because of its weakness and uselessness (for the [ritual] law made nothing perfect)" (Heb 7:18, 19). Consequently, the apostle appeals to his discouraged brethren to look away from the worn-out types of the Levitical system to their true High Priest, Jesus Christ, and His ministry for them in the heavenly temple-sanctuary.

We should be careful to note, however, that the apostle's argument in no wise depreciates *the typical significance* of the Levitical system. He will con-tinually refer to it as he points out "the better" fulfillments. Thus, both the priesthoods of the Levitical system and that of Melchizedek serve to give us a clearer understanding of the nature and scope of Christ's actual priestly ministrations in the heavenly sanctuary. See "Daniel and Revelation Committee Report," *Issues in the Book of Hebrews,* DARCOM, 4:1-3

9 The high priest was *the* mediator for all Israel; the common priests were his assistants. Essentially, the two categories coalesce into one priesthood with the common priests enabling the high priest to accomplish his ministrations which he, physically speaking, could not have accomplished alone. The high priest could perform any duty required by the office of priesthood, but the common priest was restricted from ministry in the Most Holy Place. Just as every sacrifice pointed to the cross, so every priest, and particularly the high priest, foreshadowed Christ's priesthood in the heavenly sanctuary. See Siegfried H. Horn, "Priest," SDABD 875ff.

10 It is sometimes suggested that the placing of sacrificial blood on the horns of the altars and the sprinkling of it before the veil served *to record* the sins in the sanctuary. But sin is recorded when it is committed, not when it is confessed! Since Israel understood the matter of heavenly records, it is best to see the application of the blood to the sanctuary complex as simply portraying in a ritual format the priestly pleading before God of the merits of the sacrifice in behalf of the repentant sinner.

11 The phrase "to bear iniquity" (*nāśāʼ ʻāwôn,* cf. Lev 10:17; Exod 28:38) "is used practically always in Leviticus in the sense of 'to bear sin and become responsible for it' (Lev 5:1, 17; 7:18; 10:17; 17:16; 19:8; 20:17, 19; 22:16). In Leviticus it has a negative meaning. To bear sin, to be responsible for it, means to be liable to punishment (7:18, 20, 21; 19:8). . . . But whenever *nāśāʼ ʻawôn* is used in the absolute sense, it really means to be responsible for sin and liable to punishment." "It appears to us that the ritual of the eating of the flesh clearly indicates that there is a transfer of sin in the Hebrew sacrificial system. Sin was transferred to the sacrificial victim. How was it transferred? There is only one answer to that question. Through the laying on of hands the sin of the offerer was transferred to the victim. By eating a portion of the flesh of the animal the priest bore it also" (Angel M. Rodriquez, "Transfer of Sin in Leviticus," DARCOM 3:186, 187, 188).

12 "Both ceremonies [administering the blood/eating the flesh] alike symbolized the transfer of the sin from the penitent to the sanctuary" (Ellen G. White, PP 355).

13 See "Editorial Synopsis," DARCOM 3:170, 171.

14 As humanity's High Priest, Jesus is described as "the *surety* (*egguos,* guarantee) of a better covenant [the new covenant]" (Heb 7:22). The term "surety" becomes quite personal when we realize that "Jesus stands as a continuing guarantor and that in two directions. He guarantees to men that God will fulfill his covenant of forgiveness, and *he guarantees to God that those who are in him are acceptable*" (Leon Morris, *Hebrews,* ExpBC 12:70, emphasis added. Used

by permission of Zondervan Publishing House).

"Christ has pledged Himself to be our substitute and surety, and He neglects no one. There is an inexhaustible fund of perfect obedience accruing from His obedience. In heaven His merits, His self-denial and self-sacrifice, are treasured as incense to be offered up with the prayers of His people. . . . Christ has pledged Himself to intercede in our behalf, and *the Father always hears the Son*" (Ellen G. White, SD 22, emphasis added).

15 "The great work that is wrought for the sinner who is spotted and stained by evil is the work of justification. By Him who speaketh truth he is declared righteous. The Lord imputes unto the believer the righteousness of Christ and pronounces him righteous before the universe. *He transfers his sins to Jesus, the sinner's representative, substitute, and surety.* Upon Christ He lays the iniquity of every soul that believeth. 'He hath made him to be sin for us, who knew no sin; that we might be made the righteousness of God in him' (2 Cor 5:21)" (Ellen G. White, 1SM 392, emphasis added).

16 "*Tāmîd,*" BDB 556. See also Angel M. Rodríguez, "Significance of the Cultic Language in Daniel 8:9-14," DARCOM 2:532, 533.

17 Probably named "breastpiece of judgment" because it also contained the Urim and Thummim, "the two oracular stones" the high priest employed at times to determine the will or "judgment" of God. See Num 27:21. The article apparently had no legal function and did not relate to the eschatological judgment as some have thought. The stones merely ennabled the priest to answer inquiries addressed to God on a variety of issues. See R. Alan Cole, *Exodus. The Tyndale Old Testament Commentaries,* D. J. Wiseman, ed. (Downers Grove, IL: Inter-Varsity Press, 1973), 200, 201.

18 In speaking of Christ's intercessory, priestly ministry before the Father, we do not imply that the Father is against us and that Christ seeks to persuade Him to be gracious to us. "The Father himself loves you," said Jesus (John 16:27). Because the Father and the Son function in different roles in the plan of salvation does not mean that they are at odds or that there is not perfect harmony in the plan. In *the representation* given to us in the Scriptures, God the Father seems to reveal the justice and judgment of the Deity on sin. Again, the Bible presents Christ's interceding for mercy in behalf of repentant sinners who have accepted Him as Saviour and Lord. But this intercession also reveals the mercy of the entire Godhead Who originally proposed the plan. Thus, the representation of Christ's intercession underscores again how the holy triune God has reacted to the challenge of sin in such a manner as to be consistent with both His justice and mercy.

19 "Before the vail of the most holy place was an altar of perpetual intercession, before the holy, an altar of continual atonement. By blood and by incense God was to be approached—symbols pointing to the great Mediator, through whom sinners may approach Jehovah, and through whom alone mercy and salvation

can be granted to the repentant, believing soul" (Ellen G. White, PP 353).

20 "As you near the cross of Calvary there is seen love that is without a parallel. As you by faith grasp the meaning of the sacrifice, you see yourself a sinner, condemned by a broken law. This is repentance. As you come with humble heart, you find pardon, for Christ Jesus is represented as continually standing at the altar, momentarily offering up the sacrifice for the sins of the world. He is a minister of the true tabernacle which the Lord pitched and not man. The typical shadows of the Jewish tabernacle no longer possess any virtue. A daily and yearly typical atonement is no longer to be made, but the atoning sacrifice through a mediator is essential because of the constant commission of sin. Jesus is officiating in the presence of God, offering up His shed blood, as it had been a lamb slain. Jesus presents the oblation offered for every offense and every shortcoming of the sinner. . . ."

"The religious services, the prayers, the praise, the penitent confession of sin ascend from true believers as incense to the heavenly sanctuary, but passing through the corrupt channels of humanity, they are so defiled that unless purified by blood, they can never be of value with God. They ascend not in spotless purity, and unless the Intercessor, who is at God's right hand, presents and purifies all by His righteousness, it is not acceptable to God. All incense from earthly tabernacles must be moist with the cleansing drops of the blood of Christ. He holds before the Father the censer of His own merits, in which there is no taint of earthly corruption. He gathers into this censer the prayers, the praise, and the confessions of His people, and with these He puts His own spotless righteousness. Then, perfumed with the merits of Christ's propitiation, the incense comes up before God wholly and entirely acceptable. Then gracious answers are returned.

"Oh, that all may see that everything in obedience, in penitence, in praise and thanksgiving, must be placed upon the glowing fire of the righteousness of Christ. The fragrance of this righteousness ascends like a cloud around the mercy seat" (Ellen G. White, 1SM 343, 344).

21 So, Carol L. Meyers, *The Tabernacle Menorah. American Schools of Oriental Research, Dissertation Series 2.* (Missoula, MT: Scholars Press, 1976): 174, 177, 178.

22 "*Šāqad,*" BDB 1052.

23 Just as forgiveness of sin and acceptance with God were granted in the pre-Christian Era, being based on Christ's actual atonement yet to come (see Rom 3:25, 26), so the Holy Spirit—we may reason—was permitted to move on the hearts of humankind throughout the same era, although His operations were by virtue of Christ's future, priestly-mediatorial office. See Ellen G. White, 7T 30.

24 The bread is also described in the *Hebrew text* as "holy bread" (1 Sam 21:4) because of its sacred status; as "bread of the arrangement" (1 Chr 9:32; 23:29; Neh 10:33) or simply "the arrangement"(1 Chr 28:16) because it was arranged

in "two rows," that is, in two piles of six cakes each, together with pure frankincense (Lev 24:5-9); as "the continual bread" or "continual" arrangement (Num 4:7; 2 Chr 2:4) because the cakes were regularly renewed each week, and thus lay before the Lord on the golden table continuously.

25 Insight into the symbolic significance of the bread may also be gained by comparing it with the morning and evening animal sacrifice: (a) Both cakes and lambs were viewed as "offerings by fire to the Lord" (Exod 29:41; Lev 24:9). (b) Both were offered *by* the priesthood *for* Israel. (c) Both were offered "before the Lord" (Exod 25:30; 29:42), one in the court on the bronze altar, the other within the sanctuary upon the golden table. (d) Both were continuously offered (*tāmîd*). (e) The burning of incense was associated with both (Exod 29:38-42; Lev 2:1, 2; Lev 24:7). The chief difference between the two offerings (other than one was vegetable and the other animal) seems to be that one was bloody, the other, non-bloody. If an Israelite grasped the significance of the morning and evening sacrifice (a life given for the remission of sin), he would not have regarded the non-bloody bread offering as another sacrifice for sin. It would have symbolized something other than forgiveness and reconciliation—those came through the shedding of blood.

26 "Guide Me, O Thou Great Jehovah" (hymn).

27 This is evident in the type. On the Day of Atonement the regular morning and evening sacrifice continued (and we may assume the renewing of the incense and lamps occurred at the same time). Furthermore, additional sacrifices were added on this special day. See Num 29:7-11. What would be true in the type would be true in the antitype.

7

Day of Atonement: Final Judgment

As the reader may recall from an earlier observation (ch. 5), the sanctuary parable has a three-point focus: (1) the shedding of sacrificial blood at the altar in the court; (2) priestly mediation—the manipulation of the blood, intercession at the golden altar, and other related activities in connection with the lamps and bread; (3) the ministration of final judgment. These three areas of priestly activity are interlocking; none can stand apart from the others. Together they form a complete illustration of the plan of salvation in rite and symbol.

In this chapter we will examine the high priest's last phase of ministry in the sanctuary calendar: the Day of Atonement which foreshadowed the final judgment. The primary ritual on this special day centered on the sanctuary itself, especially on the Second Apartment, the Most Holy Place.

Second Apartment: Ark of the Covenant

The "ark of the covenant," the most sacred of the sanctuary furnishings, stood in the Most Holy Place, the only physical object in the cube-shaped apartment. Essentially a chest (*'ārôn*), the ark formed a depository for the tables of stone upon which God had inscribed the Ten Commandments. Two cherubs, one at each end of the gold cover, faced each other while looking reverently downward toward the ark, their wings outspread—"overshadowing the mercy seat" (Exod 25:10-22; Deut 10:4, 5).

As a symbol, the ark was at the hub of Israelite worship. All the essential elements in redemption came together at the ark: God Himself, His Law, sacrificial blood, and priestly mediation.

In the first place, the "ark of the covenant" symbolized *God's throne.* "The Lord of hosts . . . sits enthroned on the cherubim" (2 Sam 6:2).[1] In the Most Holy Place the visible Shekinah glory, hovering between the cherubim, represented the Lord's presence. The moral law of the Ten Commandments beneath the cherubim throne attested to the divine will, the foundation of the covenant between God and His people—and the moral basis for His universal rule and government. The Law provided the worshipers an insight into the character of God in addition to stipulating His righteous requirements.[2]

Thus, the nation could grasp the truth that the throne of God—His rule and government—was one of truth, integrity, and uprightness. "The Lord reigns," Israel later sang with the psalmist, "let the earth rejoice; . . . *righteousness and justice are the foundation of his throne*" (Ps 97:1, 2; cf. Ps 9:7, 8).

Second, the presence of the Ten Commandments acknowledged *God's holiness,* imparting to His throne the attribute of *justice.* Transgression of the Law—spoken and written by the Lord at Sinai—made Israel fully aware that sin violated the personal will of the Creator; it could not be winked at (Exod 32:33; 34:7). So incompatible is the principle of sin with the principles of a holy God that divine justice requires the death of the transgressor (Ezek 18:4; Rom 6:23). On the Day of Atonement the sacrificial blood sprinkled upon the ark's cover (the mercy seat) functioned in a ritual manner to satisfy divine justice, thereby averting the execution of the death penalty charged against sinners and making the acceptance of human repentance possible.

Third, the ark reflected the divine attitude of *grace.* In actuality the entire ritual (daily and yearly) revolved around the ark. Sacrificial blood offered and mediated by the priests throughout the year made atonement for the violations of the Law. Thus, divine grace provided a substitute for repentant sinners to enable them to find forgiveness and acceptance with God. The ark's cover— with the Law beneath it, and the blood of the Day of Atonement sin offering sprinkled upon its upper surface—uniquely symbolized the meeting of divine justice and mercy, ultimately accomplished by Christ on the cross (Rom 3:24-26, NASB).[3]

The atoning blood enabled Israel to see that the throne of God—a throne of uprightness and unswerving justice—was also a throne of grace and mercy. Through the merits of sacrificial blood sin could be atoned for, could be forgiven, and could be forever removed from the nation. The reality of their present acceptance, of course, depended upon their faith in the coming Redeemer who would fulfill the type.

Fourth, the ark symbolized God's throne of *priestly mediation*. Through-out the year the priests had approached God on behalf of penitent believers: mediating the shed blood of the sacrifices and ministering through the sym-bolism of the incense, lamps, and bread. On the Day of Atonement the high priest stood within the typical throne room of God, in the immediate presence of Deity (symbolized by the Shekinah cloud). He ministered both incense and blood in a procedure which removed sin from the sanctuary and secured the approval of God for His people. Thus, the ark of the covenant came to represent to Israel the throne of mediation, intercession, and salvation through a repre-sentative priest who could reconcile God to man and man to God.

The antitype of the symbolism of the sanctuary's ritual throne is plainly evident in the NT. Christ, our high priest, "is seated at the right hand of the *throne* of the Majesty in heaven" as "a minister in the sanctuary and the true tent" (Heb 8:1, 2). It is a throne (government) grounded upon the principles of the moral law of the Ten Commandments since these precepts are the basis of the new covenant. "Christ has obtained a ministry which is as much more excellent than the old as the *covenant* he mediates is better. . . . This is the covenant that I will make . . . after those days, says the Lord: I will put my laws into their minds, and write them on their hearts, and I will be their God, and they shall be my people" (Heb 8:6-10). It is also the "throne of grace" (Heb 4:16), before which Christ is represented as always making "interces-sion" in behalf of those who seek God (Heb 7:25; 9:24).

The Day of Atonement

The yearly service—the second distinctive division of priestly ministry in the sanctuary parable—occupied only one day each year in the fall (the tenth day of the month Tishri). Known as the Day of Atonement (literally, Day of Atonements, *yôm kippurîm*),[4] it was a very solemn occasion, observed with fasting, earnest prayer, confession of sin, and cessation from secular labor (Lev 23:26-32).

The special Day of Atonement purification ritual was the only ceremony in the sanctuary system specifically requiring the ministry of the high priest (Heb 9:7). Furthermore, the yearly service was *primarily sanctuary centered*. "And when he [the high priest] has made an end of atoning for the holy place [in Lev 16, *holy place* designates the second apartment] and the tent of meeting [first apartment] and the altar [in the court], he shall present the live goat" (Lev 16:20; cf. vs. 33, first part).[5] Naturally, the penitent Israelites who trusted in God were *the beneficiaries* of the sanctuary's cleansing.[6]

We repeat, because this point is not clear in the minds of many: The daily ritual involved the cleansing and restoring of *the individual;* the yearly involved the cleansing of *the sanctuary* (with the individual being only indirectly involved, being the beneficiary of this important rite). The Day of Atonement ritual looked beyond Calvary, although its sacrificial aspects were fulfilled at Calvary. The Day of Atonement ritual looked beyond the salvation of the individual, so to speak, to the final resolution of the sin problem. Its symbolism encompassed the eradication and banishment of Satan and sin from the universe.[7]

Transfer of Sin/Responsibility

In the previous chapter we noted that the blood of a sin offering animal upon which the sins of an individual (or the congregation) had been confessed had a *double function* in the typical rites. In the first place, it secured atonement and forgiveness for the repentant sinner/congregation. And in the second place, it transferred the confessed sins and responsibility of the penitent to the sanctuary which, for the time being, assumed them. This transfer to the sanctuary (= God) introduced into the ritual parable another aspect of the plan of salvation: the process leading to the ultimate eradication of sin, its proponents, and all its effects.

Obviously, the purification ceremony engaged in by the high priest on the Day of Atonement presupposed a previous contamination of the sanctuary. "He shall make atonement for the holy place [Second Apartment], because of the [ritual] *uncleannesses [ṭum'āh]* of the people of Israel, and because of their *transgressions [pešaʻ],* all their *sins [ḥaṭṭā't]*; and so he shall do for the tent of meeting [first apartment], which abides with them in the midst of their uncleannesses. . . . And he shall sprinkle some of the blood upon [the altar in the court] . . . and cleanse it and hallow it from the *uncleannesses [ṭum'āh]* of the people of Israel" (Lev 16:16-19). "And when he has made an end of atoning [the sanctuary complex] . . . Aaron shall lay both his hands upon the head of the live goat, and confess over him all the *iniquities [ʻāwôn]* of the people of Israel, and all their transgressions [pešaʻ], all their sins [ḥaṭṭā't]" (Lev 16:20, 21).

The question that arises at this point is, How can the blood of the sin offering *cleanse* the repentant sinner, but at the same time *contaminate* the sanctuary so that the latter requires a special purification on the Day of Atonement? And, if the sin offering foreshadowed the messianic Redeemer, how could its blood have a defiling aspect? The NT always speaks of the blood of Christ in a positive manner: "the blood of Jesus his Son *cleanses* us from all sin" (1 John 1:7).

The problem does not lie in the rituals themselves, but in the examining of an Eastern system through our Western eyeglasses, as it were. Before we can make linkage with NT affirmations about the "blood" of Christ, we must understand how blood was regarded in OT antiquity. The biblical data indicates that in Hebrew thinking blood was viewed as having a dual function. It could contaminate as well as purify.[8] This paradox operates on "the principle of substitutional interchange."[9]

> The blood of the sacrifice for the sins of Israel did not have in itself a magic power for purification. Its purifying or contaminative value had to be measured according to the place and the circumstances in which it was applied. *When it had to do with persons or things that were not consecrated, it purified them. On the contrary, when it was applied to sanctified persons or objects, it contaminated them.*
>
> During the [regular religious] year the [sacrificial] blood was deposited in the place which God had sanctified with His glory—His sanctuary (Exod 29:43). In this manner sin was transferred to the sanctuary complex and contaminated it. At the end of the year, on the Day of Atonement, the paradox of the substitutional principle operated again, and the blood became the element for the purification of the sanctuary from all the sins which had contaminated it until that point. Then in the figurative ritual the sins were blotted out totally from Israel.[10]

In summary, we may say that the daily application of the blood of the sin offerings—sacrificed by repentant sinners—*legitimately* contaminated or defiled the sanctuary. But a careful reader will note that open, defiant sins that were never confessed were also said to defile the sanctuary. These included ritual uncleanness not properly cared for (Lev 15:31; Num 19:13, 20), idolatry—including the sacrifice of children (Lev 20:1-5), and all other defiant, unconfessed sins (Jer 7:8-12; Ezek 5:11).

When these hardened, rebellious sinners came to worship before the Lord in the sanctuary, He regarded them as defiling His courts:

> Declare to them their abominable deeds. For they have committed adultery, and blood is upon their hands; with their idols they have committed adultery; and they have even offered up to them for food the sons whom they had borne to me. Moreover this they have done to me: they have defiled my sanctuary on the same day and profaned my sabbaths. For when they had slaughtered their children in sacrifice to their idols, on the same day they came into my sanctuary to profane it (Ezek 23:36-39).

A reading of the references cited above clearly indicates that this kind of deliberate, unconfessed contamination of the sanctuary could only be removed by the execution of the guilty parties. No sacrifice, not even the special sacrifices of the Day of Atonement were employed to propitiate/expiate these cases of individual rebellion.[11] When such conduct developed into widespread, national apostasy, it was met by chastisements of natural disasters, foreign invasions, and captivity, but never through the sacrifices of the sanctuary system.

Although the sinning of anyone in Israel brought reproach upon the God who dwelt among His people, yet the sanctuary (= God) assumed accountability for only the repentant sinner who had through the rituals confessed his sins and who in reality had cast his burden of sin upon the Lord through the mediation of the priests.

The Yearly Ministration

Something of the importance of the yearly ministration to Judaism may be surmised from the fact that the Jewish people still celebrate the Day of Atonement as Yom Kippur. In biblical times the entire nation observed the Day of Atonement as a ceremonial sabbath, from the evening of the ninth day to the evening of the tenth (Lev 16:31; 23:32). The Day of Atonement was the second of the three public events God directed ancient Israel to observe in the fall of the year.[12] During its hours the people abstained from toil to earn a livelihood and "afflicted" ('ānāh) themselves, that is, they fasted and searched their hearts. In deep contrition they confessed their sins and waywardness from God.[13] The Day of Atonement was the only commanded fast in the entire ritual system (cf. Acts 27:9).

General rites. The day began and ended with the renewing of the regular morning and evening sacrifice, the public burnt offering which burned continuously (Exod 29:38-42). In addition to the morning sacrifice, the priests offered a larger, special burnt offering consisting of a young bull, a ram, and seven lambs—together with their required cereal offerings—and also an additional goat for a sin offering (Num 29:7-11).

The regular, daily offering and these additional sacrifices make it abundantly clear that God's mercy and forgiveness were available throughout this special day of contrition and repentance—and of judgment, as we shall see. The door of grace was swung as wide as its hinges would allow! No penitent Israelite was denied access, if he/she sincerely desired to find acceptance with God.

According to the biblical data the high priest prepared for the special rites by first bathing and dressing in his simple, linen attire. He next offered a young bull as a sin offering for himself and "for his house," probably to be understood as his associate priests (Lev 16:6, 33).[14]

After entering the Most Holy Place with a cloud of incense preceding him from his outstretched hand-held censer, the high priest sprinkles the blood of his sin offering upon the mercy seat of the ark and before it (Lev 16:11-14). In this manner he atones for his own sins and those of his fellow priests and prepares himself to minister the special purification rites. When these are completed, he will bathe again, change back into his official high priestly garb, and will offer on the altar the fat of the sin offering and two burnt offerings—one for himself and the priesthood and one for the people (Lev 16:23-25). With these sacrifices he closes his duties for the Day of Atonement.

Special rites. The special purification rites centered on two goats presented by the congregation. "He [the high priest] shall take from the congregation of the people of Israel two male goats for a sin offering" (Lev 16:5). These he placed "before the Lord." Lots were cast, "one lot for the *Lord* [*Yahweh*] and the other lot for the scapegoat [*Azazel*]" (vs. 8, KJV). The priest then sacrificed the Lord's goat "as a sin offering" (vs. 9) and brought its blood within the sanctuary where he first sprinkled some upon and before the mercy seat of the ark in the Most Holy Place (vss. 15, 16), next upon the horns of the golden altar of incense in the first apartment ("the tent of meeting," vs. 16; cf. Exod 30:10), and finally upon the altar of burnt offering and its horns, in the court (vss. 18, 19).

Thus, in ritual figures the high priest atoned for or cleansed the sanctuary complex of the confessed sins and accountability which it (= God) had for a time assumed. The live goat was then brought forward, and the high priest, in his role as Israel's priestly mediator, placed the sins and accountability (just removed from the sanctuary) upon its head. A previously appointed man then led the goat away into the wilderness where it perished.

The banishment of the live goat left the sanctuary and the people in a state of ritual purity. "And when he has made an end of atoning for the holy place [Second Apartment] and the tent of meeting [first apartment] and the altar [in the court], he shall present the live goat; and Aaron shall lay both his hands upon the head of the live goat, and confess over him all the *iniquities [ʿāwōn]* of the people of Israel, and all their transgressions [*pešaʿ*], all their *sins [ḥaṭṭāʾt];*[15] and he shall put them upon the head of the goat, and send him away into the wilderness by the hand of a man who is in readiness. The goat shall bear all their iniquities upon him to a solitary land; and he shall let the goat go in the wilderness." (Lev 16:20-22).

The purification rites atoned for and cleansed the sanctuary complex and resulted in a cleansed priesthood and people (Lev 16:33, 30). In a ritual manner it vindicated God who in His mercy had assumed the sins and accountability of His penitent people.

It is important to note that the sanctuary differed from the people (including its human priesthood) in this sense: it never had faults of its own for which it needed to be purified. The sanctuary assumed responsibility for the forgiven sins which were transferred to it. It was never itself the cause of those sins and impurities.

In a real sense, therefore, the sacrifice of the Lord's goat on the Day of Atonement was in favor of the sanctuary and was an act of vindication for it. In this manner the Day of Atonement was an affirmation of innocence so far as the sanctuary itself was concerned, because the sanctuary was in reality a representation of the throne and government of God. The One who took on the responsibility of all the sins that were deposited therein by sacrifice was the God who lived in it, and now He was being vindicated.[16]

The Scapegoat: Azazel

Before we examine the antitype to the Day of Atonement ritual, it is necessary first to identify Azazel, the Hebrew term that has come to be translated "scapegoat."[17] Many Christians today regard the two goats of the purification rite as composing a single symbol for Christ.[18] As evidence they point to the statement that the high priest took from the congregation "two male goats *for a sin offering*" (vs. 5). This, they argue, indicates the two goats made up a single sin offering.[19] They also note in the instructions these words: "The goat on which the lot fell for Azazel [scapegoat] shall be presented alive before the Lord to make *atonement [kipper]* over it" (vs. 10). Here again, they argue, is further evidence, since only Christ makes atonement.

Nevertheless, sound reasons exist for rejecting the view that the two goats together represent different aspects of the single death of Christ. Another, more reasonable position is that God, in this rite, is introducing a new facet of truth into the sanctuary parable by employing two animals.

Argument from Scripture. The Hebrew text reads literally, "One lot for Yahweh and one lot for Azazel" (Lev 16:8). Since Yahweh (God's covenant name) is a personal being, it is evident that Azazel is also a personal being. And since the casting of the lots sharply distinguishes between Yahweh and Azazel, it is also evident that these two personages stand in opposition to each other.

Arguments from reason. (a) In the ritual system two animals were never used to denote a single sacrifice. A repentant sinner might offer a sin offering and a burnt offering at the same time, but he never offered at the same time two animals to symbolize a single sin offering, or two to symbolize a single burnt offering.[20] This is presumptive evidence that the goat for Azazel was not intended to be identified with the goat for Yahweh.

(b) The goat for Azazel was not a sacrifice; its blood was not shed. Consequently, it did not bear Israel's iniquities in any *saving* manner. The rubric of the sanctuary system was, "Without the shedding of blood there is no forgiveness of sins" (Heb 9:22). The goat for Azazel was disposed of by abandoning it to the wilderness to die of itself.

(c) The sanctuary complex stood in a state of complete purification before the Azazel goat was introduced into the ritual. "When he [the high priest] *has made an end of atoning* for the holy place and the tent of meeting and the altar, he shall present the live goat" (Lev 16:20).

(d) In the Jewish pseudepigraphal book of Enoch[21] Azazel is characterized as the one who "hath taught all unrighteousness on earth" (ch. 9:6). Furthermore, "the whole earth has been corrupted through the works that were taught by Azazel: to him ascribe all sin" (ch. 10:8).[22]

When we search the Scriptures to discover a personage who stands in opposition to God and who is responsible for the origin of sin, we find abundant evidence pointing to Satan—a mighty, fallen angel. We cite two similar passages from each Testament:

1. "Then he showed me Joshua the high priest standing before the angel of the Lord, and *Satan* standing at his right hand *to accuse* him. And the Lord said to Satan, 'The Lord rebuke you, O Satan! The Lord who has chosen Jerusalem rebuke you! Is not this a brand plucked from the fire?' " (Zech 3:1, 2).

2. "And the *great dragon* was thrown down, that *ancient serpent,* who is called *the Devil* and *Satan, the deceiver of the whole world.* . . . And I heard a loud voice in heaven, saying, 'Now the salvation and the power and the kingdom of our God and the authority of his Christ have come, for *the accuser* of our brethren has been thrown down, who accuses them day and night before our God' " (Rev 12:9, 10).

The Scripture testimony is abundant that Satan, a created angel of great powers, but fallen, is the deadly enemy of God and all who belong to Him. There can be no doubt that the ritual introduces Satan—the instigator and originator of sin and rebellion against God—at this point in the Day of Atonement rite under the symbol of the goat for Azazel.

The objections. The first objection to equating Azazel with Satan is derived from the instructions that the people were to present to the high priest "two male goats for a sin offering." This is interpreted to mean that the two goats constituted a single sin offering. But the context indicates that the two animals were presented before the Lord for the purpose of selecting *one* of them to be the Lord's sin-offering goat. By casting lots the high priest determined which animal would be *the* sin offering. The priest was then to take the goat "on which the lot fell *for the Lord,*" and to "offer it *as a sin offering*" (Lev 16:9). Since the goat chosen for Azazel was never sacrificed, it obviously did not function as a sin offering.

But what about the fact that the goat for Azazel was presented to the Lord "to make atonement over it" (Lev 16:10)? The answer lies in the simple fact that the term "atonement" is used in more than one way in the Scriptures.

1. When a sin offering is sacrificed in behalf of a repentant sinner, and its blood is properly administered (and in most cases some of its flesh eaten by the priest), we can speak of "atonement" *in a saving sense* (cf. Lev 4:35, etc.). The sin of the penitent is "erased," "wiped out" *by the substitute's death.*

2. But "atonement" may also take place in *a punitive sense* when a guilty, unpardoned person forfeits his life in punishment for his offense. Two examples are presented in the book of Numbers:

a. The execution of a murderer. "Bloodshed pollutes the land, and *atonement [kpr]* cannot be made for the land on which blood has been shed, *except by the blood of the one who shed it*" (Num 35:33, NIV). Thus, Moses is saying that the punishment (execution) of the killer "atones" for his crime of murder.

b. The execution of an immoral Israelite and his Midianite paramour. While the conscience-stricken congregation wept before the tabernacle and confessed their gross idolatry in connection with the Midianite women at Baal-peor, an Israelite and his Midianite companion brazenly walked past and entered his tent. In amazement and with rising indignation the priest Phinehas seized a spear, and following them into the tent, summarily executed both. The Lord called their death an "atonement." "[Phinehas] was zealous for the honor of his God and made *atonement [kpr, piel form]* for the people of Israel." (Num 25:13, NIV). The just *punishment* of these bold sinners was viewed as atoning for the national immorality, but it did not save the 24,000 who died in a subsequent plague from the Lord.

Just as these punitive atonements of the murderer and this brazen couple removed guilt from the Israelite nation, so the goat for Azazel—bearing Israel's iniquities and accountability—rendered atonement by taking punishment, but not in a saving manner. The goat was banished from the camp to the harsh wilderness where it perished. Thus, this portion of the ritual dealing with the goat for Azazel pointed forward to the final resolution of the sin problem. Satan, as the enemy of God and His people, in the final judgment will be punished and executed as the originator and instigator of sin—fully account-able for the rebellion he introduced into God's universe.[23]

In the year-end sanctuary rites, the Lord (= sanctuary)—who had assumed the confessed sins and accountability of penitent Israelites throughout the ritual year—now clears Himself and them by placing all accountability on Azazel (Satan). Therefore, we may properly say that the Second Apartment ministra-tion of the high priest is sanctuary-centered, because the prescribed rites he carries out clear God (= sanctuary), resulting in a cleared people with the ultimate blame for sin being placed on Satan.

Two Classes of Israelites

It is important to observe that while the Day of Atonement has implications for the universe, one of its central loci is upon God's professed people. The service functioned to distinguish between two classes of God's professed people, the genuine and the false. The genuine class of believers were those Israelites who had sincerely repented of their sins throughout the year—having brought the appropriate sin offerings to the sanctuary—and who rested on this special sabbath, fasted and humbled their hearts before God in contrition and repentance. When the purification rites for the sanctuary were completed, these persons were pronounced "clean before the Lord" (Lev 16:30).

The false believers were exposed by the fact that they did not cease their daily toil on this special day, nor did they engage in fasting and soul-searching and confession of sin. In all likelihood they had neglected/rejected their religious privileges throughout the year (cf. Lev 15:31; Num 19:20), or had chosen to sin against God openly (cf. Lev 20:1-6; etc.). On the Day of Atonement such false believers were "cut off" from God's people. "It is a day of atonement, to make atonement for you before the Lord your God. For whoever is not afflicted on this same day *shall be cut off from his people*. And whoever does any work on this same day, *that person I will destroy* among his people" (Lev 23:28-30).[24]

This *separation* of the false Israelite from the genuine Israelite of faith on the Day of Atonement is a significant result of the second major priestly ministration in the sanctuary system. Both groups professed a covenant relationship with God, but the rites on this special day caused a separation to take place. In a similar manner Christ's judgment parables taught that the final judgment would remove false believers from the true:

Parable of the dragnet (Matt 13:47-49). *The gospel net,* cast into the sea of humanity, gathers both good and bad into the fellowship of God's people. But final judgment brings a sorting of the catch. Said Jesus, "So it will be at the end of the age; the angels shall come forth, and *take out the wicked from among [ek mesos] the righteous*" (NASB). Jesus is not speaking about a general separation of the wicked from the righteous, but of *the separation of false believers from true believers gathered in by the gospel net.*

Parable of the tares (Matt 13:24-30, 36-43). Jesus tells about an enemy who came at night and sowed tares on a newly-sown wheat field. When the plants developed sufficiently, the deed was discovered. However, the farmer restrained his servants from pulling up the tares, bidding them to wait until the harvest when the two species of plants could be more easily distinguished.

Christ identified the field as "the world;" the good wheat seed sown in this world represented "the sons of the kingdom," His true followers. But since the seeds of the tares were sown *only* among the wheat, it is evident that Christ had His church in mind. The church would always contain both wheat and tares, both genuine and false believers.

However, at the end of the age there would be a separation: "The Son of man will send his angels, and they will gather *out of his kingdom* all causes of sin and all evildoers, and throw them into the furnace of fire." Here again, final judgment is focused on God's professed people with the intent of separating the false from the genuine.

Parable of the wedding garment (Matt 22:1-14). In this historical parable certain previously-invited persons refuse to come to the king's "marriage feast for his son," even though twice urged to attend. Finally, the servants were sent out into the streets, and they gathered "all whom they found, *both bad and good;* so the wedding hall was filled with guests." But before the festivities begin, the king inspects His invitees. Finding a guest inappropriately attired—"without a wedding garment"—he expels him "into the outer darkness." Christ added these words in concluding the parable: "Many are called, but few are chosen."

Once more, a parable from the lips of Jesus expresses the truth that in the final judgment the Divine Inspector will examine His invited guests, He will examine His professed people. While He will reaffirm the genuine, He will separate the false from them. Israel's sanctuary parable and Jesus' judgment parables teach the same important truth: While probation continues, God's professed people will always be composed of the true and the false. But the final judgment (as in the typical Day of Atonement) will correct the situation and will separate the two. Again, we should observe that Jesus' judgment parables, like the Day of Atonement, are focused on the professed people of God, not upon the general wicked who have rejected God's grace.[25]

Final Judgment

The Day of Atonement rituals resulted in a clean sanctuary and a clean people. All "evidence" of sin and accountability had been removed from the sanctuary via the scapegoat, and the false Israelites had been "cut off" and destroyed. Because the Day of Atonement accomplished a complete disposition of sin, it is correctly viewed as the foreshadowing type of the final judgment, the divine action which will forever settle and eradicate the issue of sin.

Atonement by Judgment

The doctrinal views of many Christians do not provide any real resolution to the sin issue. They believe our salvation was accomplished at the cross and that we escape our human existence through death, entering heaven one by one by virtue of our saved, immortal souls. The future judgment day, alluded to in the commonly recited "Apostles' Creed," is viewed only as an "awards day," not as a divine investigation of their lives.

While liberal theology rejects the existence of Satan and hellfire altogether as mere myth, the popular idea is that the devils will stoke the fires of hell and eternally torment the lost. Christ dies and is resurrected, but the arch rebel of the universe continues to live on. So much for the confusion of popular religious beliefs!

However, in the rituals of the Day of Atonement, we see portrayed the deliberate and rational movements of the Deity to resolve the rebellion sin has caused and, in a just way, to lay responsibility upon the originator of sin. In the final judgment, foreshadowed in this particular ritual, *the ultimate effects* of Calvary will be seen and its objectives met. "The reason the Son of God appeared was *to destroy the works of the devil*" (1 John 3:8). "Since therefore the children share in flesh and blood, he himself likewise partook of the same nature, *that through death he might destroy him who has the power of death, that is, the devil*" (Heb 2:14).

God and His throne (= sanctuary), and those repentant persons who have placed their trust in Him through the merits of Christ, will be cleared in the final judgment. Full accountability for sin will be rolled back upon Satan, its originator. Satan, his followers, and all the effects of sin, will be banished from the universe by destruction (Matt 25:41). Atonement by judgment will, therefore, bring about a fully reconciled and harmonious universe—united in Christ (cf. Eph. 1:9, 10).

This is the objective and end result of the second and final phase of Christ's priestly, mediatorial ministration in the heavenly sanctuary. We may, therefore, describe this aspect of His work (represented by the Second Apartment, the Most Holy Place) *as a ministry of judgment and vindication.* Since the sanctuary parable presents only the essence of the final judgment in the Day of Atonement ritual, we must turn to other portions of the Scriptures for the more detailed teaching of the doctrine.

Eschatological Judgment

The final judgment, at which time all humanity will stand at the bar of the Creator, is a prominent subject in Scripture. The apostle Paul never hesitated to refer to the judgment even when speaking to pagans who did not know about the true God. "[God] has fixed a day on which he will judge the world in righteousness by a man [Jesus] whom he has appointed," he told the Athenian philosophers (Acts 17:31 cf. 24:25).

The apostle alludes to the teaching of Jesus that "The Father judges no one, but *has given all judgment to the Son,*" "and *has given him authority to execute judgment, because he is the Son of man*" (John 5:22, 27). Just as the Father created the world through the agency of the Son (Heb 1:1, 2), so He will judge the world through the agency of the Son.

All humanity—professing believers as well as unbelievers—face the final judgment: "For *we must all appear before the judgment seat of Christ,* so that each one may receive good or evil, according to what he has done in the body" (2 Cor 5:10)[26] The same court session is also called the "judgment seat of God." "For *we shall all stand before the judgment seat of God. . . . So each of us shall give account of himself to God*" (Rom 14:10, 12). No facet of our lives will be withheld from investigation: "For God will bring every deed into judgment, with every secret thing, whether good or evil" (Ecc. 12:14). "I tell you, on the day of judgment men will render account for every careless word they utter; for by your words you will be justified, and by your words you will be condemned" (Matt 12:36, 37).

Obviously, final judgment is not for the benefit of an omniscient Deity. Sin arose as a challenge to God, thrown out to Him by a creature. God could have destroyed Satan and his angels at once and settled the sin problem (as far as the Deity was concerned). But the plan of salvation had been instituted for the sake of the intelligent universe so that all created beings might be drawn willingly into agreement with God's view of sin. The moral controversy that has torn our planet began with a questioning universe. It cannot close until that same universe is satisfied with God's character, His law and government, and all His actions in dealing with the sin problem. And those actions involve His plan of salvation *and those who have professed to accept it.* So, final judgment involves God and His challenger(s) as well as rebellious humanity. But naturally, more is written in the Scriptures about humanity's relationship to the judgment (than these other matters) because we are so inextricably locked into the sin problem as sinners.

Two Options

Apart from futile attempts to earn salvation from sin by doing good works, there are really only two options that may be seriously considered: (1) Some Christians start from the premise that *salvation is obtained by divine decree.* If God predestines (decrees) a person to be saved, then he cannot resist the gospel when it comes to him, neither can he fall away and be lost after accepting it. Ultimately, there is no need for a final judgment for such a person, since his destiny is fixed before he is born. Others start this process at a later point, arguing that once a person accepts Christ as his personal Saviour and Lord, he cannot ever fall away and be lost. Christians with this kind of mind set naturally find the teaching about an investigative judgment difficult to grasp and to accept. There is simply no need for it.

(2) But, if *salvation is obtained only by faith* in the merits of Christ and the divine promises, *then the evidence for that faith and commitment must be demonstrated to an interested universe.*[27] Assurance must be given to the unfallen intelligences that God is taking into His eternal kingdom genuine believers. The books of record must be opened for impartial inspection.

The Day of Atonement purification rites do not explore these aspects of final judgment—the opening of the books of record. The major emphases of these rites are on the cleansing of the sanctuary: the clearing of God and His true people by the removal of accountability from the sanctuary, the cutting off of the false believer, and the placing of ultimate accountability for sin on the head of Satan (Azazel)—with his banishment. The prophecies of Daniel and Revelation and other portions of Scripture, added to the sanctuary parable insight, provide the Christian with a full, rounded-out biblical understanding of the final judgment, Christ's last work of high priestly ministry. This aspect of Christ's atoning priesthood will become plainer as we turn to the apocalyptic prophecies of Daniel and Revelation and other passages as well.

——————— ◆ ———————

Endnotes

1 Cf. 1 Sam 4:4; Pss 80:1; 99:1

2 Rom 7:12 cf. 1 Pet 1:16; Rev 15:3; Ps 25:8

3 The cover or lid of the ark is named the *kappōret* in the Hebrew text, commonly translated into English as the "mercy seat." Older authorities understood the word to mean a "cover." But modern scholarship rejects this meaning. See *"Kapporet,"* BDB 498. The word derives from *kipper,* "to wipe away," "to erase," "to rub out" (Gk. Septuagint, *hilastērion,* the "place of propitiation" from *hilaskomai,* "to propitiate") and alludes to the sacrificial blood of the sin offering sprinkled upon and before the ark on the Day of Atonement.

4 The plural form is thought to indicate full or complete atonement. See A. Nooradtzij, *Leviticus. Bible Student's Commentary,* Raymond Togtman, tr. (Grand Rapids: Zondervan Publishing House, 1982), 238.

5 "The distinction between the daily ritual and that of the Day of Atonement is emphasized further in the use of *kipper* and *'ēt,* the sign of the direct object. . . . The sign of the direct object is used only in the final purification or cleansing of the sanctuary on the Day of Atonement [The sign of the direct object precedes 'holy place/sanctuary,' 'tent of meeting,' 'altar,' Lev 16:20, 33, RSV]. It [the direct object sign] clearly indicates that it is the *sanctuary itself* that is to be cleansed on the Day of Atonement. In the daily sacrificial rituals the sins and impurities of individuals were atoned for and transferred to the sanctuary. The Day of Atonement now focuses upon the cleansing of that sanctuary" (Alberto R. Treiyer, "The Day of Atonement as Related to the Contamination and Purification of the Sanctuary," DARCOM 3:217, author's emphasis).

6 "It means that these rites, which cleanse both the sanctuary and altar, are relational with respect to the effects they have for the Israelites. The result of the cleansing of the sanctuary as regards the Israelites is that their cleansing is now *final* before the Lord [Lev 16:30]. This is emphasized also in another way in [Lev 16:33], where we have two usages of *kipper* followed by direct objects (sanctuary, tent of meeting, and altar). Then the *kipper 'al* construction follows to indicate that the Israelites are the ultimate beneficiaries: 'And he shall atone [*kipper + direct object*] the holy sanctuary, and the tent of meeting, and he shall atone [*kipper + direct object*] the altar, and he shall make atonement with respect to [*kipper 'al*] the priests and all the people of the assembly' (Lev 16:33)" (Gerhard F. Hasel, "Studies in Biblical Atonement II: The Day of Atonement," SA[1], 118; SA[2], 111, 112).

7 "In the ministration of the tabernacle, and of the temple that afterward took its place, the people were taught each day the great truths relative to Christ's death and ministration, and once each year their minds were carried forward to the closing events of the great controversy between Christ and Satan, the final purification of the universe from sin and sinners" (Ellen G. White, PP 358).

8 For example, the blood of a murdered man "defiles the land." But the blood of the murderer, when he is executed for this crime, makes "atonement" for the land, that is, it cleanses the land (Num 35:33, NKJV). While in this instance the same "blood" did not defile and cleanse, it does indicate that the Hebrew did not always think of blood as a cleansing agent in a positive sense. Another more striking example concerns the ashes of a red heifer employed to perform ritual cleansings (Heb 9:13). A *red* heifer was selected and slaughtered "outside the camp." After sprinkling some of its blood toward the sanctuary, the priest had the carcass burned—its skin, flesh, blood, excrement, together with cedarwood, hyssop, and scarlet stuff. The *red* hide, *crimson* yarn, *red* cedar, plus the animal's own blood clearly denote that when the ashes were mixed with water, the resultant "water for impurity" was intended to represent blood. The mixture was used to cleanse persons (or objects) who/which had become ritually unclean (Num 19:17-19). But while "the water for impurity" ceremonially cleansed the person or object upon which it was sprinkled, it defiled or rendered the person who sprinkled the solution unclean, and he was obliged to wash his clothes and remain unclean until evening (Num 19:21). Thus, "the water for impurity," which was *equated with the sacrificial blood of a sin offering* (the red heifer was called "the burnt sin offering," Num 19:17), could cleanse and defile at the same time. If the person was "unclean," the sprinkled water cleansed him. If the person was "clean" (the one who did the sprinkling), it defiled or contaminated him.

9 Treiyer, DARCOM 3:234.

10 Ibid., 235, 236, author's emphasis. In the record of the proceedings of the purification rite on the Day of Atonement no mention is made of the high priest confessing sin upon the head of the sin offering designated as the Lord's goat before slaying it. Unless this is an omission, it indicates that the blood of this particular sacrifice carried *no sin into* the sanctuary, but functioned only to remove it.

11 Ibid., 204; cf. Angel M. Rodríguez, "Transfer of Sin in Leviticus," DARCOM 3:172-177.

12 The Feast of Trumpets occurred on the first day of the seventh month (Lev 23:23-25). Since this was the first day of the "civil" year (in contrast with the religious year which began in the spring six months earlier), it came to be regarded as a New Year's Day (Rosh Hashanah). Ten days later—the 10th of the same month—the nation engaged in the solemn rites of the Day of Atonement. Finally, on the 15th to the 22nd the people celebrated the Feast of Tabernacles ("Feast of Booths") which combined the joys of harvesttime with an annual commemoration of Israel's exodus from Egypt (Lev 23:34-44).

13 Lev 16:29, 31; 23:27, 32. Cf. Isa. 58:3, 5. "To afflict" = "to fast." See " '*Ānāh*," piel form, BDB 776.

14 F. Meyrick, Leviticus. *The Pulpit Commentary,* H.D.M. Spence and Joseph S.

Excell, eds. (Chicago: Wilcox & Follett Company, nd), 4:239.

15 The Hebrew word for "sin" (*ḥaṭṭā't*) may be translated either as "sin" or as "sin offering." Consequently, Lev 16:16 may be translated "Thus [the high priest] shall make atonement for the sanctuary from the uncleannesses of the Israelites and from their transgressions for all their sin offerings." "Such a translation strongly indicates that the Day of Atonement sin offering ritual [the ministration of the blood of the Lord's goat in the two apartments of the sanctuary and to the altar in the court] functioned to cleanse the sanctuary from *only* the confessed sins of the penitent Israelites. That is, it functioned to remove the sins that had been confessed and transferred to it by means of *the sin offerings* that had been offered previously during the year" (William H. Shea, "Literary Form and Theological Function in Leviticus," DARCOM 3:165, author's emphasis. See full discussion, 158-165).

16 Treiyer, DARCOM 3:245.

17 William Tyndale (d. 1536), the English Bible translator is credited with coining the expression "scapegoat" (= escape goat). His translation of Lev 16:10 reads in part, "The goote on which the lotte fell to scape."

18 For example, see John R. W. Stott, *The Cross of Christ,* 144.

19 The earliest source of this notion is the so-called "Epistle of Barnabas," a non-inspired, "spurious" work (according to Eusebius), written sometime between the fall of Jerusalem, A.D. 70 and A.D. 135. See 7:6ff. For information on the document, see "Apostolic Fathers, III," ISBE 1:206.

20 It is sometimes suggested that in the cleansing of the leper or of a house which gave evidence of a leprouslike "disease," two birds were used as a single sacrifice (Lev 14:4-7, 34, 49-53). However, it should be noted that the birds were not the usual sacrificial birds (doves/pigeons; cf. Lev 1:14; 14:4). The slain bird was not sacrificed on the altar, nor was its blood mediated by the priest to the horns or any part of the altar in the court. In short, this particular ritual does not appear to be a normal, sacrificial ritual. The bird that was released to fly away probably symbolized the cleansed leper in the first instance, and the cleansed house in the second. Since the Day of Atonement purification rite involved a true sacrifice at the sanctuary and the priestly mediation of blood, together with the burning of the fat of the sin offering on the altar, it cannot really be equated with the nonsacrificial nature of the two-bird rite for cleansing the leper or house. Even in these rites, it seems evident that the two birds (the slain one and the living one) do *not* represent the same object. See, A. Noordtzij, *Leviticus,* 144, 145.

It has also been suggested that the morning and evening sacrifice (Exod 29:38-42) is an instance where two animals represented a single burnt offering which burned 24 hours, around the clock. But the public, daily burnt offering is not comparable to the Day of Atonement situation. If the lamb offered in the morning as a burnt offering could have continued burning around the clock for a full day, there would have been no need for a second. But just as the oil in the lamps and the incense on the golden altar had to be renewed every twelve hours to maintain their continuous activity, so the continuous burnt offering in the court had to be renewed. The two lambs that made up the daily burnt offering were not sacrificed at the same time but were spaced to keep the merits of the sacrifice always available. And in this sense they constituted a single offering.

21 This collection of apocalypses and other materials is thought to have been written during the last two centuries before Christ, but extensively edited by both Jews and Christians. See "Pseudepigrapha 1," *Dictionary of the Bible,* James Hastings, ed., rev. ed. Frederick C. Grant and H. H. Rowley, eds. (New York: Charles Scribner's Sons, 1963), 821, 822.

22 "Azazel," SDABD 97.

23 "While the sin-offering pointed to Christ as a sacrifice, and the high priest represented Christ as a mediator, the scapegoat typified Satan, the author of sin, upon whom the sins of the truly penitent will finally be placed." Ellen G. White, GC 422. "Since Satan is the originator of sin, the direct instigator of all the sins that caused the death of the Son of God, justice demands that Satan shall suffer the final punishment" (Id., PP 358).

24 Treiyer, DARCOM 3:215.

25 "By the king's examination of the guests at the feast is represented a work of judgment. The guests at the gospel feast are those who profess to serve God, those whose names are written in the book of life. But not all who profess to be Christians are true disciples. Before the final reward is given, it must be decided who are fitted to share the inheritance of the righteous. This decision must be made prior to the second coming of Christ in the clouds of heaven; for when He comes, His reward is with Him, 'to give every man according as his work shall be' " (Ellen G. White, COL 310).

26 Some cite John 5:24 as proof that a believer in Christ will never be investigated at the judgment bar of Christ. The passage reads, "Truly, truly, I say to you, he who hears my word and believes him who sent me, has eternal life; *he does not come into judgment [krisis,* judgment, condemnation] *but has passed from death to life."* Jesus, however, is not speaking of eschatological judgment, but of the new believer's *present status.* When the sinner accepts Jesus Christ as Saviour and Lord, he passes *from* "death"—a state of condemnation—to "life"—a state of acquittal and acceptance. In union with Christ he is not under divine condemnation in his present experience. Jesus' statement is similar to that of Paul's: "There is therefore *now* no *condemnation [katakrima]* for those who are in Christ Jesus" (Rom 8:1). But this wonderful union and acceptance in Christ does not deny the biblical teaching of a final judgment in which all—including the professed believer—must appear. In the case of a genuine believer, Jesus will attest the validity of the relationship before the angelic hosts (cf. Rev 3:5).

27 "The entire idea of investigative judgment . . . rests on the premise that man is

saved by faith alone. This doctrine of investigative judgment is a corrective against the extreme Calvinistic interpretations that would make salvation a matter of divine decree" (Norval F. Pease, *By Faith Alone* [Mountain View, CA: Pacific Press Publishing Association, 1962], 232).

8

Priesthood and Prophecy
Part 1

I n spite of the sanctuary's liturgical beauty, the atoning priesthood of Jesus Christ is only sketched in broad typological strokes in its rites. The plan of salvation—determined by Deity in eternity—lies evident in its shadows, awaiting antitypical fulfillment. These foreshadowed, saving acts of God, however, come alive with a vibrant reality when they are plotted on the *time grid of prophecy,* particularly the apocalyptic prophecies of Daniel and Revelation as they are fulfilled at the appointed times by Christ Himself.

The actual year the Messiah-Redeemer would appear, suffer His atoning death, and the onset of His priestly ministry in the heavenly sanctuary—as well as the commencement of His closing ministry in the final judgment—are all marked down. The prophetic time grid provides assuring evidence of God's foreknowledge of the achievement of His 'eternal purpose' to save sinners and to bring about a just and righteous end to the moral controversy that has marred the peace and happiness of the intelligent creation.[1]

Christ's Appearance and Atoning Death[2]

Specific time elements are, quite naturally, located in Daniel's prophecy in the OT as it pointed sixth century B.C. Israel toward the Messiah's future arrival. The visions of Daniel, chapters 7-9, are of particular interest here. Since the Hebrew mind tended to think from "effect or result back to its cause," we will examine these prophecies in reverse order, beginning with Daniel 9, for the sake of clarity.[3] The angel Gabriel opens his presentation to Daniel with these words:

> Seventy weeks have been decreed for your people and your holy city, to
> finish the transgression, to make an end of sin, to make atonement for iniquity,
> to bring in everlasting righteousness, to seal up vision and prophecy, and to
> anoint the most holy place (Dan 9:24, NASB).

All scholars agree that the "seventy weeks" of this prophecy—less than
a year and a half—cannot be taken literally in view of the events listed to be
accomplished. The number must be understood in some symbolic sense. And
the question is, By what method shall it be computed? The translators of the
RSV interpretively rendered it, "seventy weeks of years;" the translators of
the NIV opted for "seventy 'sevens' "—again implying a group of years. In
the body of the prophecy the larger unit (seventy weeks) is broken down to 7
weeks + 62 weeks + 1 week (= 70 weeks, vss. 25, 27). Since the Hebrew word
for "week" (vs. 27) is spelled out in its regular form ($\check{s}\bar{a}b\hat{u}\,'a$) and is translated
consistently elsewhere as "week" in the OT, we are on solid ground to hold
to the NASB translation of "weeks" for the entire period (70 weeks) and for
its constituent parts (7 weeks; 62 weeks; 1 week).[4]

The simplest method of interpretation is to follow the biblically valid
"year-day" principle in which a day in symbolic prophecy is equated to a year
of literal time (Ezek 4:6).[5] When we apply the year-day principle, we begin to
sense the significance of this special period allotted to the Jews who would
soon return from Babylonian exile to Palestine (cf. Dan 9:1, 2). Seventy weeks
x 7 days to the week = 490 prophetic days, or 490 literal years. This 490-year
era of Jewish history—both in terms of preparation for and in experiencing its
climactic events—could have been the nation's golden age, its finest hour!
The arrival of the long-hoped-for, the long-awaited Messiah would occur near
the close of this era, Gabriel announced!

Starting Point

The angel Gabriel continues:

> So you are to know and discern that from the issuing of a decree to restore
> and rebuild Jerusalem until Messiah the Prince there will be seven weeks and
> sixty-two weeks; it will be built again, with plaza and moat, even in times of
> distress. (Dan 9:25, NASB).

Three Persian kings—marvelously moved by God to release the Jews from
their Babylonian exile—repatriated all who would return to Palestine. All three
issued decrees. Cyrus the Great (539-530 B.C.) issued the original order
permitting their return and authorizing the rebuilding of the Temple at gov-

ernment expense (Ezra 1:1-4; 6:1-5). However, difficult circumstances encountered locally caused the Jews eventually to cease working on the Temple. But in the second year of the Persian king Darius I (522-486 B.C.), the prophets Haggai and Zechariah persuaded the leaders and people to begin anew on the Temple (Ezra 5:1, 2; Hag 1:1; Zech 1:1). Darius I also issued a decree reaffirming the intent of his predecessor, Cyrus, and requesting for the work to proceed at once (Ezra 6:1-12). With this official aid the work moved rapidly forward, and *the Temple* was completed about March 12, 515 B.C. (Ezra 6:15).[6]

Neither of these initial decrees dealt with the restoration of the national polity or the rebuilding of the capital, Jerusalem. But in his seventh regnal year, Artaxerxes I (465-423 B.C.) and his counselors authorized Ezra by official decree to organize the Jewish nation in harmony with the Mosaic guidelines and to install magistrates and judges to rule with authority, inflicting capital punishment if necessary (Ezra 7:11-26). Ezra evidently understood this order (to restore the functions of government) to include the rebuilding of Jerusalem. He began at once, accomplishing most of the wall and gate construction before his endeavors were thwarted (Ezra 4:7-23).

Due to a serious insurrection in the province of which Palestine was a part ("Beyond the River"), Artaxerxes I ordered the local enemies of the Jews to stop the building of the city *"until* a decree is made by me" (Ezra 4:21). Later, after peace had been restored to the province, Artaxerxes made Nehemiah, his Jewish cupbearer, governor of Judah (Neh 5:14) and authorized him to build on the city (Neh 2:1-8). The fact that Nehemiah completed the walls and gates of Jerusalem within 52 days indicates that these had already been largely put in place by Ezra before circumstances forced him to stop (Neh 6:15).

Thus, when these four Persian authorizations are examined closely, it is evident that only the initial decree of Artaxerxes I should be identified as the "decree to restore and rebuild Jerusalem" (Dan 9:25, NASB). The first two authorizations ordered and completed the rebuilding of the Temple only. But the decree of Artaxerxes I in his seventh regnal year restored the national polity, thereby permitting the rebuilding of the capital as well. This decree has the honor of being the starting point for this striking prophecy. The year for its issuance was 457 B.C.[7]

In that year Ezra led a large migration of Jews from Babylon on a four month trek back to the homeland, arriving on the first day of the 5th Jewish month. Assuming that in a month or two Ezra would have carried out the mandates of the decree and would have had sufficient time to put the legal system in place for the tiny nation, we can reasonably say that the decree was fully operational by the autumn of 457 B.C.

Messiah's Appearance

With the decree to restore the nation and its capital—identified with the decree of Artaxerxes I in 457 B.C.—we may now pinpoint the very year for the appearing of the Messiah! Gabriel continues:

> So you are to know and discern that *from* the issuing of a decree to restore and rebuild Jerusalem [457 B.C.] *until Messiah the Prince* there will be seven weeks and sixty-two weeks; it will be built again, with plaza and moat, even in times of distress (Dan 9:25, NASB).

The first unit of the 70 week prophecy, seven weeks (= 7 weeks x 7 days to the week = 49 days/years), indicates the length of time it would take to restore Jerusalem as a functioning capital—not just its walls and gates. The computation (457 B.C. minus 49 yrs. = 408 B.C.) points to 408 B.C. as the termination of this task. At present, we have no historical data to confirm this aspect of the prophecy, although both Ezra and Nehemiah surely carried on their work "in times of distress"!

Consequently, it is easier to calculate the appearance of the Messiah by simply adding the "seven weeks and sixty-two weeks" together (= 69 weeks x 7 days to the week = 483 days/years).[8] Tracing 483 years from the starting date, 457 B.C., we arrive at the fall of A.D. 27 and the appearance of "Messiah the Prince"! (483 years minus 456 [astronomical equivalent of 457 B.C.] = A.D. 27).[9]

It will be observed at once that the focus of the prophecy is not on the birth of the Messiah, but on His appearance in His official capacity. According to Luke's record "in the fifteenth year of the reign of Tiberius Caesar" [A.D. 27],[10] John the Baptist immersed Jesus of Nazareth in the Jordan river. As Jesus knelt upon the bank in prayer, "the Holy Spirit descended upon him in bodily form, as a dove, and a voice came from heaven, 'Thou art my beloved Son; with thee I am well pleased' " (Luke 3:1, 21, 22). The title, Messiah (or Christ) means literally, "Anointed One." Jesus officially began His ministry as the Messiah/Christ with the anointing of the Holy Spirit at His baptism (cf. Acts 10:38; Isa 61:1, 2; Luke 4:16-21).[11] As He opened His ministry in Galilee, Jesus announced, "*The time is fulfilled,* and the kingdom of God is at hand; repent, and believe the gospel" (Mark 1:15), an allusion to the time forecast of Daniel 9:25.[12]

Messiah's Atoning Death

Gabriel now predicts the Messiah's death:

> Then after the sixty-two weeks *the Messiah will be cut off* and have

nothing. . . . And he [the Messiah] will make a firm covenant with many for one week, but *in the middle of the week he will put a stop to sacrifice and grain offering* (Dan 9:26, 27, NASB)

The phrase referring to the "covenant," is more correctly rendered, "He will make strong a covenant for many one week."[13] The reference is to the Abrahamic/Sinaitic covenant, embedded in which were all the divine promises.[14] In the last prophetic week of the prophecy (1 week x 7 days to the week = 7 days/years) the Messiah confirmed the covenant promises to the Jewish people by means of His personal ministry and through the subsequent preaching of the apostles after His ascension (A.D. 27–A.D. 34). As the apostle Paul observes, "Christ became a servant to the circumcised [the nation of Israel] to show God's truthfulness, *in order to confirm the [covenant] promises given to the patriarchs*" (Rom. 15:8). "*When the time had fully come,* God sent forth his Son, born of woman, born under the law [that is, the Jewish system]" (Gal 4:4), but unfortunately, His "own people" did not receive Him (John 1:11).

After a short ministry of three and one-half years, our Lord was crucified ("in the middle of the week," Dan 9:27, NASB). At the moment of His death, the great inner veil of the temple was torn in two, "from top to bottom," as a violent quake shook the earth, signifying that the ancient sanctuary ritual had met its antitype in the Saviour's sacrificial death on Calvary (Matt 27:50, 51). By His supreme sacrifice on the cross—bearing the sins of the world—Christ "[made] atonement for iniquity," and "[brought] in everlasting righteousness" (Dan 9:24, NASB). If the Saviour's death occurred in the precise "middle of the week," then He died in the spring of A.D. 31 at the time of the annual Passover.

Messiah's Priesthood

Gabriel draws attention to one further event related to the Messiah: an anointing of "a most holy place" (Dan 9:24, RSV). As we have previously concluded (see ch. 1), this expression is best understood as referring to the anointing of the most sacred sanctuary in heaven, that is to say, it designates the inauguration of Christ as humanity's high priest before God in the heavenly sanctuary. Thus, according to this prophecy, in A.D. 31—subsequent to His resurrection and ascension into heaven—Christ became "a minister in the sanctuary and the true tent which is set up not by man but by the Lord" (Heb 8:2).

Prophetic Certainties

In His last conversation with His disciples on the eve of His death, Jesus said to them, "And now I have told you before it takes place, so that when it does take place, you may believe" (John 14:29). In these words Jesus touched on the divine purpose in revealing future events through prophecy: to confirm faith in God's promises. The shadow-types of the sanctuary parable functioned as a kind of prophecy for Israel. This parabolic forecast, however, was also paralleled by the direct, apocalyptic prophecies of Daniel which furnished an actual time line for some of the major events of the salvation history portrayed in the rites.

Only one Person has ever met the timing and messianic specifications called for in the 70 weeks prophecy (Dan 9), and He was Jesus of Nazareth. Jesus appeared on time, and God anointed Him by His Spirit in A.D. 27. Christ discharged His mission in three and one-half years and died an atoning death in A.D. 31, in the middle of the prophetic week as specified by the prophecy. Rising from the grave, He attested the truth of His resurrection "by many proofs" (Acts 1:3). Forty days later Christ ascended into heaven to begin His kingly reign and high priestly office in the heavenly sanctuary as once more foretold by Gabriel to the prophet Daniel.[15] These are the prophetic certainties upon which we build our faith that Jesus of Nazareth was who He claimed to be: the Christ (cf. John 8:24).

Two other related Danielic prophecies focus on Christ's priestly ministry and on the commencement of its closing phase. We turn now to examine the first of these.

Christ's Priestly Ministry Attacked

The "seventy-weeks" prophecy (Dan 9) is in reality an integral part of the previous vision given in Daniel 8, although it was given 12 years later.[16] We briefly sketch the vision of Daniel 8 now and its important time period.

Daniel 8 Vision

Daniel observes that he was "in Susa [Shushan] the capital," in the province of Elam, when he received this particular revelation (Dan 8:2). Significantly, Susa became one of the capitals of the Persian Empire (Esth 1:2). The prophet repeats three times that he saw the *vision* (*hāzôn*) at this time and place (Dan 8:1, 2).

The vision is composed of three parts: (1) The vision proper—a two-horn ram, a goat with a large horn between its eyes which breaks, four horns which emerge from the stump of the broken horn, and the appearing and activities of a "little horn" (Dan 8:3-12); (2) an audition in heaven between two holy personages (vss. 13, 14); (3) the first portion of the angel Gabriel's explanation of the vision (vss. 15-27).

Having "seen the *vision [ḥāzôn]*," Daniel has a deep concern about certain aspects of it (vs. 15). He hears a voice instructing Gabriel to explain the revelation: "Gabriel, make this man understand the *vision [mar'eh]*" (vs. 16). As we shall see, the term *mar'eh* refers to a specific part of the larger vision (*ḥāzôn*). It was the *mar'eh* segment which upset the prophet.

But Gabriel proceeds first to explain the entire vision (*ḥāzôn*) and observes its importance, "for it pertains to the appointed time of the end" (vs. 19). The ram with the two horns (the higher one coming up later) symbolized, he said, the dual kingdom of Medo-Persia, more commonly referred to as Persia, its dominant element (vs. 20). The goat with a large horn between its eyes is identified as the "king" or kingdom of Greece, and its large horn symbolized "the first king" (Alexander the Great, vs. 21). The four horns, arising from the stump of the broken horn, symbolized the "four kingdoms" that arose from Alexander's loosely forged empire upon that ruler's untimely death (vs. 22).

Any reader familiar with the four parallel visions of the book of Daniel will observe immediately that the vision of Daniel 8 follows the same sequence as the earlier dream/visions of Daniel 2 and 7 (see chart 1, Appendix D). The Ram (Medo-Persia) is the same power symbolized by the bear (Dan 7:5) and the silver breast and arms of the image (Dan 2:32, 39). The goat which eventually develops four horns is Greece, the same power symbolized by the leopard with four heads (Dan 7:6) and the bronze thighs of the image (Dan 2:32, 39).

Proceeding in the same sequence, we can see that the *activities* of the "little horn" which appear next in the Daniel 8 vision are similar to the activities of the fourth beast and its little horn (pagan/papal Rome) in the Daniel 7 vision (Dan 7:7, 8, 19-25) and (in part) with the iron legs of the image (Dan 2:33, 40).

We wish now to examine more closely the symbol of the "little horn" in Daniel 8, and its opposition to the priesthood of Jesus Christ in the heavenly sanctuary.

The little horn: pagan Rome (Dan 8:9). "Out of one of them[17] came forth a little horn, which grew exceedingly great toward the south, toward the east, and toward the glorious land" (Dan 8:9). In this manner the *horizontal* movements of pagan Rome are described as its strength grew "exceedingly great" in the Mediterranean world by military conquest: extending southward into North Africa and Egypt, eastward into Syria, and into Palestine—"the glorious land" (cf. Ezek 20:6; Ps 48:1, 2). These movements by the horn parallel Rome's military actions alluded to by the symbols of the power-shattering iron legs of the metal image (Dan 2:40) and the rapacious fourth beast with its iron teeth and bronze claws (Dan 7:7, 19). Thus, we are given in the horn's horizontal movements a symbolic summary of pagan Rome's military operations.

The little horn: papal Rome (Dan 8:10-12). The focus soon shifts to the *papal* phase of the horn as it moves into *a vertical stance* toward heaven. "It [the horn] grew great, even to the host of heaven; and some of the host of the stars it cast down to the ground, and trampled upon them" (Dan 8:10).

Gabriel explains this attack on "the stars" of heaven as an attack on God's people. "[He shall] destroy mighty men and the people of the saints" (vs. 24). This attack correlates with the predicted medieval papal persecutions pre-viously revealed in the vision of Daniel 7 (also symbolized in that vision by a "little horn"). "And as I looked, this horn made war with the saints, and prevailed over them." "He [the little horn] . . . shall wear out the saints of the Most High, . . . and they shall be given into his hand for a time, two times, and half a time" (Dan 7:21, 25 cf. Rev 13:7).[18]

Because scholars have commonly attempted to harmonize the translation of this passage to fit the Syrian Antiochus IV model, our current English translations are to some degree interpretive, favoring this view (some more, some less).[19] The sense however, of Daniel 8:11 may be paraphrased to read in the following manner: "And the horn made itself great even to the *Prince [śar]* of the *host [ṣābā']*, that is, to say, it took away from Him the *continual service [tāmîd]* and threw down the *foundation [mākôn]* of His *sanctuary [miqdāš]*."[20] The horn's action against the Prince, His people, and His sanc-tuary ministry is summarized in vs. 12. "Because of transgression, an army [host][21] was given over to the horn to oppose *the daily sacrifices [tāmîd]; and he cast truth down to the ground.* He did all this and prospered" (NKJV).

Who is the "Prince [śar] of the host" whom the horn so arrogantly opposes? According to the Scriptures the "Commander [śar] of the army [host, ṣābā'] of the Lord" (NKJV) is *a divine personage,* a heavenly being who may be worshiped (Josh 5:13-15).[22] The angel Gabriel identifies the "Prince of the host," in his explanation of the vision, as "the Prince of princes" (Dan 8:25) and later, as "Michael, your prince [śar] (Dan 10:21), and "Michael, the great prince [śar] who has charge of your people" (Dan 12:1). There is only one Divine Being who can rightfully claim such ascriptions, and He is the Messiah, the Christ. Jesus Christ is the "one mediator between God and men" (1 Tim

2:5) and the *"ruler [archōn]* of kings on earth" (Rev 1:5).

Since the papal phase of Rome functions in the Christian Era, its vertical movement against the "Prince of the host"—the "Prince of princes" is in reality an attack against Christ's royal, priestly ministry in the heavenly sanctuary (Heb 8:1, 2). This may be seen in the terse and graphic words of the paraphrase just cited above: The horn "took away from Him [the Prince] *the continual service [tāmîd]* and threw down the foundation *[mākôn]* of His sanctuary *[miqdāš]."*[23]

As we have seen earlier, the Hebrew word *tāmîd* is a very prominent term in the priestly ritual of the first apartment of the sanctuary. It is used not only in connection with the ever-burning morning and evening sacrifice, but also in connection with the ever-burning incense, lamps, the ever-present bread on the golden table, and with the names of the tribes of Israel inscribed on the stones of the breastpiece continuously borne before the Lord by the high priest. The *tāmîd* (being employed as a noun in this Daniel passage) must, therefore, refer to the whole spectrum of Christ's priestly ministration corresponding to the first apartment ministration of the Levitical priests—a ministration of reconciliation, forgiveness, and restoration of penitent sinners to God by virtue of His merits. The *foundation* of Christ's sanctuary ministry is essentially *"the grace* which [God] . . . gave us in Christ Jesus ages ago" (2 Tim 1:9, 10; cf. Eph 2:8).

Obviously, the power represented by this phase of the little horn cannot actually invade the heavenly sanctuary. But by claiming divine prerogatives, by establishing a priestly clergy between God and man who allegedly minister saving grace through a sacramental system, and by exalting the virgin Mary to a role of intercession in heaven, and by other related teachings, the papal system has for all practical purposes displaced Christ from His priestly office for centuries and has thereby marred and corrupted the great truths of salvation.[24]

An Heavenly Audition

At this point in the vision Daniel's attention is diverted to a conversation between two holy personages in the heavenly realm. They discuss the vision the prophet is seeing:

> Then I heard a holy one speaking; and another holy one said to the one that spoke, "For how long is the *vision [ḥāzôn]* concerning *the continual burnt offering [the tāmîd],* the transgression that makes desolate, and the giving over of the *sanctuary [qōdeš]* and host to be trampled under foot?" (vs. 13).

The speaker, thus addressed, turned and said directly to Daniel:

> For two thousand and three hundred evenings and mornings; then the *sanctuary [qōdeš]* shall be restored to its rightful state [*niṣdaq*] [RSV], shall be cleansed [NKJV] (vs. 14).

The question. The emphasis of the question raised by the inquirer is not on the *duration* (how long?), as our common versions render the Hebrew, but on the *termination* point of the vision (until when?). A literal translation of vs. 13 reads as follows: "*Until when ['ad-mātay]* the *vision [ḥāzôn],* the *daily/ continual* [the *tāmîd*], and the transgression desolating, to give both the sanctuary and the host a trampling?" The sense is simply, When will the vision (with its component parts—especially those aspects dealing with the horn's attack on the sanctuary ministry of the Messiah and on His people) come to an end—and what will follow?[25]

The answer. The question, "until when" (*'ad-mātay*) is answered literally, "Until [*'ad*] evening [and, vs. 26] morning two thousand and three hundred, then the sanctuary will be . . ." (vs. 14). "And [the] *vision [mar'eh] of the evening and the morning* which was told, it is true . . ." (vs. 26). This kind of expression (evening-morning) is found first in Genesis 1 where it is used by Moses to describe the 24 hour days of Creation week: "And there was evening and there was morning, one day" (vs. 5; cf. vss. 8, 13, 19, 23, 31). Thus, the Greek Septuagint (the Greek translation of the Hebrew Bible)—in both its versions of the book of Daniel—understands the expression to mean two thousand and three hundred *days.* (Literally, "Until evening and morning *days [hēmerai]* two thousand and three hundred").[26]

Since the vision of Daniel 8 is symbolic prophecy, it is reasonable to accept this time period as symbolic and to recognize its true time value (on the year-day principle) as 2300 years.[27] This conclusion is supported by the fact that the *vision (ḥāzôn,* "until when the *vision*?" vs. 13) starts at some point in the era of the Persian ram (8:1-3, 20) and proceeds successively through the era of the Greek goat (8:5, 21) and its divided states (8:22), through the era of pagan Rome (8:9, 23) and into the era of papal Rome (8:10-12, 24, 25), to terminate at some point within "the time of the end" (vss. 17, 19). This great sweep of the centuries (required by the *vision, ḥāzôn*) is clear evidence that the 2300 days = 2300 years, and nothing less.

Computing the 2300-year time period. Two different Hebrew words are used to describe different aspects of the revelation recorded in Daniel 8: *ḥāzôn* and *mar'eh.* Both are translated "vision" in our common versions. The term *ḥāzôn* is used seven times and designates the entire revelation or vision given to Daniel at Susa (vss. 1, 2, 13, 15, 17, 26b). The term *mar'eh* emphasizes the idea of an "appearance" (8:15) and is employed to designate that portion of the larger vision in which the two holy personages appeared within Daniel's view and discussed the 2300-day period and the restoring of the sanctuary (8:26a, 27). It was this *mar'eh* portion of the *ḥāzôn*-vision which especially attracted Daniel's attention and puzzled him; hence, the reason for the order to the angel-interpreter, "Gabriel, make this man understand the *vision [mar'eh]*" (8:16).

Perplexed by what he had been shown, Daniel was at first frightened by Gabriel's approach. But the angel assured him that the thrust of the prophecy did not involve the immediate future but was "for the time of the end" (vss. 17-19). First, Gabriel identified the ram, the goat, and the meaning of the four horns arising from the stump of the goat's broken horn. He then described the rise and daring actions of the little horn, asserting that it would eventually be broken by divine intervention ("by no human hand," vss. 20-25).

At this juncture Gabriel abruptly terminated his explanation, saying only that "the *vision (mar'eh)* of the "evenings and mornings" (RSV)—the 2300 evening-morning days and the righting of the sanctuary (vs. 14) was true, but Daniel was for the present to seal up the entire *vision [ḥāzôn]* "for it pertains to many days hence" (vs. 26).

The distressed prophet "was overcome and lay sick for some days" (vs. 27). He observes, "I was appalled by the *vision [mar'eh]* and did not understand it" (vs. 27). Thus, the *mar'eh* aspect of the larger vision—the 2300-day time period and its link to the sanctuary—Gabriel left unexplained. Naturally, Daniel would have associated this supposedly long delay in "cleansing/restoring" the sanctuary with the ruined Temple in Jerusalem, and he sickened at the thought.

About a dozen years later, shortly after the Persian ram's conquest of the Babylonian Empire, Daniel began to search the prophecies of Jeremiah and to plead with God to forgive His people Israel and to honor His promises to restore them to their Palestinian homeland (Dan 9:1-19). As he prayed, the prophet entered into a state of vision; Gabriel appeared before him:

> While I was still speaking in prayer, then the man Gabriel, whom I had seen in the *vision [ḥāzôn]* previously, came to me. . . . "O Daniel, I have now come forth to give you insight with understanding. . . . so give heed to the message and gain understanding of the *vision [mar'eh]*.
>
> "Seventy weeks *have been decreed [ḥātak]* for your people and your holy city, to finish the transgression, to make an end of sin, to make atonement

for iniquity, to bring in everlasting righteousness, to seal up vision and prophecy, and to anoint the most holy place.

"So you are to know and discern that from the issuing of *a decree to restore and rebuild Jerusalem* until the Messiah the Prince there will be seven weeks and sixty-two weeks . . ." (Dan 9:21-25, NASB).

It is evident from the reappearing of Gabriel and the flow of the new vision in Daniel 9 that this revelation is simply a resumption of Gabriel's explanation of the vision of Daniel 8 which he did not complete. The angel now comes to explain the *mar'eh* portion of that vision—the unexplained segment about the sanctuary and the 2300 days. "Give heed to the message," Gabriel admonishes Daniel, "and gain understanding of *the vision* [the *mar'eh*]" (Dan 9:23 cf. 8:13, 14, 16, 26a, 27). The last item Gabriel touched on in the Daniel 8 vision, but didn't explain, was *a time period* (the 2300 days). Now, in this subsequent revelation he begins with *a time period* (the 70 weeks) that will form the beginning segment of the longer span (the 2300 days).

There is a conceptual link between the two visions of Daniel 8 and 9 as well as a time element. In typical Hebrew fashion (effect to cause), the vision of Daniel 9 notes the anointing of the heavenly sanctuary (9:24), while the vision of Daniel 8 notes the cleansing or setting right of the heavenly sanctuary (8:14).[28] Thus, the evidence is more than adequate to demonstrate that the visions of Daniel 8 and 9 should be regarded as two segments dealing with the same subject and should be interpreted as a unit. In the vision of Daniel 8 no information was given the prophet to indicate either the beginning or the ending points of the 2300 prophetic days. It may be inferred, of course, that the period began during the rule of the Medo Persian ram, but no specific starting date is mentioned. As we would expect, Gabriel's continuing explanation in the vision of Daniel 9 supplies the required information. Two essential items are clearly stated:

1. "Seventy weeks [490 prophetic days] *have been decreed [ḥātak]* for your people . . ." (Dan 9:24, NASB).

The Hebrew word *ḥātak* (used only once in the OT) can mean in its concrete form "to cut," and "to cut off" or in its extended, abstract concept "to determine, decree." Both meanings are found in Mishnaic Hebrew, a development in the language dated to a millennium *after* Daniel's time. But even in Mishnaic Hebrew the concrete concept "to cut off" appears more commonly used than the abstract idea of "determine" or "decree." Since the meanings of Hebrew words developed from concrete concepts toward their more abstract ideas, it is linguistically sound to understand Gabriel to say to

Daniel (more than 500 years before Christ), "Seventy weeks have been 'cut off' for your people—to accomplish certain ends."

But from what would the 70 prophetic weeks or 490 prophetic days be cut? Since the visions of Daniel 8 and 9 form essentially one revelation, it is reasonable to infer they are cut off from the longer 2300-day period. That is, the 70 weeks (490 days) simply form the first segment of the longer span of the 2300 days.[29]

2. The second piece of information Gabriel supplies provides the starting point from which to date both time periods:

"So you are to know and discern that *from the issuing of a decree to restore and rebuild Jerusalem* until the Messiah the Prince there will be seven weeks and sixty-two weeks . . ." (Dan 9:25, NASB).

As we have observed earlier, the Persian decree that fulfilled these specifications went into effect in the fall of 457 B.C. Thus, the starting date for the 70 weeks prophecy becomes also the starting date for the longer, 2300-day span. Twenty-three hundred literal years extend from the fall of 457 B.C. to the fall of 1844. At that terminal point, according to the prediction, "the sanctuary shall be cleansed" (NKJV)/"the sanctuary shall be restored to its rightful state" (Dan 8:14, RSV).

The accuracy of the beginning date, 457 B.C., and the baptismal date of Jesus as the Christ (the Anointed One) in A.D. 27 (both dates being capable of historical verification) renders certain A.D. 34 as the end point of the 70 weeks (Dan 9:24-27) and A.D. 1844 as the end point of the 2300 days (Dan 8:14). With the termination of the latter time period, the divine action began to cleanse or to restore the sanctuary to its rightful state.

Cleansing/restoring of the sanctuary. What is meant by the expression, "then shall the sanctuary be cleansed" (NKJV) or "the sanctuary shall be restored to its rightful state" (RSV)? And what sanctuary is involved? Let us address the second question first. Two points stand out: (1) In the symbolic vision the sanctuary of the Prince appears to be located in heaven since the little horn extends itself vertically into the heavens to cast down both the *stars* who belong to the Prince—and to disrupt His priestly, sanctuary ministry (Dan 8:10-12). (2) Since in reality the prophecy deals largely with Rome's papal phase (8:10-12), the latter's attack on the sanctuary obviously comes in the Christian Era. The only sanctuary functioning in the Christian Era is the heavenly sanctuary in which Christ ministers as humanity's high priest. It is *His* priestly ministry that has been obscured by Rome's false teachings and practices. Although the "stars" designate God's people on earth, the reference to the Prince's sanctuary ministry has to point to Christ's priestly activity in the *heavenly* sanctuary, because He could not be a priest on earth (Heb. 7:14; 8:4).

The Hebrew verb translated in the two versions cited above as "cleansed"/ "restored" occurs in its passive form only once in the OT—and that occurrence is here in Daniel 8:14 (*niṣdaq*). Its active form (*ṣādaq*) carries the root meaning "to be just/righteous." Consequently, a number of modern translations have suggested such phrasing as the following: the sanctuary will "be restored" (TEV), "be properly restored" (NASB), "have its rights restored" (JB), "emerge victorious" (NEB), "be reconsecrated" (NIV), "be restored to its rightful state" (RSV). The KJV and the NKJV follow the Greek Septuagint translation of *niṣdaq* which is *katharizō*—to "cleanse" or "purify."

Here again, most translators are thinking of an Antiochus IV model—this king's desecration of the Temple and its restoration and rededication three years later by Judas Maccabeus (second century B.C.). But if we lay aside this view which requires a forcing of the Scriptures to maintain it, we will find that the Bible quite adequately explains itself.

In Daniel 8 the subject of the sanctuary forms *the conceptual framework* of the vision. For example, at the outset the ram and goat, *sacrificial animals,* are employed in the symbolism (cf. in contrast the wild beasts in Dan 7). Such words as "place/foundation" (*mākôn*, vs. 11), "sanctuary" (*miqdāš: qōdeš*, vss. 11, 13, 14), "daily"/"continual" (*tāmîd*, vs. 11, 13) are directly related to the Hebrew worship system. *Ṣādaq* is also a sanctuary term inasmuch as various forms of its root (*ṣdq*) occur numerous times in the Psalms, the "hymns" of the Hebrew service. Therefore, we are on safe ground to interpret the significance of *niṣdaq* in Daniel 8:14 within the setting of the Israelite sanctuary worship system as it foreshadows the high priestly activity of Christ in the heavenly sanctuary.[30]

Detailed studies of the biblical usages of the *ṣdq* forms, as they are used in the OT, have led to the conclusion that *niṣdaq* (Dan 8:14) is "a polychromic designation which includes within its semantic range such meanings as 'cleansing, vindicating, justifying, setting right, restoring.' . . . It appears that Daniel chose the term *niṣdaq*—a word from a root with rich and broad connotations, widely employed in judgment settings and legal procedures—in order to communicate effectively the interrelated aspects of the 'cleansing' of the heavenly sanctuary in the cosmic setting of the end-time judgment"[31]

As previously noted, the *tāmîd* ritual in the typical sanctuary related only to the priestly ministration connected with the first apartment of the sanctuary. Just so, the little horn's seizing of Christ's *tāmîd,* intercessory ministration in the heavenly sanctuary, disrupted or obscured only that facet of His work. But there are *two phases* of priestly ministration in the sanctuary. The second, major phase—typified by the ritual of the Day of Atonement—the little horn cannot touch. The Day of Atonement was the only rite in the ceremonial year that brought about the cleansing of the sanctuary, a putting of things to rights in a final manner. As we have studied earlier, the specific rite of the Day of Atonement foreshadowed the final judgment.[32]

The little horn's attack on Christ's priestly ministry does not in itself bring on the Day of Atonement judgment day. It will come in its proper time as God has designed that it should (Acts 17:31). The conversation between the holy personages, which Daniel heard in vision (Dan 8:13, 14), simply indicates that the ravages of the horn power against the "truth" would continue until the antitypical day of atonement, that is, until the day when God intervenes in final judgment. The final, eschatological judgment will indeed settle all issues related to the sin problem, including the horn's opposition to Christ's saving ministry.

Although Christ's priestly ministry in the heavenly sanctuary before the Father was clearly understood by the apostolic church, it was largely forgotten in the long ages that followed as the Christian church moved more and more from its scriptural foundation. The eventual institution of an earthly priesthood and the elevation of Mary and the "saints" as heavenly intercessors obscured and corrupted Christian understanding of Christ's mediatorial work and its importance to the plan of salvation. The sixteenth century Reformation and other spiritual movements began to correct this distortion of Scripture truth.

And now, in this "time of the end" period in which we live, the spotlight of Daniel's prophecies have focused once more on the atoning high priestly ministry of Jesus Christ. According to the visions of Daniel 8, 9, at the close of the 2300-day prophecy in 1844 Christ began His second and last phase of high priestly service—a service analogous to the typical Day of Atonement. This is a work of final judgment as we shall see more clearly as we examine in the next chapter the vision of Daniel 7.

———— ◆ ————

Endnotes

1 In some quarters it is argued that all prophecies—whether the classical prophecies of the major and minor OT prophets, or the apocalyptic prophecies of Daniel

and Revelation—should be regarded as *conditional,* as revelations of God's *purposes,* but *not of His foreknowledge.* It is argued that the possible fulfillment of any prophecy in its *primary* intent is *conditional on the obedience of God's people.* For example, the fulfillment of Daniel's predictions would depend upon Israel's steadfast obedience to God. Since Israel failed in this respect, Daniel's predictions collapsed. Any other assigned fulfillment would have to be, therefore, a reinterpretation and reapplication of these prophecies to the new condition by a later inspired writer.

   We reject this view inasmuch as it does not harmonize with the biblical data. We concur that prophecies *of divine blessing or judgment,* growing out of Israel's covenant relationship with God, are by their very nature truly conditional; their fulfillment depended upon Israel's response (see Jer 18:7-10). However, the apocalyptic prophecies of Daniel and Revelation, which essentially depict the cosmic struggle beteen good and evil and the ultimate victory and establishment of God's eternal kingdom, are revelations of His foreknowledge and His sovereignty. No failure on the part of Israel or the church can prevent the Creator from carrying out the objectives which He has revealed in these apocalyptic books. For a discussion of the issue, see William G. Johnsson, "Conditionality in Biblical Prophecy With Particular Reference to Apocalyptic," DARCOM 3:259-287.

2 For our purpose, we here limit the presentation of Daniel 9 to those points especially related to Christ's sacrifice and priesthood. For a full study, see William H. Shea, "The Prophecy of Daniel 9:24-27," DARCOM 3:75-118. For a comparison and critique of the major interpretations of this passage, see Gerhard F. Hasel, "Interpretations of the Chronology of the Seventy Weeks," DARCOM 3:3-63.

3 See, William H. Shea, "The Unity of Daniel," DARCOM 2:237. Daniel 9:24-27 presents the appearing of the Messiah the Prince, His atoning sacrifice, and entrance into His priestly ministry. Daniel 8 presents Him as the Prince of the host, ministering as priest in the heavenly sanctuary. Daniel 7 presents Him as the Son of man receiving His eternal kingdom. Thus, we see in reverse order the key activities of the Messiah: Sacrifice, Priest, and King. Ibid., 238-240.

4 The translators of the NIV are inconsistent here. The identical word which the Hebrew Masoretes vocalized as "weeks" in Dan 9:24 and Dan 10:2 (*šābu'îm*), the NIV translators have rendered as "sevens" (9:24) and "weeks" (10:2). This means their renderings of "seventy 'sevens,' " "seven 'sevens,' " "sixty-two 'sevens,' " and "one 'sevens' " are quite arbitrary. For a discussion of this translation issue, see William H. Shea, *Selected Studies in Prophetic Interpretation,* DARCOM 1:74-77. The Hebrew word for "week" is a double gender noun which shows up in its plural forms. The masculine plural (the form that appears in Daniel) emphasizes the unitary nature of the "70 weeks," linguistically denying the popular "gap" theory in this prophecy. See, Gerhard F. Hasel,

"The Hebrew Masculine Plural for "Weeks" in the Expression "Seventy Weeks" in Daniel 9:24," *AUSS* (vol. 31, no. 2), Summer 1993, 105-118. For an argument in favor of "weeks" rather than "sevens" in the translating of this prophecy, see Frank W. Hardy, "The Hebrew Singular for 'Week' in the Expression 'One Week' in Daniel 9:27," *AUSS* (vol. 32, no. 3), Autumn 1994, 197-202.

5 See Appendix B, "Year-day Principle."

6 SDABC 3:360.

7 While some continue to question the possibility of dating the seventh regnal year of Artaxerxes I (the year of his decree restoring Judah's polity by the hand of Ezra, see Ezra 7:6, 7), William Shea asserts, after a careful review of all the evidence, "There need be no doubt for anyone familiar with the available chronological sources that we have the regnal years of Artaxerxes I accurately fixed. Indeed, the dates are so well set in the cement of these sources that it is hard to imagine any kind of future discovery that could possibly move them" (William H. Shea, "When Did the Seventy Weeks of Daniel 9:24 Begin?" Appendix B, DARCOM 6:388).

The only question is whether Ezra used the Persian-Babylonian calendar that ran from spring to spring, or the Jewish civil calendar that extended from fall to fall. If he used the former, the king's decree and Ezra's return occurred in 458 B.C. If he used the Jewish fall-fall calendar, the decree and Ezra's return occurred in 457 B.C. Nehemiah's datelines concerning his affairs with Artaxerxes I (Neh 1:1; 2:1) indicate that the Jews were employing their own fall-fall calendar. Since the present "books" of Ezra and Nehemiah were considered *one* book by the Jews in Bible times, there is presumptive evidence that Ezra would have reckoned his dating of Artaxerxes I by the Jewish fall-fall calendar just as his contemporary Nehemiah did. Double-dated documents from the same 5th century B.C. times—from a Jewish colony on the island of Elephantine, in Egypt—likewise confirm the Jewish use of their fall-fall calendar. For a discussion of these documents, see Siegfried H. Horn and Lynn H. Wood, *The Chronology of Ezra 7* (Washington, DC: Review & Herald Publishing Association, 1953.

8 Some modern, English versions, following the punctuation inserted by the Masoretes (Jewish scholars who functioned after the time of Jesus), have connected the seven weeks with the Messiah and the 62 weeks with the building of the city. For example, the RSV reads in part, "from the going forth of the word to restore and build Jerusalem to the coming of an anointed one, a prince, there shall be seven weeks. Then for sixty-two weeks it shall be built again with squares and moat, but in a troubled time" (Dan 9:25). However, a careful analysis of the poetic arrangement of this passage (vss. 25, 26) links the seven weeks with the rebuilding of the city and the 62 weeks to the Messiah. "This poetic analysis rules out the Masoretic punctuation and those modern versions (RSV, NEB, AB) which pattern after it. These versions construe the phrasing to mean that the

Messiah was to come at the end of the seven-week period. . . . On the other hand the analysis confirms the ancient versions (Septuagint, Theodotion, Vulgate, Syriac) and translations which pattern after them (KJV, ASV, NASB, MLB, JB). These understand the phraseology to indicate that the Messiah was to come at the end of the second or 62-week segment of the prophecy. (The 70-week prophecy has three time segments: $7 + 62 + 1 = 70$)" (William H. Shea, "The Prophecy of Daniel 9:24-27," DARCOM 3:89-91. See also, Id., "Poetic Relationships of the Time Periods in Dan 9:25," SA[1], 277-282).

9 The B.C.-A.D. arrangement must be recognized when one makes a computation that will move from B.C. to A.D. years. There is no zero (0) in this artificial scale, and the B.C. years (Before Christ) also run in reverse to the A.D. (Anno Domini) years. For convenience, astronomers calculating across this scale give a zero value to 1 B.C. and *minus* numerals to the B.C. side of the scale as in the following diagram:

Astonomical	-4	-3	-2	-1	0	1	2	3	4
Chronological	5 B.C.	4 B.C.	3 B.C.	2 B.C.	1 B.C.	A.D. 1	A.D. 2	A.D. 3	A.D. 4

It will be observed that the "astronomical equivalent" of a B.C. date is always one number *lower* than the B.C. date. Thus, if -4 is the astronomical equivalent of 5 B.C., then -456 is the astronomical equivalent of 457 B.C. Thus, -456 (standing for 457 B.C.) must be used in subtracting (483-456) to arrive at the correct date of A.D. 27. See, S. H. Horn and L. H. Wood, *The Chronology of Ezra 7*, 27-32.

10 "Dates for Tiberius were reckoned in several different ways. What we have here in Luke 3:1 is a date formula written in an eastern style, in the Scriptures which are themselves of eastern origin. It seems reasonable, therefore, to reckon this date in the manner date formulae were employed in that region. Such a method dates Tiberius' fifteenth year to A.D. 27/28, fall-to-fall" (William H. Shea, "The Prophecy of Daniel 9:24-27," DARCOM 3:102). "If Luke was following the Syrian method as a native of Antioch, Tiberius's 'fifteenth year' would have been from the fall of A.D. 27 to the fall of A.D. 28 . . ." (Walter L. Liefeld, Luke. ExpBC 8:854. Used by permission of Zondervan Publishing House).

11 The title "Messiah" derives from the Hebrew word *Māšîaḥ;* "Christ" derives from the Greek word *Christos.* Both mean, "the Anointed One." Cf. John 1:41.

12 "The gospel message, as given by the Saviour Himself, was based on the prophecies. The 'time' which He declared to be fulfilled was the period made known by the angel Gabriel to Daniel [Dan 9:24-27]" (Ellen G. White, DA 233).

13 See William H. Shea, "The Prophecy of Daniel 9:24-27," DARCOM 3:95.

14 Cf. Ps. 105:6-11; Gal 3:16, 17.

15 For another three and one-half years the apostles continued to appeal to the Jewish nation to accept Jesus of Nazareth as the promised Messiah. But the national

leadership responded in A.D. 34 by stoning Stephen, the first Christian martyr. For an important insight into the significance of Stephen's death in connection with the closing of the 70-week prophecy, see William H. Shea, "The Prophecy of Daniel 9:24-27," DARCOM 3:80-82.

16 Some argue that if God intended for the visions of Daniel 8 and 9 to be understood as an integral unit, He would not have waited more than a decade to complete the vision of Dan 8. However, the Deity is not dependent upon the instructions of His creatures as to when to act! There is an appropriate reason indicated by the visions themselves. Although the vision of Dan 8 was given in Belshazzar's third year, *it began with a view of the Persian ram* (vss. 1-4). God simply waited until Persia had conquered the Babylonian Empire in fact before giving the vision of Dan 9 *which focused on Persia's relations with God's people*. It was when Daniel was searching the prophecies of Jeremiah (Dan 9:1, 2) and Isaiah (Isa 44:26-28; 45:1-4, 13 cf. Ezra 1:1-4) after Babylon's overthrow by Cyrus that God sent Gabriel to the prophet to announce Persia's part in restoring Judah's nationhood and its capital (Dan 9:24, 25). For a more detailed analysis for the delay in Gabriel's return to complete his explanation of Dan 8, see William H. Shea, "The Relationship Between the Prophecies of Daniel 8 and Daniel 9," SA[1], 239, 240.

17 It is commonly thought that the "little horn" (more correctly translated, "horn, which started small," NIV) issued from one of the four Greek horns, that is, from one of the Greek divisions of Alexander's empire. But, grammatically speaking, it can be demonstrated that the horn did not derive from a previous horn. Rather, it came from one of the four winds of heaven. That is, the statement is simply being made that this horn power *made its way from one of the directions of the compass*. The horn's *direction of movement* (from the west) is being emphasized rather than its place of origin. See William H. Shea, *Selected Studies on Prophetic Interpretation,* DARCOM 1:41-43; Gerhard F. Hasel, "The 'Little Horn,' the Heavenly Sanctuary, and the Time of the End: A Study of Daniel 8:9-14," DARCOM 2:387-394.

18 Four of the five verbal forms in Dan 8:9, 10 are feminine, in harmony with the feminine gender of the Hebrew word for "horn." But in vs. 11 the horn's verbal act of magnifying itself is stated in the masculine gender, probably to allude to the entity which the "horn" symbolizes. The verbal forms return to the feminine gender in vs. 12. It has been suggested that the momentary shift in gender in vs. 11 may indicate a *sequence* fulfillment for this horn's activities. If we align the vision of Dan 8 with the vision of Dan 7, it is evident that the activities of the "little" horn in Dan 8 match the activities of *the fourth beast and its little horn* in Dan 7. Consequently, it has been suggested *that Dan 8:9, 10 are fulfilled* by the pagan phase of Rome, whereas vss. 11, 12 are fulfilled by the papal or ecclesiastical phase of Rome. This sequence concept is more attractive than the idea of a dual fulfillment (a concept not found elsewhere in Daniel or Revela-

tion), but it may be putting too much weight on a temporary change of gender for the verbal action of the horn in vs. 11. The change is more obvious in Dan 8 when the horn moves away from its *horizontal* actions in vs. 9 (pagan Rome) to its *vertical* actions (papal) against the host of the stars (God's people, vs. 24) and their Prince (vss. 10-12). The emphasis on the horn in Dan 8 is on its papal aspect—a matter first announced in the previous vision of Dan 7:8, etc. For a discussion of the sequence concept, see Gerhard F. Hasel, "The 'Little Horn,' . . ." DARCOM 2:400, 401 and n.7.

19 Antiochus IV Epiphanes ruled as a Seleucid king of Syria, 175-164 B.C. Palestine was a part of his kingdom. His harsh attack upon the Jewish religion and his desecration of the Temple on December 16, 167 B.C. led to the Maccabean revolt. Hippolytus (d. ca. 236), following allusions to Antiochus in 1 Maccabees, is the first Christian commentator to identify the little horn of Dan 8 with Antiochus IV. The pagan philosopher, Porphyry (d. 304), in his work, "Against Christianity," appears to have derived his Antiochus IV (2nd century, B.C.) interpretation for the book of Daniel from the earlier writings of Hippolytus. For a discussion of the origin of the Antiochus IV Epiphanes interpretation in Daniel, see William H. Shea, "Early Development of the Antiochus Epiphanes Interpretation," DARCOM 2:256-328. For an analysis demonstrating the inappropriateness of identifying the little horn of Dan 8 with Antiochus, see Id. "Why Antiochus IV Is Not the Little Horn of Daniel 8," DARCOM 1:25-55; see also, Arthur J. Ferch, "Authorship, Theology, and Purpose of Daniel," DARCOM 2:3-83; Gerhard F. Hasel, "The 'Little Horn,' . . ." DARCOM 2:405-407.

20 See Gerhard F. Hasel, "The 'Little Horn,' . . ." DARCOM 2:405, 410.

21 The first clause of vs. 12 is obscure. Some identify the "host" of vs. 12 with the "host" of vs. 10 (cf. RSV). However, "since the term 'host' does not have the definite article (the), it seems best not to link it with the same term in the previous verses. The action of the 'host' [vs. 12] (understood as subject) is directed against 'the continuance [*tāmîd*]." Hasel, "The 'Little Horn,' . . ." DARCOM 2:416.

22 Humans are not permitted to worship either man or angel, only God. See Acts 10:25, 26; Rev 19:10; 22:8, 9.

23 Other translations read, "And *the continual burnt offering* [*tāmîd*] was taken from him" (RSV); "it removed *the regular sacrifice*, [*tāmîd*] from Him" (NASB); "the *daily sacrifices* [*tāmîd*] were taken away" (NKJV). This emphasis *on only the altar* indicates the attempt to render the passage to fit the historical Antiochus' act of desecrating the altar of burnt offering in the court of the Jewish Temple by erecting upon it a pagan altar and offering swine upon it.

24 With no intent to attack sincere believers in the Roman communion, we offer as evidence a few basic characteristics of the system that are contrary to the Scriptures. Describing the medieval papal view of grace (which continues), Williston Walker says, "Grace does not come to men indiscriminately. It has its definite channels and these are the sacraments, and the sacraments alone." *A*

History of the Christian Church, 3rd. ed. (New York: Charles Scribner's Sons, 1970), 247; "It was through the sacraments that the clergy maintained their spiritual authority over the people. By the middle of the fifteenth century the number of sacraments had been officially fixed at seven: baptism, confirmation, penance, the Eucharist (the conclusion of the ceremony of the Mass), extreme unction, marriage, and ordination (holy orders). . . . The sacramental rite eventually came to be looked upon as primarily an instrument for conveying spiritual grace, that is, for miraculously and intrinsically (*ex opere operato*) sanctifying the individual" (Harold J. Grimm, The Reformation Era, 1500-1650 [New York: The Macmillan Company, 1954], 97); "The Sacraments, which, by the ordinance of God, are a necessary means of salvation, and a plenteous source of spiritual advantage." "That the Sacraments are amongst the means of attaining righteousness and salvation, cannot be questioned" (*The Catechism of the Council of Trent,* English translation by J. Donovan [Dublin/London: Richard Coyne/Keating and Browne, 1829], 136, 138).

The following citations are taken from a Roman Catholic work: *Dignity and Duties of the Priest* by St. Alphonsus de Liguori. Eugene Grimm, ed. (Brooklyn: Redemptorist Fathers, 1927): "With regard to the power of the priests over the real body of Jesus Christ, it is of faith that when they pronounce the words of consecration the Incarnate Word has obliged himself to obey and to come into their hands under the sacramental species. . . . In obedience to the words of his priests—HOC EST CORPUS MEUM—God himself descends on the altar, that he comes wherever they call him, and as often as they call him, and places himself in their hands, even though they should be his enemies. And after having come, he remains, entirely at their disposal; they move him as they please, from one place to another; they may, if they wish, shut him up in the tabernacle, or expose him on the altar, or carry him outside the church; they may, if they choose, eat his flesh, and give him for the food of others. 'Oh, how very great is their power,' says St. Laurence Justinian, speaking of priests. 'A word falls from their lips and the body of Christ is there substantially formed from the matter of bread, and the Incarnate Word descended from heaven, is found really present on the table of the altar' " (pp. 26, 27). "The priest holds the place of the Saviour himself, when, by saying 'Ego te absolvo,' he absolves from sin. This great power, which Jesus Christ has received from his eternal Father, he has communicated to his priests. 'Jesus,' says Tertullian, 'invests the priests with his own powers' " (p. 34). "According to St. Ambrose, a priest, in absolving a sinner, performs the very office of the Holy Ghost in the sanctification of souls. . . . St. Clement, then, had reason to say that the priest is, as it were, a God on earth. . . . Innocent III. has written: 'Indeed, it is not too much to say that in view of the sublimity of their offices the priests are so many gods' " (p. 36).

Cardinal Alphonsus de Liguori, cited above, was canonized by the Roman church. His writings are viewed as presenting a summary of Catholic tradition.

The following excerpts are from his work, *The Glories of Mary* (published by the Redemptorist Fathers, Brooklyn, 1931 edition) collected by Dr. Joseph Zacchello and cited in Loraine Boettner, *Roman Catholicism* (Philadelphia: The Presbyterian and Reformed Publishing Company, 1962), 137-141. The pagination noted is from the above-mentioned edition of the work. "She is truly a mediatress of peace between sinners and God. Sinners receive pardon by . . . Mary alone" (pp. 82, 83). "Many things . . . are asked from God, and are not granted; they are asked from MARY, and are obtained," for "She . . . is even Queen of Hell, and Sovereign Mistress of the Devils" (pp. 127, 141, 143). "Mary is called . . . the gate of heaven because no one can enter that blessed kingdom without passing through HER" (p. 160). Mary "is also the Advocate of the whole human race . . . for she can do what she wills with God" (p. 193). "We often more quickly obtain what we ask by calling on the name of MARY, than by invoking that of Jesus." "She . . . is our Salvation, our Life, our Hope, our Counsel, our Refuge, our Help" (pp. 254, 257). "The whole Trinity, O MARY, gave thee a name . . . above every other name, that at Thy name, every knee should bow, of things in heaven, on earth, and under the earth" (p. 260).

25 Gerhard F. Hasel, "The 'Little Horn,' . . ." DARCOM 2:429; Angel M. Rodríguez, "The Sanctuary and Its Cleansing," *Adventist Review*, September 1994. Supplement, 7.

26 Attempts have been made to interpret the 2300 days of Dan 8:14 so as to make them fit the three year period the Temple stood profaned by Antiochus IV (25 Chislev, 167 B.C. to 25 Chislev, 164 B.C.). Some have argued that the "daily," or more specifically, the morning and evening sacrifices are being referred to in vs. 14. Since these amounted to two offerings per day, the 2300 days should be halved to make 1150 full days (for an example, see the "Good News Bible" [TEV] rendering of Dan 8:14). In response, we should note that it is an unproved assumption that vs. 14 is referring to the *tāmîd* morning and evening sacrifices. The term does not appear in the verse. Be that as it may, biblically speaking, the *tāmîd* morning and evening sacrifices were viewed as a unit. For a discussion of this issue, see Gerhard F. Hasel, "The 'Little Horn,' . . ." DARCOM 2:430-433; Siegfried J. Schwantes, " '*Ereb Boqer* of Daniel 8:14 Re-examined," DARCOM 2:462-474. "Whether the 2,300 evenings-mornings are correctly understood as whole days or incorrectly as 1,150 whole days, or whether they are taken as 6 years, 4 months, and 20 days or as 3 years, 2 months, and 10 days respectively (on the basis of a 360-day year), the fact remains that there is no historical epoch mentioned in the Book of Maccabees or in Josephus regarding Antiochus IV which corresponds with either set of figures. . . . Therefore, it seems exegetically sound to take the 2,300 evenings-mornings as 2,300 whole time periods and view them as a prophetic time period with the aid of the year-day principle known from other prophetic-symbolic time predictions" (Gerhard F. Hasel, "The 'Little Horn,' . . . " DARCOM 2:432, 433).

27 See Appendix B, "The Year-Day Principle."

28 For a discussion of the linkage between Dan 8 and 9, see Gerhard F. Hasel, "The 'Little Horn' . . ." DARCOM 2:436-439; Willaim H. Shea, "Unity of Daniel," DARCOM 2:227-230; Id., "The Relationship Between the Prophecies of Daniel 8 and Daniel 9," SA[1], 228-250.

29 See William H. Shea, "The Prophecy of Daniel 9:24-27," DARCOM 3:105-108 and for his more detailed study in "The Relationship Between the Prophecies of Daniel 8 and Daniel 9," SA[1], 228-250. See chart 3, Appendix D.

30 See Angel M. Rodríguez, "Significance of the Cultic Language in Daniel 8:9-14," DARCOM 2:527-549.

31 Gerhard F. Hasel, "The 'Little Horn' . . ." DARCOM 2:453, 454. For another discussion ot this term, see also Niels-Erik Andreasen, "Translation of *Niṣdaq/ Katharisthēsetai* in Daniel 8:14," DARCOM 2:475-496.

32 The question is sometimes asked whether Hebrews 9:23 is applicable to the antitypical day of atonement/final judgment setting which began in 1844. The verse reads as follows: "Therefore it was necessary for *the copies* of the things in the heavens [the earthly sanctuaries] to be *cleansed* [*katharizō*] with these [animal sacrifices], but the heavenly things [the heavenly sanctuary] themselves with better sacrifices [Christ's sacrifice] than these" (NASB). Some argue that the passage simply teaches that the heavenly sanctuary was cleansed at the time of Christ's death on the cross in A.D. 31. But such a position ignores the fact of Christ's priestly ministration which began subsequent to His death and resurrection. More important, the position fails to note that no sacrifice ever stood alone. The offering of a sacrifice required two procedures: (1) the slaying of the animal and the offering of the required parts on the altar; (2) the application or mediation of its blood/merits by the attending priest. Calvary provided the antitypical, sacrificial aspect of every offering, including that of the Lord's goat on the Day of Atonement. And Christ's priestly ministry mediates or applies the merits of His sacrifice in the heavenly sanctuary. "All the 'work' of Heaven is done on the basis of Calvary and is an application of its significance. Hebrews 9:23 (in context) contains both the ideas of Christ's efficacious death and the application of its merits—whether such is to be applied at the justification of a sinner who accepts God's salvation or whether applied in the final judgment to reaffirm the true believer and to vindicate God's authority and sovereignty before the universe. The cross event did not cleanse the heavenly sanctuary at the moment of the Saviour's death, but it did provide the basis upon which Christ, as man's high priest, could mediate His merits and bring about a total reconciliation of the universe (cf. Eph 1:10; Col. 1:20) and thus restore the heavenly sanctuary and government of God 'to its rightful state' (Dan 8:14, RSV)" ("Daniel and Revelation Committee Report," DARCOM 4:9).

9

Priesthood and Prophecy
Part 2

Continuing to move in the Hebraic mode of effect to cause, we come to *Daniel's* own initial vision (Dan 7). This foundational revelation is likewise locked into Nebuchadnezzar's dream of the metal image (Dan 2) and the prophet's second vision (Dan 8) as we have demonstrated above in remarks on the latter revelation.

In the Daniel 7 vision four wild beasts arise in succession from the sea: a lion with eagle's wings; a bear rising up on one side first, while chewing on three ribs; a four-headed leopard with four wings; and finally, a predator with ten horns, iron teeth, and claws of bronze—unlike anything in nature (Dan 7:1-7). As the prophet watches, an eleventh horn emerges from the beast's head with "eyes like the eyes of a man, and a mouth speaking great things" (vs. 8). This "humanized" horn pushes three others out of its way and becomes "greater than its fellows" (vss. 20, 21). Speaking great words against God, the horn attempts to change His times and the law, and it makes "war" against His people for an extended period of time (prophetically spelled out as "a time, two times, and half a time" (vss. 8, 20, 21, 25).[1]

According to the angel interpreter (probably Gabriel), the fourth beast symbolized "a fourth kingdom on earth" (Dan 7:23). Since the image dream given to Nebuchadnezzar (Dan 2) and the two visions given to Daniel (Dan 7 and 8) are parallels, and since Daniel and Gabriel have identified by name the first three of these "world" powers, it is not difficult—on historicist principles—to identify the subsequent two powers symbolized in the Daniel 7 vision:

1. Lion = Babylon (cf. Dan 2:37, 38)
2. Bear = Medo-Persia (cf. Dan 8:3, 20)

3. Leopard = Greece (cf. Dan 8:5, 21)
4. Predator with 10 horns = pagan Rome
5. Little horn with human eyes and mouth = papal Rome[2]

After the portrayal of the origin and career of the little horn, Daniel is given a view of the final judgment as it convenes in heaven (Dan 7:9, 10, 13, 14). The prophet describes the moving scene which rivets his attention heavenward:

> As I looked, thrones were placed and one that was ancient of days took his seat; his raiment was white as snow, and the hair of his head like pure wool; his throne was fiery flames, its wheels were burning fire. A stream of fire issued and came forth from before him; a thousand thousands served him, and ten thousand times ten thousand stood before him; *the court sat in judgment, and the books were opened.* . . .

> I saw in the night visions, and behold, with the clouds of heaven there came one like a son of man, and he came to the Ancient of Days and was presented before him. And to him was given dominion and glory and kingdom, that all peoples, nations, and languages should serve him; his dominion is an everlasting dominion, which will not pass away, and his kingdom one that shall not be destroyed.

The essential points in the Daniel 7 vision are covered three times, a fact which underscores its importance: (1) the vision proper, vss. 2-14, (2) Daniel's inquiry to know "the truth concerning all this," and the angel's brief interpretation, vss. 15-18, (3) Daniel's second, more extended inquiry, and the angel's more extended interpretation, vss. 19-27.

In Daniel's second question and the angel's response, more is said about the horn, the judgment, and the eternal kingdom:

> **Daniel:** As I looked, this horn made war with the saints, and prevailed over them, until the Ancient of Days came, and *judgment was given for the saints of the Most High,* and the time came when the saints received the kingdom (vss. 21, 22).

> **Angel:** He [the little horn] shall speak words against the Most High, and shall wear out the saints of the Most High, and shall think to change the times and the law; and they shall be given into his hand for a time, two times, and half a time. But *the court shall sit in judgment, and his dominion shall be taken away,* to be consumed and destroyed to the end. And the kingdom and the dominion and the greatness of the kingdoms under the whole heaven shall be given to the people of the saints of the Most High (vss. 25-27).

Judgment and Christ's Kingdom

With the salient aspects of the vision before us in the above textual summarizations, four important observations may be made which impact upon the meaning and significance of this revelation:

1. The judgment scene (Dan 7) and the cleansing/restoring of the heavenly sanctuary (Dan 8) *describe the same event.* This fact can be observed by simply paralleling the two visions:

Daniel 7	Daniel 8
1. Lion (Babylon)	1. . . .
2. Bear (Medo-Persia)	2. Ram (Medo-Persia)

3. Leopard (Greece)
    4 heads (Empire divided)
	3. Goat (Greece)
	    4 horns (Empire divided)

4. Predator with 10 horns (pagan Rome)	4. Little horn (pagan Rome phase, vs. 9)
5. Horn with eyes/mouth (papal Rome)	5. Little horn (papal Rome phase, vss. 10-12)
6. JUDGMENT	6. CLEANSING OF SANCTUARY

Since both the judgment and the cleansing/restoring of the sanctuary occur *in the same place (heaven),* and commence evidently *at the same time* (at some point after 1798, according to Daniel 7—more precisely, in 1844, according to Daniel 8, 9), it is evident that both visions are portraying the same event. Each vision, in its own way, is describing the nature of Christ's second phase of high priestly ministry, the closing work of His priesthood.

2. The vision (Daniel 7) portrays several aspects *of the final, eschatological judgment.* This heavenly court session is not dealing with some minor issue on earth. Rather, it is one facet of the final judgment itself. This is demonstrated by the fact that *at its close Christ and His people will receive the eternal kingdom.* The controversy between good and evil has reached its climactic end. Obviously, the final judgment precedes the granting and reception of Christ's eternal dominion and kingdom.

This truth effects the interpretation of the prophecy. It means that all biblical passages dealing with the final judgment may be properly brought to bear on this prophecy, because it provides only one segment of information on the subject, albeit a most important segment.

3. *The Day of Atonement* rite must be allowed to shed light on its antitype, the final judgment. This is true for two reasons: (1) This sanctuary rite foreshadowed the eschatological judgment. Moreover, as we have noted, (2) the cleansing/restoring of the heavenly sanctuary (portrayed in the Daniel 8 parallel) is *the same event* as the final judgment scene presented in Daniel 7. Consequently, the sanctuary types have a proper input here.

4. The Daniel 7 session of final judgment occurs in heaven before Christ's second coming. It is at the close of this court session that the Son of man (Christ) is awarded His kingdom and dominion (vss. 13, 14). Since this award is made in heaven, this aspect of the final judgment may be rightfully designated its "preadvent judgment" phase. When Christ returns, He comes, not as "a man of sorrows" (Isa 53:3), but as "King of kings and Lord of lords" in the glory and majesty of His kingdom (Rev 19:16).

Who Will Be Judged?

The Books

That the preadvent judgment is also an "investigative" phase of the final judgment is evident from the notice that when "the court sat in judgment," "the *books* were opened" (vs. 10). The "books" are not listed by name, but in Daniel's fourth line of prophecy mention appears to be made of the book of life.

> At that time shall arise Michael, the great prince who has charge of your people. And there shall be a time of trouble, such as never has been since there was a nation till that time; but at that time your people shall be delivered, *every one whose name shall be found written in the book.* And many of those who sleep in the dust of the earth shall awake, some to everlasting life, and some to shame and everlasting contempt (Dan 12:1, 2).

According to the NT no general resurrection of either the righteous or the unrighteous occurs *before* the second coming of Christ. Gabriel's reference to the deliverance of those "found written in the book" must allude to the prior examination of their names carried out in the preadvent phase of final judgment described in Daniel 7. Those "found written in the book" must refer to those followers of God who have been attested and reaffirmed as God's genuine people and numbered as true citizens of Christ's eternal kingdom (cf. Dan 7:22, 27).

Both Testaments make reference to books or records kept in heaven.[3] Two general categories are mentioned: (1) records of human thoughts, words, and deeds, and (2) a "book of life" that registers the names of persons who have yielded to the wooing of the divine Spirit and have entered into the worship and service of God.

The significant fact, with regard to the "book of life" is that *names can be removed as well as added.* For example, observe God's response to Moses' intercession for Israel at Sinai:

> So Moses returned to the Lord and said, "Alas, this people have sinned a great sin; they have made for themselves gods of gold. But now, if thou wilt forgive their sin—and if not, blot me, I pray thee, out of thy book which thou hast written." But the Lord said to Moses, *"Whoever has sinned against me, him will I blot out of my book"* (Exod 32:31-33).

Jesus implies a similar removal in the prophecy of Revelation:

> He who conquers shall be clad thus in white garments, and *I will not blot his name out of the book of life* (Rev 3:5).

As may be seen from even a casual reading of the Daniel 7 vision, no human being—not even a representative of the "little horn" power—appears in person before this court. God is in heaven; man is on earth. This "audit" takes place by means of the "books" of record.

Insight From the Sanctuary Types

We have observed in an earlier chapter dealing with the Day of Atonement that the primary rite on that special occasion foreshadowed the final, eschatological judgment. It needs now to be pointed out that the rite pertained to God's professed people, Israel, and *not* to the non-Jewish nations around them.

Two classes of Israelites were distinguished on this special day: (1) one class, who had throughout the year repented of and confessed their sins, offering the specified sacrifices, and who now maintained a sincere spirit of contrition during the Day of Atonement; and (2) another class who had not repented and confessed their wrongs, or who had backslidden, and who now refused to humble themselves before God in heart-searching and contrition (see Lev. 23:29, 30). The former saw their confessed sins and accountability removed from the sanctuary and in figure placed on the Azazel goat which was led away to perish in the wilderness; the latter were "cut off" from the Lord's people and executed.

In other words, the Day of Atonement, among other things, was *a day of separation.* False Israelites were separated from genuine Israelites. The false were destroyed, the genuine were confirmed in the congregation of the Lord. Although the Day of Atonement ceremony did not have a "book of life" as part of the rite, it did proceed on the premise that all Israel were God's people and were written in His "book" (Exod 32:32, 33). In ordaining the separation of the false from the genuine Israelite on the Day of Atonement, God directed the carrying out in essence of His decree, "Whoever has sinned against me, him will I blot out of my book" (Exod 32:33).

Thus, we may safely affirm that the preadvent phase of final judgment/ cleansing-restoring of the heavenly sanctuary in Daniel 7, 8 deals primarily with the professed followers of God—spiritual Israel (cf. Gal 6:16)—who are recorded in "the book of life." The enemies of God who have *never* submitted to His Spirit, are obviously not recorded in God's "book of life." Another, later phase of final judgment will deal with this class.[4]

When Daniel says in his inquiry of Gabriel, "The Ancient of Days came, and *judgment* [sentence] was given for [that is, in favor of] the saints of the Most High" (Dan 7:22), we may rightly conclude that these persons are attested as genuine believers in the preadvent judgment and are retained "in the book [of life]" (Dan 12:1).

If this prophecy merely portrayed a trial of the wicked horn, it would not be necessary for the divine Judge to render a sentence in favor of His people. Sentence would be passed on the persecuting horn, not on them. But this vision is not dealing simply with a persecuting power. This is a vision of the *final* judgment which, in all its phases, will review the life of every individual before it is over.[5]

Christ's Priestly Role in the Judgment

A thoughtful reading of the "judgment" segments of Daniel 7 (vss. 9, 10, 13, 14, 22, 26) reveals a striking omission: No description of the Court's activities is recorded! The focus is on the beginning of the judgment and on its conclusion, but nothing is said about the actual process of the session. Christ's reception of His eternal kingdom is noted (vss. 13, 14), but all other reference to His part in this important event is omitted. We must turn to other Scripture passages to discover Christ's high priestly role in this final event in the heavenly sanctuary. We first list four passages under two general headings which affirm His office as judge:

1. The incarnation and atoning death qualified Jesus Christ to become humanity's judge.

The Father judges no one, but has given all judgment to the Son, . . . and has given him *authority [exousia]* to execute judgment, *because he is the Son of man* (John 5:22, 27).[6]

And he commanded us [Peter and the other apostles] to preach to the people, and to testify that *he [Jesus Christ] is the one ordained by God* to be judge of the living and the dead (Acts 10:42).

2. God "judges" the world (just as He created it) by the agency of Christ.

Because he [God] has fixed a day on which *he will judge the world in righteousness by a man [Jesus Christ] whom he has appointed,* and of this he has given assurance to all men by raising him from the dead (Acts 17:31).

On that day when, according to my gospel, *God judges the secrets of men by Christ Jesus* (Rom 2:16).

The following passages in particular refer to Christ's intercessory role as high priest in the final judgment:

He who conquers shall be clad thus in white garments, and *I [Jesus Christ] will not blot his name out of the book of life; I will confess his name. before my Father and before his angel* (Rev 3:5).

In concluding (by final judgment) the moral controversy which has savaged our world, God must show to the loyal universe of intelligent beings why it is safe to take into His eternal kingdom repentant sinners who have professed to be His followers.

When the records of a genuine believer are opened in the preadvent judgment, Jesus, our high priestly advocate, will say (according to Rev 3:5), Father, angels, loyal universe—Here are the records. Yes, this person is a sinner, and here is the full evidence of his waywardness. But see also his repentance and confession, and his whole-hearted acceptance of Me as his Saviour and Lord, and My pardon. See the evidence from the record of his life that he is truly in union with Me. I claim him as My own child. He has faithfully endured until the end with Me. My blood, My blood, Father, covers him and blots out the record of his sins! In this manner Christ confesses a genuine believer "before [his] Father and before his angels," and secures the right to blot out the records of his/her sins.[7]

Another judgment passage indicates how the priestly Christ will have to relate to false claimants upon His grace. To clarify His point, we place beside it a pertinent statement by the apostle Paul.

> Not every one who says to me, "Lord, Lord," shall enter the kingdom
> of heaven, *but he who does the will of my Father* who is in heaven. *On that
> day* [the day of judgment] many will say to me, "Lord, Lord, did we not
> prophesy in your name, and cast out demons in your name, and do many
> mighty works in your name?" And then will I declare to them, "I never knew
> you; depart from me, you evildoers" (Matt 7:21-23).

> For it is not the hearers of the law who are righteous before God, *but the
> doers of the law who will be justified* (Rom 2:13).

In such cases as Christ refers to, He will be unable to intercede the merits
of His sinless life and atoning death in their behalf. Consequently, the willfully
disobedient will be removed from the "book of life" regardless of their
profession.

A third passage, dealing with Christ's priestly role in the final judgment
reads as follows:

> Who will bring any charge against God's elect? It is God who justifies.
> Who is to condemn? It is Christ Jesus, who died, yes, who was raised, who
> is at the right hand of God, who indeed intercedes for us (Rom 8:33, 34,
> NRSV).

Some Christians have difficulty accepting the biblical doctrine of a preadvent phase of final judgment that would remove false believers from the "book
of life." Such generally hold a doctrine of Calvinist derivation, popularly
expressed as "once saved, always saved." Once justified, it is argued, the
believer may backslide, but he can never fall away and be lost. Although this
is a false teaching on assurance,[8] there is a true doctrine of assurance, and the
believer who remains in daily union with Jesus Christ has no need to fear the
final judgment.[9]

It has been pointed out by George Eldon Ladd that "justification is *both*
a past event in history and a future eschatological event. . . . This is why Paul
says that even believers, who *have been* justified, must appear before the
judgment seat of God (Rom 14:10), which is the judgment seat of Christ (2 Cor
5:10). The decree of acquittal which was pronounced over us at the cross must
be confirmed by God's verdict in the day of judgment." (Author's emphasis).[10]

Commenting on Romans 8:33, 34 (cited above), he adds:

> These words picture the elect-believer on the day of judgment standing
> before God. God asks, "who can bring any charge that will lead to this man's
> condemnation?" His enemies, his sins, the devil all speak out with words of

condemnation. But that is not the last word. Christ speaks in the believer's defense, recalling that in his suffering and death on the cross, justification was achieved. No voice can prevail over the voice of Christ who defends. But it is not only Jesus who died, but Christ Jesus who was raised from the dead and who *lives to make intercession to God* for the believers. Indeed, we are justified by his resurrection [Rom 4:25]: for if the justification of the cross is a proleptic announcement of the eschatological acquittal, but if Christ has not been raised to defend his people in the eschatological judgment, then the whole doctrine of justification is a figment of the imagination. (Author's emphasis).[11]

From this brief review of Christ's priestly role in the preadvent, sanctuary phase of final judgment, we see that He acts to separate false believers from the genuine and to reaffirm the justification of the latter by His intercession before the Father and the loyal angels and inhabitants of other worlds. The "books" or records, now fully open, enable Him to do this before the unfallen intelligences of heaven.

The Little Horn and Final Judgment

The question we wish to address now is, What part does the "little horn" have in this preadvent phase of the judgment? We believe the typical Day of Atonement rite will also assist us here to determine the truth on this point. First we cite the pertinent passage:

He [the little horn] shall speak words against the Most High, and shall wear out the saints of the Most High, and shall think to change the times and the law; and they shall be given into his hand for a time, two times, and half a time. *But the court shall sit in judgment, and his dominion shall be taken away, to be consumed and destroyed to the end* (Dan 7:25, 26).

Since the days of the Christian writer, Irenaeus (ca. 130-ca. 202), Christians in general have held that the entities described as "the little horn" (Dan 7), the seven-headed, ten-horned leopard beast (Rev 13), and "the man of lawlessness" (2 Thess 2) represented *the same power*—the antichrist.[12] To these three, we may with propriety add the "little horn" of Daniel 8:10-12 since it parallels the little horn of Daniel 7.

Many modern Christians identify the antichrist of these passages—as did the early church fathers—with *a single individual* who will appear at the end of the age as a great persecutor. On the other hand the sixteenth century Reformers identified the antichrist as *a system of Christian apostasy,* sitting already in the temple of the church, namely, the papal system. Our interest here at this point is to observe the characteristics of this antichrist power as may be summarized from the four passages mentioned above and to determine how this "agency" relates to the preadvent phase of final judgment.

Characteristics. (1) The antichrist power attacks *God's law and truth* (Dan 7:25; 8:12).

(2) The antichrist power defames *God's character, misrepresenting Him* (Dan 7:25; cf. Rev 13:6).

(3) The antichrist power *seeks self-autonomy*—usurps God's place in His church; reaches for world dominion (Dan 7:8, 26, 27; Rev 13:3, 7, 8; 2 Thess 2:4).

(4) The antichrist power *perverts the provisions of the plan of salvation* by casting down Christ's priestly, sanctuary ministry, blaspheming His sanctuary dwelling (Dan 8:10-13; Rev 13:6).

(5) The antichrist power *attacks and destroys God's true people* (Dan 7:25; Rev 13:7).

The reader may recall that we discussed four of these points as "issues" which *Satan (Lucifer) raised in his revolt* against the Creator (see ch. 4). It will be recalled that Lucifer challenged the necessity of God's Law, questioned His character for imposing such on the creation, sought to be independent of God, and denied that God could be both just and merciful at the same time (the very heart of the plan of salvation). Furthermore, his rebellion drew a third of the angels away from the Creator to their eternal ruin and destruction (Rev 12:4; 2 Pet 2:4).

Although Satan and the angels he deceived were expelled from heaven, it is evident from our summarization of the characteristics of the antichrist power that Satan has continued his warfare against God with the same challenges. There is some adaptation to the human situation, but the same basic issues are pressed against God's law, character, and the union of His justice and mercy.

The archrebel. Satan's first attempts on earth to continue his controversy, begun in heaven, was through the corrupting influences of paganism. The OT records Satan's persistent attempts, and often success, to ruin the faith of Israel through the rites and practices of pagan idolatry. Later he would be even more successful in his deceptions through the enormous and pervasive influence of an apostate Christianity.

In the remarkable prophecy of Revelation 12 God discloses (among other things) the real power behind both the forces of paganism and apostate Christianity. In vision the apostle John is shown the symbol of a woman about to give birth to a child (vss. 1, 2). A large, red, seven-headed dragon stands nearby to devour the child (vss. 3, 4). The woman (symbolizing God's people) gives birth to a boy (the Christ) who is "caught up to God and to his throne" (vs. 5). Defeated in his attempt to destroy the child, the dragon turns on the woman, who flees from its onslaught into the wilderness for 3½ times, that is, 1260 days—in reality, 1260 years (vss. 6, 14). The dragon attempts to drown her by a flood of waters issuing from its mouth, but is unsuccessful (vss. 15, 16).

Who does the dragon represent? And what events do these attacks on the child and woman represent? The prophecy is clear on both points: (1) The dragon is identified as "the Devil and Satan, the deceiver of the whole world" (vs.9). (2) The man child symbolizes Christ; the woman symbolizes God's people. It was through the agency of its *pagan Roman head* that the dragon (Satan) attempted to destroy Christ at His birth and at Calvary (Herod the Great; Pontius Pilate); and it was through the agency of its *papal, Roman head* that the dragon (Satan) attempted to destroy the church during the 1260 years it was "given into his hand" (Dan 7:25). Satan, then, the archrebel, is the real power behind these forces. Through paganism and apostate Christianity he has continued on earth his war against the government of God.

A Wider View

Satan's Conviction

If in the preadvent phase of the final judgemt, sitting in heaven since 1844, God's genuine people are attested and retained in the "book of life," and false believers are removed (Dan 7:10, 22; 12:1; cf. Lev 23:29, 30); and if the Court condemns the antichrist horn, removing its dominion and decreeing its destruction (7:26); and if this same Court awards the eternal dominion and kingdom of this world to Christ, the Son of man and His genuine people (7:13, 14, 27), then it is strongly implied that Satan, the real power behind the antichrist (Rev 12:3, 4, 6, 9, 13, 14) and the usurper of the dominion of this world (cf. Luke 4:5, 6), will likewise come under final review in this preadvent Assize.

The typical Day of Atonement confirms and portrays this wider view of the preadvent judgment in the figure of the Azazel goat. Throughout the ritual year repenting Israelites offered their sin offerings. In the mediation of the sacrificial blood/or flesh within the sanctuary precincts their confessed sins and accountability were transferred to it. In effect, the sanctuary (the Lord who dwelt there) assumed accountability for these repentant believers. Thus, on the Day of Atonement, when the blood of the Lord's goat cleansed the sanctuary of this assumed accountability and placed it on the head of the Azazel goat (banished to the wilderness), *God Himself* was figuratively being vindicated or cleared, and the blame for sin was being laid upon Satan.

> In a real sense, therefore, the sacrifice of the Lord's goat on the Day of Atonement was in favor of the sanctuary and was an act of vindication for it. In this manner the Day of Atonement was an affirmation of innocence so far as the sanctuary itself was concerned, because the sanctuary was in reality a representation of the throne and government of God. The One who took on the responsibility of all the sins that were deposited therein by sacrifice was the God who lived in it, and now He was being vindicated.[13]

Thus, there are two definite links of the antichrist horn to the preadvent phase of the final judgment portrayed in the visions of Daniel 7 and 8. First, in a general way, the horn is a symbol of millions of professing believers who would all be recorded in the "book of life" and who would thereby come under review. Second, as a corporate entity, the horn represents an agency that *Satan* has used to promote the same challenges against God that he earlier raised in heaven.

Now, if the Court is to judge and take away the horn's dominion, then Satan, who manipulates this agency, must also come in review. The time has come for the Deity to settle the great moral controversy which this apostate, archangel began, and to settle once and for all the issues he raised in the beginning and has continued to foster through paganism and apostate Christianity. These agencies will meet their destruction (cf. Dan 7:11, 26), and so will their author-creator.

We must keep our reasoning straight here. The controversy which began with *God* does not merely end with the judgment of *man.* If it began with God, it must end with God. That is, if the great moral controversy which has troubled our universe for millennia began with false accusations against the Deity, it can only terminate—with a secure universe—if the Deity is cleared or vindicated of these charges. In actuality, God "cannot" reaffirm the justification of His genuine, repentant people unless He Himself and His plan of salvation are acknowledged by the loyal universe as true and just, and the same loyal intelligences agree with God that Satan is a wicked rebel and his accusations against God are false. The ultimate purpose of final judgment is not simply to vindicate an omniscient Deity, but also to draw all created intelligences both loyal and redeemed—and the lost—into a willing agreement with God and His view of matters.

It is evident, then, that the Azazel goat of the Day of Atonement rite (Lev. 16) and the antichrist-little horn (Dan 7/8) are definitely linked together. Both typically and symbolically, they represent Satan, the originator of sin. Their association by type (Day of Atonement) and by prophecy (Dan 7, 8) with the final judgment as it begins in heaven strongly indicates that *the preadvent phase* functions:

1. To clear God of all accusations raised against His character, law, and government, and to demonstrate His mercy and justice as revealed in the plan of salvation.

2. To attest and retain the genuine followers of God in the "book of life," and to blot out the records of their pardoned sins.

3. To remove both the false and the unfaithful believers from the "book of life."

4. To secure the final condemnation of Satan and all his agencies by the loyal, unfallen universe, and to decree their destruction.

These positive actions of the preadvent judgment may be inferred to have been confirmed prior to Christ's second coming by noting the events that take place at His return:

1. The general resurrection of the righteous dead. The preadvent judgment determined *who among the dead of the past millennia* would rise in the "first resurrection" (Rev 20:4, 6).

2. The translation of the righteous living. The preadvent judgment determined *who among the last generation of the living would be gathered by the angels* to Christ (Matt 24:30, 31).

3. The arrest and imprisonment of Satan in this ruined earth for a 1000 years. The preadvent judgment convicted Satan and determined his arrest, confinement, and destruction (Rev 20:1-3, 10).

God's Vindication

The key term in the prophecy of Daniel 7 is "dominion" (8 times, vss. 6, 12, 14, 26, 27). The implicit, underlying question is, Who shall have the dominion, the sovereign rulership over this world? Shall the forces of apostasy (displayed by wild beasts and horns) control the earth and the saints? Shall Satan continue his rebellion against his Creator through these agencies endlessly? Or, shall Christ recover His dominion, put down the usurper, and assume His authority as this world's rightful Sovereign? These are crucial questions the final judgment will resolve.

The controversy between God and Satan, beginning in heaven as a gigantic revolt against divine authority and continuing upon the earth, especially through the agency of apostate Christianity, will be settled once and for all by the actions of the heavenly Court *prior* to Christ's second coming.

In connection with Daniel 7, 8, the Day of Atonement types, and the general biblical data on the final judgment, it can be seen that the Court's sentence in the preadvent session is given not only in favor of the attested saints, but first and foremost of all in favor of God. This requires, at the same time, a full condemnation of Satan, his accusations and agencies. The heavenly sanctuary is cleansed of its records of sin and restored to its rightful state. God and His throne stand vindicated, His character unassailable, His true people likewise approved and secure in His grace.

We may inquire, What has led the loyal universe of unfallen angels and the sinless inhabitants of other worlds to agree at this time of judgment with God's view of Satan and sin—a view that in time both the redeemed and the lost will also confirm? Two reasons for this agreement may be safely inferred:

Sin's fruitage. The millennia-long rebellion against the Creator and His will—conceived and instigated by Lucifer—has resulted only in enormous ruin, unfathomable devastation both to fallen angels and to the human race, culminating in eternal death. Attempting to live independently of the Creator has not produced the promised state of endless happiness and well-being assured by Lucifer.

Salvation's fruitage. The Creator's revelation of the plan of salvation to save sinful humanity has disclosed depths in the divine character heretofore uncomprehended by the intelligent creation. The plan is embodied in the sacrificial, atoning death of Christ:

a. In the cross of Christ stands revealed God's awesome holiness—the justice and rightness of His character, law, and government which guarantees the security of the universe.

b. In the cross of Christ stands revealed God's unparalled love for sinners, His merciful forgiveness, acceptance, and transforming grace and power. Blest Father! Blest Son! Blest Holy Spirit!

Three Phases of Final Judgment

The major aspects of the final judgment are enfolded within the typical Day of Atonement ritual just as an oak is enfolded within an acorn. This can be easily seen by examining the accompanying sketch.[14] The three parts of the ceremonial sequence, (1) the removal of confessed sin and accountability from the sanctuary, (2) the banishment of the Azazel goat to the wilderness, and (3) the clean camp—are analogous to the three phases of final judgment explained elsewhere in the prophecies and other parts of the Scriptures.

Preadvent/Investigative Phase

The removal of confessed sin and accountability from the sanctuary on the ritual Day of Atonement relates in the antitype to the important, preadvent judgment phase in the heavenly sanctuary prior to Christ's return (Dan 7-9, 12). This investigative phase focuses on the names recorded in the "book of life," just as the Day of Atonement focused on the removal of the confessed sins of penitent Israelites from the sanctuary and the separating of impenitent Israelites from the congregation. Just so, false believers will be removed from the "book of life," and the faith and justification of genuine believers and their union with Christ will be reaffirmed before the loyal universe, and the records of their pardoned sins will be blotted out.

The propriety of removing the confessed sins and accountability (in figure) from the Lord (= the sanctuary) who had assumed them and the placing of the same upon the Azazel goat (symbolizing Satan), indicates that in the antitypical, preadvent judgment, God will be vindicated, cleared of all the accusations Satan has made, and that Satan himself will be fully exposed as the archrebel in the universe and his destruction decreed. Satan will be seen as the originator and instigator of sin and rebellion against God. Conducted in heaven, the preadvent/investigative phase of final judgment will fully satisfy the loyal angels and the inhabitants of other worlds regarding God's character and dealings with the sin problem.

Millennial Review Phase

The banishment of the Azazel goat to the wilderness, bearing accountability for sin in a punitive sense, is analogous to Satan's millennial imprisonment on this ruined earth while the second phase of the final judgment takes place in heaven. The prophet describes this phase in these words:

> Then *I saw thrones, and those seated on them were given authority to judge.* I also saw the souls of those who had been beheaded for their testimony to Jesus and for the word of God. They had not worshiped the beast or its image and had not received its mark on their foreheads or their hands. They came to life and reigned with Christ a thousand years. . . . Blessed and holy are those who share in the first resurrection . . . they will be priests of God and of Christ, and they will reign with him a thousand years (Rev 20:4-6, NRSV).

It is altogether fitting that in this second phase of final judgment, the once persecuted followers of God should lead out in "judging" their former oppressors. The tables are turned!

The apostle Paul adjusts the focus more sharply on this phase of final judgment in his letter to the Corinthian church, "Do you not know that *the saints will judge the world?* ... Do you not know that *we are to judge angels?*" (1 Cor 6:2, 3). This latter reference to angels includes Satan together with the angels he led away in his revolt against God. They cannot escape "the judgment of the great day" (Jude 6).

The probation of Satan and the fallen angels closed with their expulsion from heaven (cf. Rev 12:7-9). Human probation closed with the conclusion of the preadvent judgment, just prior to Christ's second coming (Rev 22:11, 12). Consequently, the millennial phase of final judgment consists only in a review of the records. No decision can be rendered now that would give these impenitent, intelligent beings eternal life, or even an extension of another probationary period.

But such a "review" permits the redeemed to examine in detail all the issues involved in the great moral controversy which has so long troubled the universe. They will see that Satan and his angels had no grounds for their rebellion, and they will be enabled to see why this person or that person was ultimately lost. They will see all the means God used to persuade Satan and the other angels to remain loyal, and how He sought in every way to draw human sinners to repentance and eternal salvation. God will answer all the questions and the saved will be satisfied about God's fairness and mercy and will verify the justice of their punishment and death.[15]

Executive Phase (Close of the Millennium)

Finally, the clean sanctuary and camp is analogous to the results of the executive phase of final judgment in which impenitent sinners will also be led to a total and rightful understanding of the issues, the rightness of God, and the true nature of their rebellion. This takes place at the close of the millennium, after the resurrection of the wicked dead, and as Satan—momentarily freed from his "imprisonment"—attempts to lead the armies of the lost to attack the "Holy City" which has settled on the earth, having come down from God out of heaven with all the throngs of the redeemed.

> Then I saw a great white throne and him who sat upon it; from his presence earth and sky fled away, and no place was found for them. And I saw the dead, great and small, standing before the throne, and books were opened. Also another book was opened, which is the book of life. And the

dead were judged by what was written in the books, by what they had done. And the sea gave up the dead in it, Death and Hades [the grave] gave up the dead in them, and all were judged by what they had done. Then Death and Hades [the grave] were thrown into the lake of fire. *This is the second death,* the lake of fire; and if any one's name was not found written in the book of life, he was thrown into the lake of fire (Rev 20:11-15).

And the devil who had deceived them was thrown into the lake of fire and sulphur . . . (Rev 20:10).

Jesus Christ also spoke about this executive phase of the final judgment which closes the millennial period:

Before him [the Son of man] will be gathered all the nations, and he will separate them one from another as a shepherd separates the sheep from the goats, and he will place the sheep at his right hand, but the goats at the left. Then the King will say to those at his right hand, "Come, O blessed of my Father, inherit the kingdom prepared for you from the foundation of the world;" . . . Then he will say to those at his left hand, "Depart from me, you cursed, into the eternal fire prepared for the devil and his angels." . . . And they will go away into eternal punishment, but the righteous into eternal life (Matt 25:32-46).[16]

The *executive* phase of the final judgment involves the total human race as well as the fallen angels. It is at this point that the sentences determined in the first two phases of the final judgment are executed. The impenitent are punished and destroyed (the "second death," from which there is no resurrection). The earth is purified by fire and is made anew and awarded to the redeemed as their eternal home.

It is easily seen that the three phases of the final judgment cover the whole of Christ's Second Apartment, priestly ministration of judgment and vindication. It may also be seen that this protracted judgment is designed to secure the willing consent of all created intelligences.

Observe that the first phase—the preadvent judgment convened in the heavenly sanctuary—allows the unfallen universe of angels and the inhabitants of other worlds to understand fully the issues of the great moral controversy. They alone are present at this session. The second phase—the millennial review, also conducted in heaven—allows an extended period of time to satisfy the redeemed on all questions pertaining to sin and salvation. Finally, the executive phase, which takes place on earth, allows even the impenitent to understand the significance of their personal choices in the light of God's repeated offers of mercy and forgiveness.

The plan of salvation has been laid so carefully, so comprehensively and fairly that the universe of intelligent beings—whether loyal and unfallen, redeemed, or lost—will confess in the final judgment that God is right and true in all His dealings, and that Satan and his accusations and those who have joined with his rebellion—angel and human—are wrong. "For Scripture says," declares the apostle Paul, "As I live, says the Lord, to me every knee shall bow and every tongue acknowledge God" (Rom 14:11, NEB).

Epilogue

In the prophecies of Daniel 7-9 we see both remarkable fulfillments and forecasts. We see that Jesus Christ appeared on time to carry out His messianic mission (A.D. 27)—especially to make atonement for the sins of the race on Calvary (A.D. 31). Upon His resurrection and ascension that same year He entered into His high priestly ministry in the heavenly sanctuary. In A.D. 1844 He entered into His second phase of ministration, the antitypical day of atonement—the final judgment. The types clearly teach that God's grace is still available to repentant sinners throughout both phases of Christ's priestly ministry. Nevertheless, since 1844 the world has been living in the solemn era of His closing work in heaven, in "the hour of [God's] judgment" (Rev 4:6, 7). And the appeal is especially urgent to our judgment-bound generation, "Consider Jesus, the apostle and high priest of our confession" (Heb 3:1).

The atoning priestly ministry of Jesus Christ has always had one primary objective, to remove the sin barrier between the Creator and the intelligent creation.

> For in him [Jesus Christ] all the fullness of God was pleased to dwell, and through him God was pleased to *reconcile* (*apokatallassō*) to himself all things, whether on earth or in heaven, by making peace through the blood of his cross (Col 1:19, 20, NRSV).

> He [God] has made known to us his hidden purpose—such was his will and pleasure determined beforehand in Christ—to be put into effect when the time was ripe: namely, that the universe, all in heaven and on earth, might be brought into a unity in Christ (Eph 1:9, 10, NEB).

With the cessation of the executive phase of the final judgment (Rev 20:11-15) and the creation of a "new" heaven and earth (Rev 21:1-5) as the home of the redeemed—the divine plan of salvation attains its full consummation. Satan and the fallen angels, impenitent sinners, and all the effects of sin no longer exist. While the wonder of divine grace—so freely lavished upon us—will ever be our study and song, Christ will no longer function in His mediational, priestly office. Face to face communion will replace His gracious intercession (Rev 22:3, 4), and in this sense the "temple" of that world-to-come will be "the Lord God the Almighty and the Lamb" (Rev 21:22).

As we observed at the beginning of our study, Christ was established (after His resurrection and ascension) upon the divine throne in heaven as humanity's king-priest. In this manner He will reign in His mediatorial capacity until the close of the executive phase of the final judgment at which time He will make a surprising change in His role.

The apostle Paul reveals this change: "Then comes the end, *when he hands over the kingdom to God the Father,* after he has destroyed every ruler and every authority and power. For he must reign until he has put all his enemies under his feet. . . . When all things are subjected to him, *then the Son himself will also be subjected to the one who [God the Father] put all things in subjection under him, so that God may be all in all*" (1 Cor 15:24-28, NRSV). The Deity will no longer reign over the earth through the mediatorial office of Christ, but will do so directly. And Jesus Christ will forever retain His humanity as the representative head of the redeemed race and co-ruler (Rev 22:1, 3).

Wonder of wonders! We marvel at the condescension of the Deity Who sacrificed Themselves for our eternal salvation and bow in awe! Even now, we are moved by such amazing love to join our voices ahead of time in the universal ascription of praise the whole creation will shout on that glad day of triumph:

> Worthy is the Lamb, the Lamb that was slain, to receive all power and wealth, wisdom and might, honour and glory and praise! . . . Praise and honour, glory and might, to him who sits on the throne and to the Lamb for ever and ever! (Rev 5:12, 13, NEB).

———————◆———————

Endnotes

1 Stated in symbolic phrases as 3½ prophetic times/years, this same period is repeated in Rev 12:14 where it is also defined as 1260 prophetic days (vs. 6).

The subject of the persecution of God's people by the same power is dealt with in both prophecies. Thus, for 1260 years (computed on the year-day principle) God's people suffered intermittently at the hands of this authority (cf. Dan 7:21, 25; Rev 12:6, 14; 13:1-10). See chart 2, Appendix D.

2 Daniel's prophecy does not deal with individuals, but with powers and systems. While there are many genuine Christians in the Roman communion, the prophecies portray the papal *system* as an apostasy from the true religion of the Scriptures. The following points may be noted as the basis for identifying the little horn of Dan 7 with the papacy: (1) The horn's origin is in western Europe. This may be seen by the fact that it arises *among* the 10 horns of the beast, the divisions carved from the western portion of the empire by various Germanic tribes (vs. 8). (2) The horn arises after the 10 horns are established, that is *after A.D. 476,* the date usually assigned to western Rome's final dissolution (vss. 7, 8, 20, 24). (3) The horn is responsible for uprooting three of these new kingdoms (vss. 8, 20, 24). (4) The horn's attitude toward God. It speaks arrogant words against God (vss. 8, 20, 25 cf. Rev 13:5; 2 Thess 2:3, 4). (5) The horn's attitude toward God's Law. The horn-power would attempt to make changes in the Ten Commandments by its own authority (vs. 25). (6) The horn's attitude toward God's people. The horn would make war against them and would persecute them (vss. 21, 25). (7) God's people would be especially subject to this persecution for a specific period of time. This period is prophetically symbolized as 3½ times/years = 1260 days which on the year-day principle = 1260 years (vs. 25 cf. Rev 12:6, 14).

Only one religiopolitical power can fit these identifying marks in the Christian Era and that is the Roman papal system. The papacy developed in Europe. The pope's position as head of all Christian churches was legally defined by the Code of the Roman emperor Justinian in 534—and became a practical reality in 538 when the Ostrogoths were driven from Rome, the last of three Arian, anti-Catholic powers to be removed through papal and emperor cooperation. The papacy has in the past, and continues to this day, to make great claims for its authority to speak and act for God within the temple of the Christian church (see ch. 8, n. 24 for a small sample of its "great words"). Rome continues to claim that it modified the Ten Commandments and champions Sunday sacredness as an emblem of its authority in religious matters, although the fourth precept calls humanity to worship the Creator on the Sabbath, the seventh-day of the week. History records that the papacy persecuted millions who differed from its doctrine during the Middle Ages—a fact that the modern papacy admits in part. Extending the medieval heyday of the papacy for 1260 years from 538, we arrive at 1798, the year that the French government sought to break the political power of the papacy over Europe by taking the reigning pope into captivity. Revelation 13:1-10 parallels the prophecy of the little horn presented in Daniel 7 and adds additional identifying data. Following historicist principles, we have clear evidence that the little horn of Daniel 7 symbolizes not Antiochus IV, but the Roman papacy. For a further analysis of these identifying marks, see SDABC 4:818-838; LeRoy Edwin Froom, *The Prophetic Faith of Our Fathers* (Washington, DC: Review and Herald, 1950), 1:492-517.

3 For example, OT: Exod 32:32, 33; Pss. 56:8; 69:28; 139:16; Isa 4:3; Mal. 3:16; Dan 12:1; NT: Luke 10:20; Phil 4:3; Heb 12:23; Rev 3:5; 13:8; 17:8; 20:12, 15; 21:27. In reality, the Deity does not deal with huge ledgers and ink pens, nor with electronic computers! The Bible writers can only speak to us in human terms, but the point is being made: God is all-knowing; nothing is unnoticed or forgotten that pertains to each individual of His human creation.

4 It should be emphasized again that the judgment scene of Dan 7 is not a minor investigation into the activities of the little horn. On the contrary, the data indicates clearly that the vision is portraying a segment of the final judgment that deals with all the large, pertinent issues of the sin problem and concludes by awarding the eternal kingdom of this world to Christ as its rightful Sovereign. Second, one aspect of the little horn is the fact that it represents a religious organization whose leaders and people are composed of professing Christians. Hence, this facet of final judgment is a religious investigation and not a secular one, and it deals with professed Christians whether persecutors or persecuted.

While the vision of the final judgment in Dan 7 makes its own contribution to the whole subject of final judgment, we must not forget that the vision of Dan 8 and the Day of Atonement ritual of the sanctuary have their particular input into our understanding of the subject. We must permit all biblical references on the subject of the final judgment to inform us of the total truth, lest we willingly deceive ourselves and thereby fail to grasp the truth on this important biblical teaching.

5 We must not forget that professed believers are indeed involved in the final judgment. See, Rom 14:10-12; 2 Cor 5:10, etc.

6 Cf. also Matt 20:28; Heb 2:9. "The Father has also committed to [Christ] the execution of judgment. That this should be so is reasonable, for the Son of God, a divine being, is also the Son of man, a human being, who has resisted temptation (Heb. 4:15), borne sin vicariously, and tasted death. Yet He is triumphant in the great controversy with Satan. No other being in the universe is thus qualified to pass eternal judgment upon men, and no other being can glorify and vindicate God by that judgment" (SDABC 5:952, 953).

7 Ellen G. White describes Christ's priestly ministry in behalf of all genuine believers in the preadvent phase of final judgment in this manner: "Jesus does not excuse their sins, but shows their penitence and faith, and, claiming for them forgiveness, He lifts His wounded hands before the Father and the holy angels, saying: 'I know them by name. I have graven them on the palms of My hands' " (GC 484).

8 Cf. 1 Cor 9:27; 2 Pet 2:20-22; 3:17; Heb 6:4-8; 10:26, 27; Matt 13:5-7, 20-22.

9 Cf. John 10:27-29; 1 John 5:11-13; 2 Tim 4:6-8.
10 George Eldon Ladd, *I Believe in the Resurrection* (Grand Rapids: William B. Eerdmans Publishing Company, 1975), 148. The author is not holding a brief for automatic, universal salvation by the expression, "The decree of acquittal which was pronounced over us at the cross. . . ." He explains his view on a previous page: "Paul teaches justification as a present reality grounded in the death of Christ, to be received by sinners by faith (Rom 3:21-31)." (147).
11 Ibid., 148.
12 See, LeRoy Edwin Froom, *The Prophetic Faith of Our Fathers* (Washington, DC: Review and Herald, 1950-1954), 1:246-248.
13 Alberto R. Treiyer, "The Day of Atonement . . ." DARCOM 3:245.
14 See chart 4, Appendix D.
15 For a brief overview of the theological significance of the millennial review phase of the final judgment, see, Joel Badina, "The Millennium," DARCOM 7:241, 242.
16 The English translations, "forever," "for ever and ever," and "everlasting/eternal" are renderings for the Greek noun *aiōn* and its related adjective *aiōnios* respectively. Their basic idea is one of *duration,* a period of uninterrupted time. The concept of "endlessness" is not inherent in these terms. The *length* of time involved may or may not be endless, but derives from the *nature* of the object or person described by these terms. God "alone" has immortality (1 Tim 6:16). The Gospel reveals how sinful mortals, doomed to die, may receive immortality through faith in Jesus Christ (2 Tim 1:9, 10). God will bestow the gift of immortality on all the redeemed at the second coming of Christ (1 Cor 15:51-57). Thus, when the Scriptures speak of the eternal God or of the redeemed entering into eternal life, it speaks of "endlessness," because God's nature is immortal and He has bestowed the same upon the redeemed. But neither Satan and his evil angels nor wicked human beings are immortal by nature. They will be punished according to their sinful deeds and will then perish. The wages of sin is death (Rom 6:23), the "second death" (Rev 20:14, 15; 21:8).

10

Questions About Christ's Priesthood

The two-phase, priestly ministry of Jesus Christ in the heavenly sanctuary is attention-arresting because it serves in so many ways to clarify the great plan of salvation—the sinner's only hope—which the Trinity devised in eternity for our redemption. Due to the constraints of space, we conclude this survey of our Lord's priesthood by speaking to a few questions that are sometimes raised.

Christ's Priesthood and Heaven's Last Appeal

Time of the End

According to Daniel's prophecy the "little horn" power would make "war with the saints" and would prevail over them (7:21) and would "wear out the saints of the Most High" (7:25). God's people would "be given into his hand for a time, two times, and half a time" (7:25), a chronological expresssion equal to 1260 prophetic days, or 1260 years on the year-day principle (cf. Rev 12:6,14). This period of the medieval persecutions of God's people (A.D. 538-1798) brought the inhabitants of our world to a new prophetic era, "the time of the end." In Daniel's fourth line of prophecy, Gabriel explains this point to the prophet, alluding first to the persecutions of the previous era:

> And those among the people who are wise shall make many understand, though they shall fall by sword and flame, by captivity and plunder, for some days. When they fall, they shall receive a little help. . . . And some of those

who are wise shall fall, to refine and to cleanse them and to make them white, *until the time of the end ['ad-'ēt qēṣ],* for it is yet for the time appointed (Dan 11:33-35).

The expression, "the time of the end," occurs several times in Daniel's prophecies (8:17; 11:35, 40; 12:4, 9). "In the book of Daniel the time of the end is not the end of time, as if it were a point in time when all things come to their conclusion. On the contrary, the time of the end in the book of Daniel is a period of time. . . . Events occur in that period of time."[1] We may infer, therefore, from the passage cited above (Dan 11:33-35) that "the time of the end" began in 1798 at the conclusion of the 1260 years allotted to the little horn's persecuting activity.

We would naturally expect such a span—designated as "the time of the end"—to extend from its beginning point to the close of human probation. Thus, on historicist principles of interpretation, the prophecies of Daniel alert us to the truth that since 1798 the planet has been passing through its final era of human history, "the time of the end."

From the viewpoint of biblical prophecy, what may we expect to happen during this last allotment of human probation? We note three prominent activities:

Activities During "the Time of the End"

Daniel 12:4. *A renewed interest and study of the prophecies of Daniel would take place.* This would naturally serve to clarify as well the book of Revelation, its companion NT apocalyptic prophecy. Gabriel assured Daniel that this would be true: "But you, Daniel, shut up the words, and seal the book, *until the time of the end.* Many shall run to and fro, and *knowledge shall increase*"(Dan 12:4).

During the midquarters of the eighteenth century a great religious awakening occurred in the American colonies, starting under the revival preaching of T. J. Frelinghuysen and Gilbert Tennent, and continuing under Jonathan Edwards, and especially George Whitefield (d. 1770).[2] This revival of spirituality was followed in the Old World in the next century by what is sometimes referred to as "the Advent Awakening," stimulated by the renewed study of the prophecies of Daniel. The Advent Awakening crossed the Atlantic ocean to form a more definite movement in the New World.

The nineteenth century also came to be known as the "missionary century" with the birth of foreign missions outreach—a movement which has continued throughout the twentieth century, becoming ever more global as it works hand in hand with Bible societies, which were established in the early nineteenth century to provide the Scriptures in "everyman's" language.[3] With the collapse of certain anti-Christian ideologies in the last decades of the twentieth century, doors have miraculously swung open to the rapid preaching of the gospel to many lands long closed to the teachings of the Christian Scriptures.

Daniel 8:17. *In 1844 Christ's second phase of priestly ministry in the heavenly sanctuary, the preadvent phase of the final judgment would commence* (Dan 7:9-14; 8:14). Gabriel pointed to the occurrence of this solemn, heavenly activity during this period when he informed Daniel, "Understand, O son of man, that *the vision is for the time of the end.*"

Revelation 14:6-14. *Heaven's final appeal to the peoples of this world would be given while Christ engaged in His preadvent judgment ministry.* The biblical support for this view lies in the following remarkable prophecy of Revelation:

> Then I saw another angel flying in midheaven, with an eternal gospel to proclaim to those who dwell on earth, to every nation and tribe and tongue and people; and he said with a loud voice, "Fear God and give him glory, for *the hour of his judment has come;* and worship him who made heaven and earth, the sea and the fountains of water."
>
> Another angel, a second, followed, saying, "Fallen, fallen is Babylon the great, she who made all nations drink the wine of her impure passion."
>
> And another angel, a third, followed them, saying with a loud voice, "If any one worships the beast and its image, and receives a mark on his forehead or on his hand, he also shall drink the wine of God's wrath, poured unmixed into the cup of his anger, and he shall be tormented with fire and sulphur in the presence of the holy angels and in the presence of the Lamb. . . ."
>
> Here is a call for the endurance of the saints, those who keep the commandments of God and the faith of Jesus. . . .
>
> Then I looked, and lo, a white cloud, and seated on the cloud one like a son of man, with a golden crown on his head, and a sharp sickle in his hand.

Inasmuch as humans have been commissioned to proclaim the gospel (Matt 24:14; 28:18-20), we may regard these three angels as symbols of Christians moving throughout the world to share the good news of salvation. It is obvious that these "angels" fly in "the time of the end," because their ministry is immediately prior to the Second Coming of Christ (Rev 14:14). It is also clear that since the first angel bears the "everlasting gospel," he would continue to "fly" until the close of human probation. Since that is so, the other two angels will in turn eventually join the first, so that the three in time virtually form one final message: the everlasting gospel with certain end-time emphases on the fall of "Babylon" and "the mark of the beast."

But when did these messages start? The answer is supplied by the "first" angel who announces, "Fear God and give him glory, for *the hour of his judgment has come*; and worship him who made heaven and earth, the sea and the fountains of water" (Rev 14:7).

Here is a paradox. The angel announces that the moment of God's final judgment has arrived—"has come," indeed, is here! That would normally mean the *end* of human probation, the cessation of all gospel activity. Yet, the same angel is busy proclaiming "the eternal gospel" to "every" nation, tribe, tongue, and people—a task that would take considerable time in reality! Furthermore, two other angel messages must follow along and join the first before Christ actually appears. Thus, the paradox is that the gospel is being spread worldwide (with certain end-time emphases), calling humanity back to the Creator *at the same time* the final judgment is in session!

The resolution to the paradox is that the first angel's message is referring to *the commencement of the preadvent phase of the judgment in the heavenly sanctuary which began its work in 1844 according to Daniel 7-9.*[4] In other words, this first message which began to be proclaimed historically a little before 1844, announces, in effect, the beginning of Christ's second phase of high priestly ministry which commenced at the close of the 2300-year prophecy, a ministry of judgment and vindication. And while He is employed in His judgment task in heaven, His remnant people (Rev 12:17) are carrying God's final gospel appeal to "every nation and tribe and tongue and people" on earth. This paradox was already foreshadowed in the Day of Atonement ritual itself. Throughout this ritual of judgment, salvation was available—portrayed by the ever-burning daily sacrifice and the ever-burning incense.

The question naturally arises, How can final judgment and offers of salvation run side by side? The answer is implied by the Scriptures themselves. As we have observed earlier, the preadvent judgment phase centers on professing followers of God whose names are recorded in the "book of life." Except for the last generation who will be living at the time of Christ's return, the rest who are recorded in that book are dead, asleep in their graves. Christ, our high priest, is also "ordained to be judge of the living *and the dead*" (Acts 10:42). Thus, while the messages of the three angels began to move out across the world to the vast populations of the living in the mid-nineteenth century (1844), Christ's priestly judgment began with the generations of *the dead* who had at some point during their lives professed to be followers of God, probably starting with Abel, the first recorded to die.

Why has it taken the heavenly Court so long to carry out its task in the preadvent judgment? some ask. First, we must recall with the apostle Peter that "time"—as we think of it—has no meaning to an *eternal* Deity. "Do not ignore this one fact, beloved, that with the Lord one day is as a thousand years, and a thousand years as one day" (2 Pet 3:8; cf. Ps 90:4). Furthermore, just as Jesus said to His disciples, so He would say to modern Christians, "It is not for you to know times or seasons which the Father has fixed by his own authority" (Acts 1:7). The fact that the Deity will indeed judge the human family is sufficient for us (Acts 17:31).

One thing is crystal clear, however, to God's remnant people: The Gospel Commission—in this "hour of his judgment"—demands that the gospel must be taken to "every nation and tribe and tongue and people" (Rev 14:6). The task is global. The "yeast" of God's last appeal must be implanted in every people group so that it may permeate every culture.

Modern economics and trade agreements have shrunk the earth to a global "village." In our day rapid transit, high tech electronics, radio, TV, and satellite communications make it possible for the Lord's end-time appeals to "fly," as it were, to the vast populations of earth. There is judgment-urgency to stir the church to fulfill its divine orders, because one day—in God's arrangement—the preadvent judgment will move from the cases of the dead to the last living generation.

Thus, during "the time of the end," two important activities occur which impact on each other. In heaven, the preadvent phase of final judgment moves forward, clearing God and His genuine people, condemning Satan and his polices, and removing the false from the "book of life"—beginning with the first generation of the dead. On earth, God's remnant people are active in carrying the "everlasting gospel" with its end-time emphases in a global endeavor to reach every people group. When both activities are accomplished the end will come. Such a world mission focus will naturally involve a period of time even under the harvest-ripening showers of the promised "latter rain" of the Holy Spirit (cf. also Rev 18:1-5).

The Process of Judging in the Heavenly Court

Appearance/Audit?

How do I personally appear in the preadvent judgment? The apostle Paul states that "each of us shall give account of himself to God" (Rom 14:12). How is this possible?

Although the Scriptures make many references to the final judgment, their silence in regard to *the process* is remarkable. In the clearest description of the heavenly judgment (Dan 7:9, 10,13, 14) the focus is only on its beginning and ending. As we have previously observed regarding the vision of Daniel 7, no reference is made to Christ's role in the Session, neither does the prophet see individuals standing in a line waiting their turn to appear before the Judge.

Since the preadvent phase of final judgment occurs in heaven, and since all whose names are in the "book of life" are in their graves except for professing believers in the present, living generation, we may safely infer that each person who "stands" before the Judge, "stands" by means of his/her records. The thoughts, motives, actions are all there in the records and will "answer" for the individual. None are bodily present.

Will an individual know when his/her name is presented to the Court? Neither the dead nor the living will know, nor is it necessary to know. On this point we do well to recall the admonition, "Consider Jesus, the . . . *high priest* of our confession" (Heb 3:1). Just as the ancient high priest represented all Israel "upon his heart"—typified by the breastpiece—so Jesus Christ as our high priest and judge represents every genuine child of God recorded in the "book of life." Whenever the time comes for our names to be presented, He will be there to intercede His merits and to reaffirm our justification. He entreats us to "abide" in Him, to remain in a vital union with Him, as a living branch remains in union with the living Vine (John 15:1-11). Such persons He can present before His Father "with exceeding joy" (Jude 24, NKJV).

Judgment of the Living

Could an individual, presently living, have his/her name brought up today before the Court? On what basis would such a person be judged if he/she had many more years to live and could conceivably change in the future from a nominal believer to a genuine one, or could backslide and give up the faith altogether?

Here again, the Scriptures are silent. However, if we may infer from its general teachings and examples, we would reject the idea suggested by some that God would judge such a person on the basis of His foreknowledge of that person's future actions. In others words, it is suggested that God, in His omniscience, simply looks down to the end of the individual's life and sees what their final decisions will be. Then He judges them on the basis of this foreknowledge. If this were the process, we would have a form of predestination, a divine judgment *before* a human decision.

But the biblical data always presents God's acts of judgment as *following* upon human determined and settled choices. The "day of the Lord," so prominent in the OT, was a kind of local judgment and close of probation on a city or nation. It always came *after* that city or nation had rejected God and turned from Him. The Flood and the destruction of Sodom and Gomorrah came *after* the inhabitants of the world and of those cities had cast off all allegiance to the Creator.

Consequently, in harmony with the biblical accounts, it may be suggested that if the case of a *living* person were to come up in the preadvent judgment, it would be a person who had sinned away his day of grace, who had committed the "unpardonable sin" (Matt 12:31, 32), that is to say, his/her personal decision was already fixed. In other words, in light of the biblical principles and experiences, it does not seem a righteous action on the part of God to judge and fix the destiny of a living person as long as that individual could properly exercise his/her choice as a free moral agent.

More likely, the judgment of the living will occur somewhat simultaneously when the last, living generation is faced with a destiny-determining issue. Such a planet-wide issue is foretold in Revelation 12-16. It is the final conflict over the Law of God, as it centers on the enforcing of "the mark of the beast." Whom will we obey?—the church-state union (image of the beast) which will enforce the "mark" under penalty of boycott and death (Rev 13:11-17), or God, who warns that the recipient of the "mark" will be severely punished and destroyed (Rev 14:9-12).[5]

The last living generation on this earth will have to make a decision either for the state/church confederation or for God. It will be an individual choice, and it will be a final choice. Following that conflict and decision time, the preadvent judgment will close, fixing forever the destiny not only of the dead but of the last living generation as well. The righteous Judge in heaven will say—and the loyal universe will concur—" 'Let the evildoer still do evil, and the filthy still be filthy, and the righteous still do right, and the holy still be holy.' 'Behold, I am coming soon, bringing my recompense, to repay every one for what he has done' " (Rev 22:11, 12).[6]

The Preadvent Judgment and the Final Generation

It has been argued by some that "the cleansing of the sanctuary in heaven is dependent upon the cleansing of God's people on earth. How important, then, that God's people be holy and without blame! In them every sin must be burned out, so that they will be able to stand in the sight of a holy God and live with the devouring fire.'"[7] This view is generally buttressed by John's description of the 144,000, the symbolism for the last living generation of the righteous. John notes, among other things, "In their mouth no lie was found, for they are spotless" (Rev 14:5).

While this position presents a high view of sanctification, it seems to this writer to be out of harmony with the Scriptures on at least two counts:

1. Theologically, it makes the Deity subject to humanity, when it is really the other way around. No human, nor group of humans can "tie" God's hands, so to speak, nor dictate His program. The preadvent judgment (the cleansing/restoring of the heavenly sanctuary, Dan 7, 8) began in 1844 just when God determined it should begin. It will close when God determines to close it. The Father "has fixed by his own authority" the times and seasons (Acts 1:7). Unpreparedness on the part of God's people cannot in itself delay the completion of the preadvent judgment.

2. Theologically, the statement appears to create two different plans of salvation. If sin is "burned out" of the last living generation of genuine believers in such a manner that these can live in the presence of "the devouring fire" of a holy God, how will all the other generations of the redeemed—from Adam to this last group—live in the presence of the same God? Does the fact that they are said to be "spotless" mean that they have attained to a state of holiness greater than all the rest of the innumerable throng of the redeemed? We must remember that *all* the saved are commanded to "strive . . . for the *holiness* [sanctification, *hagiasmos*] *without which no one will see the Lord*" (Heb 12:14).

Only One Plan of Salvation

The Scriptures know of only *one plan* of salvation. There is one God, one Law, one Saviour from sin. The last generation of genuine believers will be saved on the same basis as the first generation of genuine believers. No child of God is saved on the basis of a certain level of achieved character development, but on the basis of God's magnificent grace (Eph 2:8-10). Of course, the *fruits* of a redeemed life provide the evidence that a repentant sinner has truly laid hold of divine grace. When a believer's character reflects the character of Christ, it attests to his/her genuine commitment to Christ (Jas 2:14-26) [8] The real issue in the preadvent judgment is not whether the genuine believer can present a faultless record of achievement in character growth, but whether he/she is in a vital, growing union with Jesus Christ (John 15:4-6). It is the dead branch that the pruning shears of the judgment cuts away.

The truth is that all generations of the redeemed will enter into eternal life "spotless," because they have received the gift of Christ's imputed righteousness as well as His inwrought righteousness. This is seen in the general, biblical texts that speak with regard to *all* believers, and not specifically about the last generation of God's people. Two may be cited:

> Christ loved *the church* and gave himself up for her, that he might sanctify her, having cleansed her by the washing of water with the word, that he might present the church to himself in splendor, *without spot* or wrinkle or any such thing, that she might be *holy and without blemish* (Eph 5:25-27).

> Now to him who is able to keep you from falling and to present you *without blemish* before the presence of his glory with rejoicing (Jude 24).

Some of the redeemed will have grown only a little in sanctified living (for example, the thief who was saved as he hung, dying on a cross beside Christ). Then, again, some of the redeemed, through their long fellowship with Christ, will have incorporated the virtues of a godly life to a high degree (like the apostle John). But both classes—and all in between—will stand "spotless" before God because of the imputed righteousness of Christ. Or, we may express it in John's language borrowed from the sanctuary ritual: "If we walk in the light, as he is in the light, we have fellowship with one another, and *the blood of Jesus his Son cleanses us from all* sin" (1 John 1:7).[9]

The last generation of genuine believers are special in terms of their loyalty and steadfastness to God under extremely difficult circumstances. They will reveal God's character and message in a final appeal to an entire world united in brazen opposition to the Creator. We can scarcely grasp the tremendous pressures under which they will endure in this final witness for God. Nevertheless, in terms of their personal salvation, they will be saved as all other sinners are saved: by grace, through their faith in the merits of Jesus Christ, their Saviour and Lord.[10]

While we disagree with the idea that "the cleansing of the sanctuary in heaven is dependent upon the cleansing of God's people on earth," it is evident that the worldwide announcement that the preadvent judgment is presently in session (Rev 14:6, 7), places a strong emphasis upon the ethical requirements of the gospel. "To be living in such a time, when this judgment is transpiring in heaven, is a sobering thought. It should have an effect upon the way the people of God live."[11] It is not God's purpose to "scare" sinners into His kingdom, but to arrest their attention to the seriousness of their condition as sinful creatures and awaken them to their real needs and their future destiny in this moral universe in which they live. A truly converted sinner, motivated by supreme love for God, will "make every effort" to put away all known sin from his/her life (1 Pet 2:1) and to incorporate every grace into the character through submission to the working of the Holy Spirit (2 Pet 1:5-8; 3:18).

In the nation of Israel God designed the ritual Day of Atonement as "a time of holy convocation," as "a sabbath of solemn rest," in which they were to "afflict [themselves]" (Lev 23:26-32). As we have seen earlier on, the Day of Atonement was a day of fasting, a special occasion for genuine Israelites to humble themselves before God in repentance and confession, a time for serious searching and contrition of heart, resulting in the making of all things right with God and man.

In the antitypical day of atonement, we cannot literally fast throughout this extended period. But the "fast" still signifies a call to repentance, contrition of soul, the confession and putting away of sin from the life. "In like manner, all who would have their names retained in the book of life, should now, in the few remaining days of their probation, afflict their souls before God by sorrow for sin and true repentance. There must be deep, faithful searching of heart. The light, frivolous spirit indulged by so many professed Christians must be put away. There is earnest warfare before all who would subdue the evil tendencies that strive for the mastery. The work of preparation is an individual work. We are not saved in groups."[12]

"Internalized Sanctuary"—Dangers

In recent years some very sincere persons have sought to free themselves from the pervasiveness of sin by "internalizing the sanctuary." They see themselves as seeking a "Most Holy Place experience" by daily praying God to reveal and remove every sin from their inner selves as it is brought to mind. This process seems laudable on the surface, but it carries serious dangers with it.

In the first place, this heavy concentration on one's sinfulness *can lead the believer into the depths of despair.* "The heart is deceitful above all things, and desperately corrupt; who can understand it?" (Jer 17:9). Our carnal natures are capable of bubbling up with an endless stream of evil, even if no overt act is committed (cf. Matt 15:18-20).

Second, this searching of the alleged Most Holy Place of the heart to expel sin *can lead to a form of self-righteousness.* What if no sin presents itself to my consciousness as I pray today and tomorrow? Have I reached a state of sinlessness? I may think so. But I am on dangerous ground to think so, as the Scriptures say, "If we say we have no sin, we deceive ourselves, and the truth is not in us" (1 John 1:8). Even as a repentant sinner, I will always stand in need of grace, *I can never stand righteously independent of God.*

Third, "internalizing" the sanctuary by centering earnest thought on personal sin and weakness can prove dangerous to a healthly spiritual experience. It can turn us away from the truth of the objective ministry of our High Priest in the heavenly sanctuary and all the important teachings related to it. More serious is the danger that in shifting faith's focus from Christ to our sins and defects we separate ourselves from Christ Himself. We may think sincerely, thereby, to obtain a true knowledge of ourselves. But that knowledge can be devastating and can blind us to the Saviour's ability to save. There is only one safe way to obtain knowledge of ourselves:

> *In one way only can a true knowledge of self be obtained. We must behold Christ.* It is ignorance of Him that makes men so uplifted in their own righteousness. When we contemplate His purity and excellence, we shall see our own weakness and poverty and defects as they really are. We shall see ourselves lost and hopeless, clad in garments of self-righteousness, like every other sinner. *We shall see that if we are ever saved, it will not be through our own goodness, but through God's infinite grace.*[13]

When the believer's thoughts are centered on the Saviour, his/her sins are naturally disclosed, but there is hope in this approach inasmuch as *under the Holy Sprit we are drawn into a deeper attachment to Him and His grace* rather than to despair over our multiple sins and defects.

> *A life in Christ is a life of restfulness.* There may be no ectasy of feeling, but there should be an abiding, peaceful trust. *Your hope is not in yourself; it is in Christ.* Your weakness is united to His strength, your ignorance to His wisdom, your fraility to His enduring might. *So you are not to look to yourself, not to let the mind dwell upon self, but look to Christ.* Let the mind dwell upon His love, upon the beauty, the perfection, of His character. Christ in His self-denial, Christ in His humiliation, Christ in His purity and holiness, Christ in His matchless love—this is the subject for the soul's contemplation. It is by loving Him, copying Him, depending wholly upon Him, that you are transformed into His likeness.[14]

We repeat, the most serious danger resulting from constant introspection is that it diverts the attention from the living Christ in the heavenly sanctuary, that in reality it prevents a true union of the believer with the Lord.

> *When the mind dwells upon self, it is turned away from Christ, the source of strength and life. Hence it is Satan's constant effort to keep the attention*

diverted from the Saviour and thus prevent the union and communion of the soul with Christ. The pleasures of the world, life's cares and perplexities and sorrows, the faults of others, *or your own faults and imperfections*—to any or all of these he will seek to divert the mind. Do not be misled by his devices. Many who are really conscientious, and who desire to live for God, he too often leads to dwell upon their own faults and weaknesses, and thus by separating them from Christ he hopes to gain the victory. *We should not make self the center and indulge anxiety and fear as to whether we shall be saved.* All this turns the soul away from the Source of our strength. Commit the keeping of your soul to God, and trust in Him. Talk and think of Jesus. Let self be lost in him. . . . If you will leave yourself in His hands, he will bring you off more than conqueror through Him that has loved you.[15]

The believer whose life is centered on Christ and who lives wholly for God (Deut 6:5) need never fear that he/she will fail to resist and overcome "sin which clings so closely" (Heb 12:1). The apostle Paul expresses his confidence to us in this generation as he did to the Philippians in the first, "I am sure that he who began a good work in you will bring it to completion at the day of Jesus Christ" (Phil 1:6).

Judgment and the Doctrine of Assurance

Does the preadvent judgment, prefigured by the sanctuary types of the Day of Atonement and foretold by the apocalyptic prophecies of Daniel 7, 8, jeopardize a genuine believer's assurance of salvation in Jesus Christ? By no means! Both the doctrines of salvation and judgment are biblical teachings and include the doctrine of Christ's priesthood. They are not at odds with each other. Actually, in the matter of salvation and judgment, the options can be reduced to three positions held by Christians. However, only one of these can be correct and in harmony with Scripture. We list them:

1. When the repentant sinner accepts Jesus Christ as Saviour and Lord, he/she is eternally saved and can never fall away and be lost. This position— held by many Protestant Christians—we believe is contrary to the plainest teachings of the Scriptures. It simply nullifies the biblical doctrine of final judgment.

2. Although viewed as a child of God and saved, at death the believer must go through an indefinite period of suffering in Purgatory as temporal punishment for committed, but absolved, sins before entering heaven. This period can be shortened by the application of the merits of the Mass and/or

indulgences. This nonscriptural position of Roman Catholicism likewise invalidates a true, final judgment.

3. The repentant sinner who receives Jesus Christ as Saviour and Lord is forgiven and accepted, and stands justified and saved before God. In the preadvent phase of final judgment the genuine believer's union with Christ and previous justification are reaffirmed by Christ before the loyal universe, and his/her name is retained in the "book of life. The false professor is removed from the same. We believe this is the biblical teaching of the comprehensive doctrine of Christ's priesthood. It is the belief held by Seventh-day Adventists.

Far from robbing the genuine believer of assurance in Christ, His atoning priesthood sustains confidence. The sanctuary types illustrate and clarify the plan of salvation, and the penitent rejoices to grasp the reality of Christ's substitutionary death for his/her sins as prefigured in its sacrifices. Faith reaches upward to find stability in a *living* Christ, the believer's priestly Advocate who ministers in the very presence of the holy God for us.

As we humbly "walk" in union with the Lord, we believers may be fully assured that Christ not only intercedes in our behalf, but in the awesome, preadvent judgment now in session, He will represent us and reaffirm our justification and faith in God before the loyal universe. We cannot escape final judgment, but what greater assurance can genuine believers have than to know by faith that Christ is both our personal Saviour and high priest, and that His last ministry in the heavenly sanctuary courts is on our behalf?

> *If Christ is my Saviour, my sacrifice, my atonement, then I shall never perish. Believing on Him, I have life forevermore.* Oh, that all who believe the truth would believe in Jesus as their own Saviour. I do not mean that cheap faith unsupported by works, but that earnest, living, constant, abiding faith, that eats the flesh and drinks the blood of the Son of God. I want not only to be pardoned for the transgression of God's holy law, but I want to be lifted into the sunshine of God's countenance. Not simply to be admitted to heaven, but to have an abundant entrance.[16]

———— ◆ ————

Endnotes

1 William H. Shea, "Time Prophecies of Daniel 12 and Revelation 12, 13" DAR-COM 6:340.

2 Bruce L. Shelley, "The Great Awakenings," NIDCC 428-429.

3 See LeRoy E. Froom, *Movement of Destiny* (Washington, DC: Review and Herald, 1971), 56-58.

4 Some argue that the "judgment" announced by the first angel's message (Rev 14:6, 7) refers to an imminent judgment on "Babylon the great" (Rev 17:1) and does not refer to the preadvent phase of final judgment as foretold in Dan 7-8. It needs only to be noted in reply that the antichrist power symbolized by the little horns of Dan 7, 8, the seven-headed leopard of Rev 13:1-10, and the "man of lawlessness" of 2 Thess 2 is also symbolized in a large measure by "Babylon the great." As we have already demonstrated, the antichrist power will be judged in the preadvent judgment, a fact foreshadowed in the sanctuary type of the Azazel goat. Consequently, the message of the first angel, announcing a judgment functioning in probationary time, is referring to the Dan 7, 8 preadvent judgment; there is no other.

5 Space prevents a discussion of this final conflict over the Law of God—over obedience to God's seal of the Sabbath or to the beast's "mark." For interested readers, see C. Mervyn Maxwell, "The Mark of the Beast," DARCOM 7:41-132; Ellen G. White, "God's Law Immutable," GC 433-450.

6 For a useful editorial on this subject, see Raymond F. Cottrell, "The Judgment of the Living," RH, August 8, 1963, p. 13.

7 M. L. Andreasen, *The Sanctuary Service,* 2nd. rev. (Washington, DC: Review and Herald Publishing Association, 1947), 321.

8 For an in-depth study of this subject area, see Ivan T. Blazen, "Justification and Judgment, DARCOM 3:339-388.

9 See Appendix A, "The ABCs of Personal Salvation" for a biblical overview on how the sinner is saved through Christ.

10 In connection with the last generation of God's people it is sometimes argued that Christ cannot return the second time until a sizable group demonstrates that the divine Law can be fully and perfectly kept, that this is the required evidence that God is right and Satan wrong—in terms of obedience to the divine will. But there is no Scripture support for this view to my knowledge. The demonstration of obedience that is being sought has already been obtained by Christ's sinless life. As Ellen G. White has stated it: *"Every soul may say: 'By His perfect obedience He has satisfied the claims of the law, and my only hope is found in looking to Him as my substitute and surety, who obeyed the law perfectly for me. By faith in His merits I am free from the condemnation of the law. He clothes me with His righteousness, which answers all the demands of the law.* I am complete in Him who brings in everlasting righteousness. He presents me to God in the spotless garment of which no thread was woven by any human agent. All is of Christ, and all the glory, honor, and majesty are to be given to the Lamb of God, which taketh away the sins of the world' " (1SM 396, emphasis added).

11 William H. Shea, "Theological Importance of the Preadvent Judgment," DAR-

COM 3:331.
12 Ellen G. White, GC 490.
13 Ellen G. White, COL 159, emphasis added.
14 Ellen G. White, SC 70, 71, emphasis added.
15 Ibid., 71, 72.
16 Ellen G. White, 2SM 381, emphasis added.

Appendix A

The ABCs of Personal Salvation[1]

What God Has Done for Us

As sinners we are helpless to effect our own salvation. The good news of the Christian message is about what God has done for us through Jesus Christ. One of the great summary texts in the NT centers on this divine activity in our behalf:

"For our sake he [God] made him [Jesus Christ] to be sin who knew no sin, so that in him we might become the righteousness of God" (2 Cor 5:21).

Note the points made:

1. Jesus "knew" no sin. In these few words the apostle declares the absolute sinlessness of the Saviour's life. This is a mystery we cannot fathom—that He lived among us "holy, blameless, unstained" (Heb 7:26).

2. God made Jesus to be sin for our sake. Now the apostle points to the vicarious nature of the Saviour's death. The guilt of the sins of humankind was accounted to Him as if it were His own, and He bore Heaven's judgment on sin in our stead. "The Lord has laid on him the iniquity of us all" (Isa 53:6). "He himself bore our sins in his body on the tree" (1 Pet 2:24). "For Christ also died for sins once for all, the righteous for the unrighteous" (1 Pet 3:18).

3. God makes an exchange with us. The significance of this statement is that just as our sins were accounted to Christ as though they were His, so His righteousness (His obedience) is accounted to us as though it were ours! The merits of Christ's sinless life and His atoning death are imputed to the believer who, drawn by the Spirit, reaches out to embrace the Redeemer.

"Therefore, if any one is in Christ, he is a new creation; the old has passed away, behold, the new has come" (2 Cor 5:17).

Accepting Christ as Saviour and Lord

Human Need, Divine Grace

Many are attracted to Christ, but because of convictions of unworthiness, hesitate to commit themselves. Bad habits, we reason, must first be changed and a more virtuous character developed before we become Christians.

But such a concept prevents us from receiving and experiencing the converting, transforming power of divine grace. We do not realize that Heaven's salvation is designed for sinners. "Those who are well have no need of a physician, but those who are sick," declares the world's Redeemer. "I came not to call the righteous, but sinners" (Mark 2:17). And He assures, "him who comes to me I will not cast out" (John 6:37).

The fact is, Heaven can do nothing for those who consider themselves good enough to be saved! Salvation is a matter of divine grace, not of human goodness. "For *by grace* you have been saved through faith; and this is not your own doing, it is the gift of God" (Eph 2:8).

Grace is God's loving, merciful attitude toward undeserving human beings, and His power to save them from their sins. It is estrangement from God, and enslavement to sin—not righteous deeds—that make the sinner the object of God's loving concern.

In contrasting the prayer of the convicted and distressed publican ("God be merciful to me a sinner!") with that of the self-righteous Pharisee ("God, I thank thee that I am not like other men"), Jesus said of the publican, "I tell you, this man went down to his house justified rather than the other" (Luke 18:10-14).

The ABCs of salvation *begin when we realize we are not good.* Man was created in the image of God (Gen. 1:27), but that image has been marred and defaced. "All have sinned and fall short of the glory of God" (Rom 3:23). Our minds are bent on sin and rebellion against God and righteousness.

Both the Old and New Testaments declare emphatically man's alienation from God. "The heart is deceitful above all things, and desperately corrupt; who can understand it?" (Jer 17:9). "The mind that is set on the flesh is hostile to God; it does not submit to God's law, indeed it cannot" (Rom 8:7).

Our education, culture, and social conventions may appear to hide this attitude, but in Heaven's sight these are but a thin veneer bonded by the human will upon an unregenerated heart. A moral man who trusts in his own uprightness will fail in his pride to find true peace of heart. Such a man was the wealthy Nicodemus, whose complacent, legalistic religious life Christ shattered. Fixing His soul-reading gaze upon the rabbi, Christ solemnly disclosed Christianity's great truth and miracle: the new birth. "Unless one is born anew, he cannot see the kingdom of God" (John 3:3).

The apostle Paul characterized man's nature this way:

> For I delight in the law of God, in my inmost self, but I see in my members another law at war with the law of my mind and making me captive to the law of sin which dwells in my members. Wretched man that I am! Who will deliver me from this body of death? (Rom 7:22-24).

The apostle answers his own heart cry in the subsequent verse, "Thanks be to God through Jesus Christ our Lord!"

We cannot feel convicted about our sinful condition and our need for salvation, however, unless the Holy Spirit impresses these matters upon our minds (John 16:7-11). The apostle Paul asks, "Do you not know that God's kindness is meant to lead you to repentance?" (Rom 2:4). Just as bread dough will not rise of itself, so divine grace, like yeast in the dough, must permeate our lives, working out the miracle of change. We, in our own endeavors, can no more change our wayward moral nature than the leopard can change its spots (Jer 13:23).

The New Birth

At this point we ask, How does God go about making sinners into new creations? How are sinners transformed in mind so as to have the same outlook as their heavenly Father?

This change is so fundamental that Christ depicts it as a *new* birth and life. "Do not marvel that I said to you, 'You must be born anew.' The wind blows where it wills, and you hear the sound of it, but you do not know whence it comes or whither it goes; so it is with every one who is born of the Spirit" (John 3:7, 8).

When we surrender the will to Christ's control, He produces within us characters and lives that resemble His own. Thus sinners become citizens of His kingdom.

While the process of the new birth is a mystery of divine grace, yet God has outlined the simple steps we are to take to cooperate with His plan.

Repentance. "Repent therefore, and turn again," the apostle Peter exhorted his convicted hearers, "that your sins may be blotted out" (Acts 3:19).

True repentance implies sorrow for our sins and a turning away from them (2 Cor 7:10). Repentance involves (as the Greek word *metanoia* indicates) a basic change of mind—a change of understanding and attitude toward God, ourselves, and others—that naturally leads to a new pattern of living. Hence, true repentance leads to a genuine conversion, a turning around from the old life of sin to pursue a new course in Christ.

Confession. Coming to Christ in heartfelt repentance, we are prompted by the Holy Spirit to acknowledge and confess our sins and guilt. There can be no redemption if we stoutly justify our waywardness and deny our sins. Declares the prophet to the ancient sinners of Judah, "Only acknowledge your guilt, that you rebelled against the Lord your God" (Jer 3:13). This is a timeless appeal to all sinners. The wise man supports this universal truth, "He who conceals his transgressions will not prosper, but he who confesses and forsakes them will obtain mercy" (Prov 28:13).

When we come to God in repentance, confessing our sins and reaching out to accept Jesus Christ as our only Saviour from sin and our Lord, we are confronted with one of the Bible's most reassuring promises, "If we confess our sins, he is faithful and just, and will forgive our sins and cleanse us from all unrighteousness" (1 John 1:9). The honor of the throne of Heaven undergirds this heart-warming promise. And God fulfills His word at the moment the sinner accepts it. Heaven avers, "Though your sins are like scarlet, they shall be as white as snow; though they are red like crimson, they shall become like wool" (Isa 1:18).

We need not look for some great emotional flight of feeling as evidence that we have been accepted by God. Here is where some would-be Christians become discouraged and are tempted to seek an emotional experience with groups who pursue a religion of feeling. A new convert may—or may not— have a great upheaval of emotion at the moment of his/her conversion. God has called us to move by principle and not by impulse. He invites us to live by faith in Him—not by our feelings.

Faith is simply trusting God, taking Him at His word. Faith says, "God's promises are true. I have met His conditions, and He has forgiven me and has accepted me as His child. These are the facts, not because I feel anything, but because He promised."

Justification: God's Response to the Penitent

God's acceptance of a repentant sinner—as we have discussed above—is presented by the apostle Paul under the headings of "justification" and "sanctification," two topics which, unfortunately, are sometimes misunderstood by even professing Christians. We will summarize their essential elements in the following remarks.

The apostle declares of repentant sinners, "They are *justified* by his grace as a gift, through the redemption which is in Christ Jesus" (Rom 3:24). To "justify" someone in the biblical sense means that God pardons and declares that person righteous, without fault before Him. The word is legal terminology and carries the sense of "acquittal" (cf. Deut 25:1). On what basis, therefore, can God declare a penitent sinner righteous and acquit him/her?

When, under the wooing of the Holy Spirit, we are drawn to trust in Christ as our Saviour, repenting and confessing our sins and surrendering our wills to His Lordship, God does three wonderful things:

1. He freely forgives our past sins. This is done on the basis of Christ's substitutionary death on the cross which has fully met the requirements of divine justice and atoned for human sin.

2. He imputes (accounts) to us the perfect obedience of His Son. This is done on the basis of Christ's sinless life (Rom 4:1-8; 2 Cor 5:21; 1 Cor 1:30). Christ's perfect character stands in place of our imperfect ones. His perfect obedience stands in place of our failures.

> Righteousness is obedience to the law. The law demands righteousness, and this the sinner owes to the law; but he is incapable of rendering it. The only way in which he can attain to righteousness is through faith. By faith he can bring to God the merits of Christ, and *the Lord places the obedience of His Son to the sinner's account.* Christ's righteousness is accepted in place of man's failure, and God receives, pardons, justifies, the repentant, believing soul, treats him as though he were righteous, and loves him as He loves His Son. This is how faith is accounted righteousness.[2]

3. He adopts us as children into His family. This is done on the basis of our acceptance of Christ as Saviour and Lord (John 1:12; Gal 3:26; 4:5, 6). As penitent sinners, forgiven in Christ, accounted obedient in Christ, we are fully accepted as sons and daughters of God and receive all the privileges of this relationship (cf. Rom 8:14-17).

Forgiven and covered by the free gift of Christ's righteousness, we stand before God as His children. Finding no fault in us (by virtue of our union with Christ), He graciously acquits us, declaring us righteous before Him.

> He lived a sinless life. He died for us, and now He offers to take our sins and give us His righteousness. If you give yourself to Him, and accept Him

as your Saviour, then, sinful as your life may have been, for His sake you are accounted righteous. Christ's character stands in place of your character, and you are accepted before God just as if you had not sinned.[3]

Sanctification: The Believer's Response to Grace

The agency used by the Holy Spirit to bring about the new birth and life in union with Jesus Christ is the Word of God, the Holy Scriptures. The apostle Peter says that new Christians "have been born anew, not of perishable seed but of imperishable, through the living and abiding word of God" (1 Pet 1:23).

Standing in union with Christ, justified before God, and belonging to God's family does not eliminate the need for spiritual growth in divine knowledge and right living. The past has been forgiven, but God intends to restore in man His "image" which sin defaced. The Word of God, which, under the Holy Spirit, brought about the new birth, is still the agency for developing a Christlike character in each believer.

> More than this, Christ changes the heart. He abides in your heart by faith. You are to maintain this connection with Christ by faith and the continual surrender of your will to Him; and so long as you do this, He will work in you to will and to do according to His good pleasure. So you may say, "The life which I now live in the flesh I live by the faith of the Son of God, who loved me, and gave Himself for me." Galatians 2:20. . . . Then with Christ working in you, you will manifest the same spirit and the same works—works of righteousness, obedience.[4]

For most conservative Christians, including Seventh-day Adventists, the doctrine of justification by faith—how a sinner is saved by faith in Jesus Christ—is relatively easy to understand. But there is considerable confusion over the doctrine of sanctification—the biblical teaching on growing up spiritually in union with Christ. Many Christians view the living of a sanctified life as a continuous battle against temptation and sin—a battle and a march, a battle and a march. On the other hand many Christians believe that complete freedom from the power of sin—and even from the desire to sin—can be obtained in this life. These Reformed and Wesleyan perspectives on the subject of sanctification mingle within our own Adventist communion.

It is easy to move to extremes on this subject. Speaking of certain false views on sanctification, Ellen White wrote many years ago:

> There is in the religious world a theory of sanctification which is false

in itself and dangerous in its influence. In many cases those who profess sanctification do not possess the genuine article. Their sanctification consists in talk and will worship. Those who are really seeking to perfect Christian character will never indulge the thought they are sinless. Their lives may be irreproachable, they may be living representatives of the truth which they have accepted; but the more they discipline their minds to dwell upon the character of Christ, and the nearer they approach to His divine image, the more clearly will they discern its spotless perfection, and the more deeply will they feel their own defects.

When persons claim that they are sanctified, they give sufficient evidence that they are far from being holy. They fail to see their own weakness and destitution. They look upon themselves as reflecting the image of Christ, because they have no true knowledge of Him. The greater the distance between them and their Saviour, the more righteous they appear in their own eyes.[5]

The English verbs and nouns—"to sanctify/hallow," "to consecrate/dedicate," "sanctification/holiness," and "saint"—translate from either the Hebrew or Greek terms and carry the distinctive idea, "to separate." For example, when God "sanctified" or "hallowed" the seventh-day Sabbath, He simply separated it from the other six days—He set it apart for a holy use (Gen. 2:3; Exod 20:11).

Moses was told to "consecrate" the firstborn, that is, to set them apart for a special service to God (Exod 13:2). When Eleazar the son of Abinadab was "consecrated," he was simply separated or set apart to care for the ark of the covenant which had been left at his father's house after its return by the Philistines (1 Sam 7:1). However, with respect to personal salvation from sin, these terms are viewed in the Scriptures from two different perspectives: (1) sanctification as a status or standing before God, and (2) sanctification as a process or growth.

Sanctification as a Standing Before God

When a penitent sinner accepts Jesus as his/her personal Saviour and Lord, he/she is *separated* from the kingdom of Satan and brought into God's kingdom. "[God] has delivered us from the dominion of darkness and transferred us to the kingdom of his beloved Son" (Col 1:13).

Thus, many NT passages view sanctification as a *past act*—as an event already accomplished. For example, the apostle Paul tells King Agrippa that God sent him to the Gentiles to turn them "from darkness to light and from the power of Satan to God, that they may receive forgiveness of sins and a place among those who *are sanctified* [literally, *have been sanctified and are presently in a state of sanctification*] by faith in me" (Acts 26:18). The Corinthian Christians are greeted as those "who *have been sanctified* in Christ Jesus" (1 Cor 1:2, NASB). Although some of them had come out of gross sins, they were now viewed as sanctified. "And such [sinners] were some of you; but you were washed, but you *were sanctified*, but you were justified in the name of the Lord Jesus Christ, and in the Spirit of our God" (1 Cor 6:11, NASB).

These passages, which regard sanctification as a past act, are recalling the moment when repentant sinners became believers in Christ and *were separated* by His power from the world to join His own kingdom. The open, public moment when this occurred would have been at the time of their baptism when they plainly declared their allegiance to God.

In the NT the believer is commonly referred to as a "saint." Many of Paul's letters address the believers as "saints" (cf. 2 Cor 1:1; Eph 1:1; Phil 1:1, etc.). This expression is not used to describe the sinlessness of these people. It simply recognizes their standing or status before God, they are *separated ones*. A saint is a person who has been separated from the world and now belongs to God.

From this viewpoint sanctification is not a goal toward which one strives. Rather, it is a standing the believer already possesses, having left the world to become a member of God's family. As a Christian, the believer has been set apart for fellowship with God.

In this biblical view, therefore, justification and sanctification-as-a-standing before God are two sides of the same coin of Christian experience. *Justification* emphasizes the fact that the penitent who has entered into union with Christ has been pardoned and declared righteous before God. Because of Christ's merits, his/her sins have been forgiven, and the obedience of Christ has been accounted to him/her. The believer stands justified—faultless and accepted in God's sight. On the other hand *sanctification-as-a-standing* before God emphasizes the fact that this same, justified believer has been separated from the world and set apart for God. As a separated one (saint), he/she belongs wholly to God. In this sense Ellen G. White says, "We may claim sanctification."[6]

Sanctification as a Process/Growth

The Scriptures consistently portray the beginning of a penitent sinner's relationship with God as *the start of a new life*. "Therefore, if any one is in Christ, he is a new creation" (2 Cor 5:17). So radically different are the principles of God's kingdom from those of Satan's that the believer is said to be "born anew" (John 3:7). Like "newborn babes," new Christians are to nurse on "the pure spiritual milk" of God's Word, so that they may "grow up" (1 Pet 2:2). As in nature, so in the spiritual realm, babies must either grow or perish. And so the constant appeal of Scripture to the children of God is, "*Grow* in the grace and knowledge of our Lord and Savior Jesus Christ" (2 Pet 3:18). "Speaking the truth in love, we are *to grow up* in every way into him who is the head, into Christ" (Eph 4:15).

To speak about growing spiritually is just another way to describe the sanctification process. If the Christian's baptism is seen as the *initial* and public separation of the sinner from Satan's kingdom to submission to the kingship of Christ (sanctification as a standing), then sanctification *as a process* may be seen as the *daily* and private separation from sin, the cleaving to that which is good and holy and the rejecting of that which is evil—after the believer's baptism. As the Christian continues to mature in spiritual understanding, as he/she reaches out to know the Father's will more extensively, he/she becomes more sensitive to what is right and wrong.

Such spiritual development will mean a daily crucifixion of the will to God, a daily surrender to His Lordship. The apostle Paul says in a literal rendering of Romans 6:11, "[*Keep on considering*] yourselves dead to sin and alive to God in Christ Jesus." This indicates a continuous process of reaffirming one's personal commitment to God. Ellen G. White alludes to this in her familiar words:

> Consecrate [a synonym for sanctify] yourself to God in the morning; make this your very first work. . . . Thus day by day you may be giving your life into the hands of God, and thus your life will be molded more and more after the life of Christ.[7]

Most of the biblical passages touching on the subject of sanctification view it as a process, as a continual separation from sin. "This is the will of God, your sanctification," the apostle Paul declares to his Thessalonian converts. He continues by showing that God is calling them to live morally pure lives and not to copy the licentiousness of their pagan environment (1 Thess 4:3-8). He closes the letter with a prayer for their full growth in holiness, "May the God of peace himself sanctify you wholly [separate you wholly from sin]; and may your spirit and soul and body be kept sound and blameless at the coming of our Lord Jesus Christ." And he assures them, "He who calls you is faithful, and he will do it" (1 Thess 5:23, 24). Thus, it is clear that the Christian is to be mentally, physically, and spiritually set apart to the worship and service of

God, and that he/she is to pursue and refine this ideal continuously.

Progressive or instantaneous. Some Christians believe that sanctification is meant to be an instantaneous experience rather than a process. In this sense they make it a second work of grace which occurs subsequent to the Christian's justification and initial acceptance with God. This view is sometimes referred to as "the second blessing."But the Scriptures never view *sanctification-as-a-growth* as being instantaneous. This, in itself, is a contradiction in terms. Instead, the Christian is challenged to "*Strive* for peace with all men, and *for holiness* without which no one will see the Lord" (Heb 12:14).

Note how the apostle Paul describes his Christian experience:

> Not that I have already obtained this or am already perfect; but I press on to make it my own, because Christ Jesus has made me his own. Brethren, I do not consider that I have made it my own; but one thing I do, forgetting what lies behind and straining forward to what lies ahead, I press on toward the goal for the prize of the upward call of God in Christ Jesus (Phil 3:12-14).

The metaphor is striking. The apostle sees himself as a runner in the great race of life—running toward the goal. There is no stopping along the way. *The track is as long as his life.* Nothing suggests that the goal is only halfway or three-quarters of the way down the track—at some point *before* his life ends. The implication is that there is never any point this side of death or the coming of Christ at which a believer may stop and say, I have achieved the full spiritual development I am capable of attaining, and I am now sinless. Ellen White's comments on this aspect are plain:

> This sanctification is a progressive work, and an advance from one stage of perfection to another.[8]

> So long as Satan reigns, we shall have self to subdue, besetting sins to overcome; so long as life shall last, there will be no stopping place, no point which we can reach and say, I have fully attained. Sanctification is the result of lifelong obedience.[9]

> Even the most perfect Christian may increase continually in the knowledge and love of God.[10]

> The germination of the seed represents the beginning of spiritual life, and the development of the plant is a beautiful figure of Christian growth. As in nature, so in grace; there can be no life without growth. The plant must either grow or die. As its growth is silent and imperceptible, but continuous, so is the development of the Christian life. At every stage of development

our life may be perfect; yet if God's purpose for us is fulfilled, there will be continual advancement. Sanctification is the work of a lifetime. As our opportunities multiply, our experience will enlarge, and our knowledge increase. We shall become strong to bear responsibility, and our maturity will be in proportion to our privileges.[11]

Wholeness for God. As a doctrine, sanctification is rather easy to explain in its broad terms; as a lifestyle, however, it is not always easy to practice. The Christian is constantly confronted on all sides by the world's temptations, the flesh, and the devil. The term "flesh" implies the repentant sinner's own baggage of inherited evil propensities and acquired bad habits. While the miracle of the new birth brings about a radical new outlook and motivation, it does not in this present life destroy our carnality. Rather, the Lord Jesus' ruling in the heart suppresses and subordinates our bent to sin by the operation of the Holy Spirit. That is why Christ's admonition to the disciples is also applicable to us: "Watch and pray that you may not enter into temptation; the spirit indeed is willing, but the flesh is weak" (Matt 26:41).

In Christ's prayer, just before His arrest in Gethsemane, He said, "For their sake [the disciples'] I consecrate [sanctify] myself" (John 17:19). Christ is not admitting sinfulness here, but is stressing the way He lived as a model for the disciples. He consecrated/sanctified Himself in the sense that He daily dedicated Himself wholly to God. And that is really what *holiness* or *sanctification* (same word in the Greek) is all about. Holiness is wholeness for God—every day serving God with all the heart, mind, and strength. In Gethsemane, as Jesus struggled with the great temptation to abandon mankind to its fate, one refrain ran through His prayers, "Not my will, but thine [the Father's], be done" (Luke 22:42).

This principle by which our Saviour lived and prayed summarizes the essence of sanctification as a process or growth. Note Ellen White's definition:

> On one occasion I spoke in reference to genuine sanctification, which is nothing less than *a daily dying to self and daily conformity to the will of God*. . . . Paul's sanctification was a constant conflict with self. Said he, "I die daily." 1 Cor. 15:31. His will and his desires every day conflicted with duty and the will of God. Instead of following inclination, he did the will of God, however unpleasant and crucifying to his nature.[12]

"The followers of Christ are to become like Him—by the grace of God to form characters in harmony with the principles of His holy law."[13]

An operation of the Holy Spirit. Neither justification nor sanctification is an achievement of human effort, although the believer responds wholeheartedly in faith and obedience to God's grace. The operation of the Holy Spirit is everywhere present in the saving process, wooing and trans- forming.

> For if you live according to the flesh you will die, but if *by the Spirit you put to death the deeds of the body* you will live. For all who are led by the Spirit of God are sons of God (Rom 8:13, 14).

The Spirit employs the Word of God in His mysterious miracle of transformation. Jesus prayed God to "Sanctify them in the truth; thy word is truth" (John 17:17). The Scriptures are a mighty, cleansing agency when they are applied by the hand of the Spirit.

> How can a young man keep his way pure? By guarding it according to thy word (Ps 119:9).

> Having purified your souls by your obedience to the truth for a sincere love of the brethren, love one another earnestly from the heart (1 Pet 1:22).

The apostle Paul cites the biblical principle that operates in this area of spiritual growth, "Do not be overcome by evil, but *overcome evil with good*" (Rom 12:21). In this process of restoring the image of God from within (cf. Col 3:10) the Spirit directs the follower of God to focus his/her thoughts on what is good and wholesome (cf. Phil 4:8), particularly to meditating upon the Saviour. The cultivating of holy thoughts—of upright and wholesome thought patterns—is to root out and crowd out the unholy. We become like the One whom we choose to think about. "We all, with unveiled face, beholding the glory of the Lord, *are being changed into his likeness* from one degree of glory to another; for this comes from the Lord who is the Spirit" (2 Cor 3:18).

> A life in Christ is a life of restfulness. There may be no ecstasy of feeling, but there should be an abiding, peaceful trust. Your hope is not in yourself; it is in Christ. Your weakness is united to His strength, your ignorance to His wisdom, your frailty to His enduring might. So you are not to look to yourself, not to let the mind dwell upon self, but look to Christ. Let the mind dwell upon His love, upon the beauty, the perfection, of His character. Christ in His self-denial, Christ in His humiliation, Christ in His purity and holiness, Christ in His matchless love—this is the subject for the soul's contemplation. it is by loving Him, copying Him, depending wholly upon Him, that you are to be transformed into His likeness.[14]

It was said of Christ, "Thou hast loved righteousness and hated lawless-ness" (Heb 1:9). This same attitude toward sin and righteousness is developed by the Spirit in the Christian. We come to love the things we once hated, and to hate the things we once loved. New tastes, ideals, perspectives, and attitudes develop toward God and our fellow beings.

> All true obedience comes from the heart. It was heart work with Christ. And if we consent, He will so identify Himself with our thoughts and aims, so blend our hearts and minds into conformity to His will, that when obeying Him we shall be but carrying out our own impulses. The will, refined and sanctified, will find its highest delight in doing His service. When we know God as it is our privilege to know Him, our life will be a life of continual obedience. Through an appreciation of the character of Christ, through communion with God, sin will become hateful to us.[15]

Always growing—always accepted. Does this mean, then, that sinless perfection is obtainable in this life? The Scriptures set a high ideal. The apostle Peter says, "But as he who called you is holy, be holy yourselves in all your conduct; since it is written, 'You shall be holy, for I am holy' " (1 Pet 1:15, 16). No higher standard could be set—and grace is provided for its spiritual attainment.

Yet, at the same time, a warning is sounded: "If we say we have no sin, we deceive ourselves, and the truth is not in us" (1 John 1:8). "My little children, I am writing this to you so that you may not sin; but if any one does sin, we have an advocate with the Father, Jesus Christ the righteous; and he is the expiation for our sins" (1 John 2:1, 2).

Perhaps, the tension between the ideal ("You shall be holy, for I am holy") and the actual experience ("there is no man who does not sin," 1 Kgs 8:46) is only apparent and not real—if the Christian truly maintains a bond of union with Jesus Christ.

We have noted that from a biblical viewpoint sanctification is both a standing with God and a process. When the believer enters into union with Christ, he/she stands before God both justified and sanctified, clothed in the imputed obedience/righteousness of Christ. By grace the believer has been put right with God and consecrated wholly to Him. The believer is a "saint"—a separated or dedicated one. It is in this sense (by divine grace) that the believer attains the ideal placed before him/her: "You shall be holy, for I am holy."

In vital union with Christ and under the umbrella of his/her justification and sanctification-as-a-status—"perfect in Christ"—the believer continues to grow spiritually, to live the sanctified life, daily yielding the human will to the will of God. This character growth knows no termination point prior to death or the coming of Christ. As long as the Christian lives, knowledge will widen, understanding will mature, repentance will deepen. Thus, during each moment of a continuously developing growth, the Christian has the assurance of God's acceptance for Christ's sake.[16]

Assurances

Becoming a Christian, entering into a lifelong bond of union with Christ, brings peace and joy to the believer because human beings were made to enjoy fellowship with their Creator.

> Come to me, all who labor and are heavy laden, and I will give you rest. Take my yoke upon you, and learn from me; for I am gentle and lowly in heart, and you will find rest for your souls. For my yoke is easy, and my burden is light (Matt 11:28-30).

Commitment to Jesus Christ brings unity of purpose to the individual and greatly simplifies the issues of life.

> The surrender of all our powers to God greatly simplifies the problem of life. It weakens and cuts short a thousand struggles with the passions of the natural heart.[17]

Anchoring to Christ, the eternal Rock, brings stability to believers who would otherwise be tossed to and fro on the tides and currents of life's uncertainties. When trials like wind and storm surge about, the Christian can say with the apostle, "I know whom I have believed and I am convinced that He is able to guard what I have entrusted to Him until that day" (2 Tim 1:12, NASB).

The Christian experiences a new life in every way (cf. 2 Cor 5:17). Being at peace with God (Rom 5:1) removes the tensions which heretofore placed the unregenerated sinner at odds with the Creator. Jesus said of us sinners, "I came that they may have life, and have it abundantly" (John 10:10). We list some of the divine assurances that form the basis for Christian happiness and security:

1. Life in Christ brings freedom from guilt and remorse. "Take heart, my son; your sins are forgiven." (Matt 9:2. Cf. Isa 1:18; 1 John 1:9; Prov 28:13).

2. Life in Christ brings freedom from the tyrannical rule of sin. "There is therefore now no condemnation for those who are in Christ Jesus. For the law of the Spirit of life in Christ Jesus has set me free from the law of sin and death" (Rom 8:1, 2).

3. Life in Christ brings freedom from the fear of death. (Cf. Heb 2:14, 15). The Christian grasps the blessed assurance of eternal life as a reality. "And this is the testimony, that God gave us eternal life, and this life is in his Son. He who has the Son has life; he who has not the Son of God has not life. I write this to you who believe in the name of the Son of God, that you may know that you have eternal life" (1 John 5:11-13).

Although the Christian dies as do all human beings, yet he/she falls asleep in death with the certain hope that the Lord will awaken His children at the resurrection when He comes the second time (John 6:39, 40; 1 Thess 4:16-18).

4. Life in Christ brings freedom from corroding care and fear of want. "My God will supply every need of yours according to his riches in glory in Christ Jesus" (Phil 4:19). He who provides for the earth and its teeming life in field and forest says:

> Do not be anxious, saying, "What shall we eat?" or "What shall we drink?" or "What shall we wear?" For the Gentiles seek all these things; and your heavenly Father knows that you need them all. But seek first his kingdom and his righteousness, and all these things shall be yours as well (Matt 6:31-33).

Little wonder that the apostle Paul "decided to know nothing among [the Corinthians] except Jesus Christ and him crucified" (1 Cor 2:2). In the dying form of the Son of God, the Christian sees Heaven reaching out to embrace lost humanity and draw it back to the Father's heart. The cross says to every sinner, "You are of infinite worth to God." In one sense, God does not see sinful men and women as they are, but as they may become in Christ. Grace sees worth even in a devil-possessed Mary Magdalene, a dishonest tax collector like Zacchaeus, a nameless dying thief, an accused adulteress. No person is worthless in God's sight.

The Christian finds genuine security in Christ. His "life is hid with Christ in God" (Col 3:3). Although perplexities may shadow the path and clouds of sorrow and grief envelop, nothing can really hurt the believer permanently. The Christian trusts the Father, knowing "that in everything God works for good with those who love him, who are called according to his purpose" (Rom 8:28).

Whether the Christian lives until Christ's return, or is allowed to fall asleep in death, he/she has this certain promise from the lips of the Saviour:

> My sheep hear my voice, and I know them, and they follow me; and I give them eternal life, and they shall never perish, and no one shall snatch

them out of my hand. My Father, who has given them to me, is greater than all, and no one is able to snatch them out of the Father's hand (John 10:27-29).

For the Christian, the life of heaven begins here. The Scriptures describe it as a "fellowship" with God—as "a walk" with the Father and the Son. The apostle John wrote, "That which we have seen and heard we proclaim also to you, so that you may have fellowship with us; and our fellowship is with the Father and with his Son Jesus Christ. . . . If we walk in the light, as he is in the light, we have fellowship with one another, and the blood of Jesus his Son cleanses us from all sin" (1 John 1:3, 7). And the apostle Paul adds this portrayal of the new Christian's experience, "You are no longer strangers and sojourners, but you are fellow citizens with the saints and members of the household of God" (Eph 2:19). Home! Home at last!

———— ♦ ————

Endnotes

1 Adapted from the author's article, "Walking in the Light: An Overview of the Doctrine of Salvation in Christ," *Journal of Adventist Education,* December, 1983–January, 1984, 17-34.
2 Ellen G. White Comments, SDABC 6:1073, emphasis added; "The great work that is wrought for the sinner who is spotted and stained by evil is the work of justification. *By Him who speaketh truth he is declared righteous.* The Lord imputes unto the believer the righteousness of Christ and pronounces him righteous before the universe. He transfers his sins to Jesus, the sinner's representative, substitute, and surety. Upon Christ He lays the iniquity of every soul that believeth. 'He hath made him to be sin for us, who knew no sin; that we might be made the righteousness of God in him' (2 Cor 5:21)" (Id., 1SM 392, emphasis added); "Every soul may say: 'By His perfect obedience He has satisfied the claims of the law, and my only hope is found in looking to Him as my substitute and surety, who obeyed the law perfectly for me. By faith in His merits I am free from the condemnation of the law. He clothes me with His righteousness, which answers all the demands of the law. I am complete in Him who brings in everlasting righteousness. He presents me to God in the spotless garment of which no thread was woven by any human agent. All is of Christ, and all the glory, honor, and majesty are to be given to the Lamb of God, which taketh away the sins of the world' " (Id., 1SM 396).
3 Id., SC 62.

 4 Ibid., 62, 63.
 5 Id., SL 7.
 6 Id., 2SM 32.
 7 Id., SC 70, 71.
 8 Id., ML 250.
 9 Id., AA 560, 561.
10 Id., 1T 340.
11 Id., COL 65, 66.
12 Id., LS 237, emphasis added.
13 Id., GC 469.
14 Id., SC 70, 71.
15 Id., DA 668.
16 Id., AA 560-562.
17 Id., MYP 30.

Appendix B

The Year-Day Principle

How shall the time periods in the apocalyptic prophecies of Daniel and Revelation be understood? Proponents of the preterist/historical-critical and futurist schools of interpretation take the time expressions to denote literal time. On the other hand interpreters of the historicist school view the time expressions as symbolic units designed to indicate much longer periods of literal, historical time. Furthermore, the historicist holds that these time units are to be unlocked with a key commonly known as the "year-day principle." On this basis, one symbolic day represents one literal, historical year.

Thus, the year-day principle is an integral presupposition of the historicist method of prophetic interpretation, a method which sees the prophecies of Daniel and Revelation unrolling in fulfillment across the centuries from the times of Daniel and John until the establishment of God's eternal kingdom. The most recent treatment of this subject among Seventh-day Adventists has been written by William H. Shea in *Selected Studies on Prophetic Interpretation,* DARCOM 1:56-93.

For the benefit of those readers who may not have access to this work, we summarize as far as is practical in a limited space Dr. Shea's reasoned position that the year-day principle is a biblically grounded concept, a divinely designed method for unlocking the significance of the apocalyptic time periods.

General Considerations

Both the preterist/historical-critical and futurist schools of interpretation empty the Christian Era of nearly all input from the books of Daniel and

Revelation. They thereby wipe it clean of prophetic significance.

The former "school" relegates the book of Daniel to the second century B.C. and the book of Revelation to the first centuries A.D. The latter applies the last "week" of seven years, broken off from Daniel's 70-week prophecy (Dan 9), to the end of the world, during which time most of the book of Revelation finds its fulfillment. In this manner Daniel and Revelation are muted and prevented from addressing the church and the world of the Christian Era.

This is in marked contrast with the OT Scriptures which record the mighty acts of God in His conflict with evil and provide prophetic evaluations of their character. The historicist approach is able to continue this OT pattern by employing the year-day principle, thereby permitting the prophecies of Daniel and Revelation to point out and to interpret significant events in the moral controversy between good and evil during the centuries of the Christian Era as well as at its beginning and end.

Time prophecies in the Bible often deal with periods of adversity which usually turn for the better at their close. In the historical narratives we may list as examples the 120 years allotted to limit the wickedness of the antediluvian world (Gen 6:3), the 400 years of Israelite oppression in Egypt (Gen 15:13), and the 70 years of Babylonian captivity (Jer 25:11).

In the apocalyptic prophecies three time periods ($3\frac{1}{2}$ times/years = 42 months = 1260 days) are mentioned seven times altogether as an extreme period of persecution of God's people. If the latter are interpreted as literal time years), then there is considerable disparity between the length of apocalyptic time periods of hardship and the time periods of adversity in the historical narratives. Actually, the magnitude of the events and predicted persecutions described in the prophecies of Daniel and Revelation require that their expressed, short time-units be understood to represent much greater lengths of historical time.

Symbolic Time

Even a casual reader of Daniel and Revelation observes at once the marked difference between these apocalyptic prophecies and those recorded by the classical prophets (the so-called "major" and "minor" prophets). The messages of the former are couched in symbols (beasts, horns, women, sea-monsters, etc.). Consequently, it is reasonable to infer that the apocalyptic time periods are also symbolic in nature.

The careful reader will also observe that these periods are expressed in unusual time units. For example, it is not normal biblical language to speak of a length of time as "a time, two times, and half a time" (Dan 7:25), nor even to refer to the same era as "one thousand two hundred and sixty days" (Rev 12:6, 14). If Daniel or John had expressed himself in a nonsymbolic manner, he simply would have said, "three years and six months" (cf. Jas 5:17). The expressing of time units in an unusual manner suggests their symbolic quality and the need to discover their literal intent.

"In contrast to statements about time in classical prophecies, apocalyptic employs symbolic numbers with symbolic time units in symbolic contexts. These factors converge to indicate that these references should be understood as standing for symbolic and not literal time."[1]

The most striking evidence that the short, symbolic time units of apocalyptic prophecy stand for periods of longer, historical time is the 70-week prophecy recorded in Daniel 9. All schools of prophetic interpretation are agreed that the events foretold in this prophecy (Dan 9:24-27) could not have been reached and accomplished if the period is regarded as 70 *literal* weeks. According to its internal requirements the prophecy begins at some point during the Persian rule, spans the succeeding Greek era, and extends into the reign of the Roman Empire as far as the crucifixion of Christ and a little beyond. Although historical-critical and futurist scholars deny the application of the year-day principle to the 70-week prophecy, they still must treat it as a symbol or statement of something other than what the Masoretes vocalized it to say expressly, 70 *weeks*.

Like the 70 weeks, the 2300-day unit (Dan 8) must be regarded as a symbolic time unit of a much longer historical time span. It also begins in the days of Persian rule and extends through the Greek era, the Roman era, through the period of the medieval papacy to a point which Daniel describes as "the time of the end." Obviously, this longest of the prophetic periods is a symbolic time unit that must be unlocked for its longer significance and is not to be taken simply as a period of six-plus literal years.

The Year-for-a-Day Concept

General Use of Day/Year Terms

Considerable biblical data is available to demonstrate that long before the writing of the apocalyptic book of Daniel, a general relationship between the terms for "day" and "year" had become deeply ingrained in Hebrew thought.

The concept appears to have had its roots (biblically speaking) in the first recorded genealogy (Gen 5), in such repeated phrases as the following: "Thus

all the *days* that Adam lived were nine hundred and thirty *years;* and he died."
"Thus all the *days* of Seth were nine hundred and twelve *years;* and he died."
An early *prophecy* links these two time elements. Speaking of the wickedness
of man prior to the Flood, God said, "My spirit shall not abide in man for ever,
for he is flesh, but his *days* shall be a hundred and twenty *years*" (Gen 6:3).

At times the word "days" (in the plural) was used to stand for a "year"
when an annual event like the Passover was designated. For example, the Lord
commanded, "You shall therefore keep this ordinance [Passover] at its appointed time *from year to year*" (literally, "from days to days," Exod 13:10).
The expression, "a *yearly* sacrifice" was expressed literally as "the sacrifice
of the *days*" (1 Sam 20:6). Hannah took to Samuel, who lived at Shiloh, a new
robe *each year* (literally, "from days to days," 1 Sam 2:19).

It became a custom for young Israelite women to mourn *yearly* (literally,
"from days to days") for Jephthah's daughter. The record also adds that they
sorrowed four days "in the year" (*šānāh*). Here we have an equation between
"days" ("from days to days") made directly with the word for "year" (*šānāh*,
Judg 11:40).

Apart from its use with annual events, the plural noun was sometimes
employed as a substitute for "year." For example, in the Israelite exodus the
people journeyed only when the cloud lifted from the tabernacle. Consequently, they remained encamped as long as the cloud remained stationary,
"whether it was two days or a month or *a year*" [literally, "days," Num 9:22,
NASB]. David remained in the land of the Philistines "a *year* [literally, 'days']
and four months" (1 Sam 27:7).

Old Testament poetry, like its prose, yields the same evidence. The two
time expressions were often paralleled in the Hebrew phrasing.

> Are thy *days* as the *days* of man,
> or thy *years* as man's *years*? (Job 10:5).

> The wicked man writhes in pain all his *days,*
> through all the *years* that are laid up for the ruthless (Job 15:20).

> I consider the *days* of old,
> I remember the *years* long ago (Ps 77:5).

> For all our *days* pass away under thy wrath,
> our *years* come to an end like a sigh (Ps 90:9).

"The close and particular relationship between 'days' and 'years' that is
found both in the prose and poetry of the OT provides a background for the

more specific application of this type of thought in apocalyptic time prophecies."[2]

Specific Use of the Year-Day Principle

The earliest passage in which the year-day principle is reflected occurs in the Levitical legislation dealing with the sabbatical year of land rest and with the related institution of the jubilee (Lev 25:1-12). The first piece of legislation provided for retaining the land's productivity; the latter legislation prevented the land from being permanently alienated from its original owner and heirs.

> **The sabbatical year.** "When you come into the land which I give you, *the land shall keep a sabbath* to the Lord. Six years you shall sow your field, and six years you shall prune your vineyard, and gather in its fruits; but in *the seventh year* there shall be *a sabbath of solemn rest* for the land" (Lev 25:2-4).

It is evident from this instruction that the sabbatical year (the last or seventh year in a block of seven years) is modeled from the weekly Sabbath. Just as six days of labor were to be followed by the seventh day of Sabbath rest, so six years of farming were to be followed by a seventh year of sabbath rest for the land. The seventh-day Sabbath was to be a Sabbath of "solemn rest" (Lev 23:3); likewise the seventh year, the sabbatical year, was to be a sabbath of "solemn rest" for the land (Lev 25:4, 5). Thus, we have in the institution of the sabbatical year an early application of a year-day principle: the Sabbath *day* and its six preceding working days function to pattern the sabbatical *year* and its six preceding farming years.

The jubilee year. The jubilee year marked the end of a period of fifty years composed of seven sabbatical year groupings. A literal reading of the opening lines of the legislation (Lev 25:8) reads as follows:

> You shall count seven *sabbaths of years,* seven years seven times, and to you *the days* of the seven sabbaths of years shall be *forty-nine years. . . .* (vs. 8).

> And you shall hallow the fiftieth year, and proclaim liberty throughout the land to all its inhabitants; it shall be a jubilee for you, when each of you shall return to his property and each of you shall return to his family (Lev 25:10).

It is not certain whether the fiftieth year was a free-standing year *after which* the count began on the next series of 49 years, or whether the fiftieth year was actually *the first year* in the count of the next series of 49 years. However, for our purpose, it is not necessary to resolve that uncertainty, although the evidence from Qumran indicates that some Jews at least regarded the 70-week (490 days) prophecy of Daniel 9:24-27 as containing 10 jubilees (10 x 49 = 490).

The expression, "sabbaths of years," refers back to the institution of the sabbatical year of rest for the land and its six preceding farming years which in turn was modeled from the seventh-day Sabbath rest and its preceding six working days. Seven of these Sabbatical Year groupings of years were allocated to form a jubilee period of 49 years. The significance here is that Moses employs the year-day principle directly in this computation of the jubilee period: "*The days* of the seven sabbaths of years [the Sabbatical groupings of seven years] shall be to you forty-nine *years* . . . " (Lev 25:8). The "days" of these seven groupings are now explicitly said to represent the "years" of the jubilee period. Furthermore, "one could almost say that the time period involved in Dan 9:24-27 [the 70-week prophecy] was modeled after the jubilee legislation."[3]

Prophetic judgments. Two passages—similar in that they deal with the theme of God's judgments—provide further insights into the biblical application of the year-day principle.

1. Numbers 14:34. Because the migrating Israelites accepted the false, majority report of the spies Moses had sent to survey Palestine and refused to trust in God's promised leading, He sentenced them to wander in the wilderness 40 years, a year for each day the spies had spent in exploration.

> According to the number of the days in which you spied out the land, forty days, *for every day a year*, you shall bear your iniquity, forty years, and you shall know my displeasure (Num 14:34).

In this instance, God's prophetic judgment is calibrated in terms of the year-day principle, a day for a year. It will be noted that in the application a *past day* [the past 40 days of exploration] is employed to represent a *future year* [the 40 years of wandering were yet to be experienced]. As we shall see, this simply means that the year-day principle could be adapted and applied in more than one way.

2. Ezekiel 4:4-6. In the sixth century B.C. God directed Ezekiel to act out a parable to represent the impending siege and conquest of Jerusalem and the exile of the survivors into Babylonian captivity. A model of the city was constructed before which the prophet was to lie a total of 430 days as though living in a state of siege. These "days" [390 for the northern kingdom + 40 for the southern kingdom] served to represent the appalling sinful condition of both kingdoms during the divided monarchy, because of which their exile had been decreed.

When this passage in Ezekiel is compared with the pronounced judgment in Numbers 14:34, striking similarities can be seen. We place the two passages together in a somewhat literal translation. The italicized phrases denote the similarity of language in the two passages:

> According to *the number of the days* which you spied out the land, *forty days, day for the year, day for the year, you shall bear your evil* forty years (Num 14:34).

> *The number of the days* you lie on your side, and *you shall bear their evil.* I have given you the years of their evil according to a number of *days,* three hundred and ninety days, and *you shall bear the evil* of the house of Israel. . . . and *you shall bear the evil* of the house of Judah *forty days, day for the year, day for the year* I have given you (Ezek 4:4-6).

The similarity of the expressions, the bearing of evil and the identical repetition of the time element—"day for the year, day for the year," indicates that the divine instruction given to Ezekiel is drawn directly from the phraseology of Numbers 14:34. The year-day principle expressed in both passages is linguistically the same.

However, there is a significant difference in the manner in which the year-day principle has been applied. In Numbers 14 *past days* have been used to represent *future years.* In Ezekiel 4 it is just the reverse: *past years* have been used to represent the *future days* of the prophet's enacted parable.

"Ezekiel does not say 'year for the day,' when Numbers says 'day for the year.' The latter phraseology ('day for the year, day for the year') appears in *both* passages, *stated in the same manner.* There is no difference between them in this regard even though their historico-chronological application differs. This fact demonstrates the point that the same year-day principle could be employed in different ways on different occasions.

"The symbolic 'days' present in apocalyptic prophecy refer to events that were to take place in the future from the prophet's time. The application of the same year-day principle of these symbolic 'days' can be seen, therefore, as one more way this principle could be applied."[4]

Apocalyptic prophecy. As we have observed earlier, apocalyptic prophecy, such as is found in Daniel and Revelation, is couched in thorough-going symbolism. Consequently, its time periods are also expressed in a symbolic manner. The most striking of these is the 70-week prophecy of Daniel 9:24-27 which foretold, among other things, the advent and atoning death of the Messiah.

1. The 70-week prophecy. Scholars of all persuasions agree that 70 literal weeks (less than a year and a half of actual time) are not sufficient to reach to the events predicted and to accomplish what was envisioned. It is thus a crucial question how the time period should be determined.

As the Hebrew text presently stands, the Masoretes (Jewish scholars who flourished between A.D. 500-900) have vocalized the key time element as "seventy weeks." This larger span is composed of three smaller units, likewise vocalized as "weeks"—7 weeks, 62 weeks, 1 week. Since this prophecy spans kingdoms (beginning in Persian times and extending through the Greek period into the Roman era including the crucifixion of Christ), it is most natural to apply the year-day principle to unlock its actual length in historical years. On this basis the 70 weeks equal 490 symbolic days (70 weeks x 7 days to a week = 490 days) or 490 literal years, and 69 weeks or 483 literal years extend from the starting point to the Messiah, leaving one week for His ministry—and that of His apostles—to the Jewish nation.

However, those scholars who espouse the preterist/historical-critical or futurist approach argue for a purely numerical kind of translation, such as "seventy weeks of years" (RSV) or "seventy sevens," or some other expression that would suggest a simple statement of literal time rather than symbolic time needing to be decoded. In this manner they would separate this distinctive prophecy from the time symbolic elements of other apocalyptic prophecies. Consequently, they drop the Masoretic vocalization for "week(s)" and attempt to work out some other way to get a long period of literal time without using the year-day principle.

It has been demonstrated, however, that these attempts are not linguistically sound. The Hebrew word for "week" is derived as a specialized term from the word for "seven," and is spelled with the Hebrew letter *waw* functioning as a *u*-vowel letter. This spelling or pointing with a *u*-vowel and translation as "week" is consistent throughout the Scriptures. Consequently, it is both inconsistent and arbitrary to give the word in Daniel 9:24-27 a numerical value such as "sevens," "besevened," "heptads," or "hebdomads."

Even if one dropped the Masoretic vocalization, the consonantal forms that introduce this prophecy (vs. 24) would have to be translated as "seventy seventies," not "seventy sevens," as some scholars have observed—a meaningless expression. The fact that the term for the seventieth week in vs. 27 is stated twice in the singular and fully spelled with its *u*-letter vowel clearly demonstrates that the other time units written in the plural (70, 7, 62) should also be understood as "weeks" as the Masoretes have vocalized them.

As 70 *weeks* (with its constituent parts, 7 weeks + 62 weeks + 1 week), the prophecy inherently carries along with it the year-day principle, one symbolic day standing for one literal, historical year. Starting in the Persian period from the established date of 457 B.C. (the seventh regnal year of Artaxerxes I and his decree establishing the Jewish national polity; see Dan 9:25; Ezra 7), 69 prophetic weeks or 483 literal years extends to A.D. 27, the fifteenth year of Tiberius Caesar (a date capable of verification) and the baptism and anointing of Jesus of Nazareth as the Christ (Luke 3:1, 21). The subsequent events called for in the prophecy, Christ's atoning death and the end of the full 70 weeks—A.D. 31, 34—follow respectively in harmony with the data required by the prophecy. In this clear-cut prediction, with its verifiable parts, the year-day principle is pragmatically confirmed.

2. Twenty-three hundred days. As we have demonstrated in our remarks on Daniel 8, the 2300-day prediction (Dan 8:14) is an integral part of the vision of Daniel 9. The starting point for the 70-week prophecy (457 B.C.) is the starting point for the 2300-day prophecy as well. If the year-day principle is applicable to the former, so it is to the latter. Only the operation of a year-day principle could trace this longest of apocalyptic prophecies which begins during the Persian rule and extends through the succeeding Grecian and Roman kingdoms, and down through the era of the medieval papacy into earth's last period, "the time of the end." The prophecy itself requires such a principle to reach its true, ultimate fulfillment: the autumn of 1844. Thus, 2300 symbolic days are properly interpreted as 2300 literal, historical years.

3. Days/years (Dan 8 & 11). Commentators are in general agreement that the literal, historical events described in the vision of Daniel 11, 12 provide an interpretation of the symbolic figures and events presented in the vision of Daniel 8. Because of its literal description, the Daniel 11 account gives us an insight into the *nature* of the *symbolic days* (the 2300 days) of Daniel 8.

As we have observed above, the 2300 days span several successive eras of political rule, one of these being the Grecian era inclusive of its divided condition after Alexander's death. In Daniel 11 reference is made to certain *years* in connection with the reigns of three kings (two Seleucid and one Egyptian).

"After *some years* they shall make an alliance" is identified with the reign of Antiochus II (Dan 11:6); "For the king of the north shall again raise a multitude greater than the former; and after *some years* he shall come on with a great army and abundant supplies" is identified with Antiochus III (Dan 11:13); "And for *some years* he shall refrain from attacking the king of the north" is identified with the Egyptian ruler, Ptolemy III (Dan 11:8).

Since the vision of Daniel 11 is explaining in literal language some of the events that would take place during the same span of time covered by the symbolic vision of Daniel 8, these references to literal, historical years demonstrate that the 2300 symbolic days obviously represent literal, historical years. Twenty-three hundred literal days (6 plus years) could not begin to cover the "years" of these three kings, not even to speak of the eras of Persia, Rome, and the medieval Roman papacy! The comparison of the historical "years" of certain kings in Daniel 11 with the symbolic time unit of the 2300 days in Daniel 8 provides another biblical confirmation of the validity of the year day principle.

Conclusion

It is evident to any reader that the apocalyptic prophecies of Daniel and Revelation are written largely in symbolic language. This notable feature includes their time periods which call attention to their symbolism by being expressed in unusual time units and are too short to allow the events being portrayed to be accomplished. Thus, it is evident that these short, symbolic time units must be interpreted by a sound principle that will unlock their symbolism.

The biblical data—both prose and poetry—amply demonstrate that the Hebrew mind-set from earliest times associated year-day relationships. Thus, it was only natural for such a method of stating time periods to be employed in both legislation and prophecy.

The first application of a year-day principle occurs in the legislation regarding the sabbatical year and the jubilee year, the latter period of 49 years being based on the *days* in seven weeks of *years*. In the realm of classical prophecy Numbers 14:34 and Ezekiel 4:4-6 demonstrate that the year-day principle could be used to equate a past day for a future year, or a past year for a future day respectively. The 70-week prophecy (Dan 9) strikingly displays an apocalyptic application of the year-day principle in which a future, symbolic day stands for a future, literal year. The accurate fulfillment of the time elements of this prophecy confirms the validity of the year-day principle as the biblical key to unlock symbolic time units in apocalyptic prophecy.

Because internal evidence demonstrates that the prophecies of the 70 weeks (Dan 9) and the 2300 days (Dan 8) span many centuries, their short time units must be understood as symbolic of much longer periods of actual historical time. The year-day principle is thus a required tool to unlock the time units of the prophecies of Daniel and Revelation so they may present their important messages to the peoples who live—and who will yet live in the Christian Era. Unlocking the time periods of Daniel 7-9 especially enables both Daniel and Revelation to proclaim God's judgment-hour warning to our present modern world and to offer His final invitation of grace.

———— ◆ ————

Endnotes

1 William H. Shea, Selected Studies on Prophetic Interpretation, DARCOM 1:62.
2 Ibid., 69.
3 Ibid., 72.
4 Ibid., 74.

Appendix C

Israel's Sanctuaries

Introduction

Israel's sanctuaries were not built as residences for a priestly caste, nor were they conceived to bring renown to the architects and skilled craftsmen who erected them. Nor were they intended to be monuments to perpetuate the memory of the rulers who oversaw their construction, even when their names did indeed become associated with the structures.

Israel's sanctuaries were not unique in form, but they were unique in the sense that their rituals portrayed the great truths of the plan of salvation as laid by the divine Creator. By means of these sacred edifices and their rites God determined to disclose to the populations of the world the good news of His way out of the darkness and despair of human enslavement to sin and satanic agencies.

"My house," God declared, "shall be called a house of prayer for all peoples" (Isa 56:7). He intended that the nations of earth would seek saving truth at His sanctuary, and that they would say to one another, "Come, let us go up to the mountain of the Lord, to the house of the God of Jacob; that he may teach us his ways and that we may walk in his paths" (Isa 2:3).

For the benefit of those readers unacquainted with the physical features of the Hebrew sanctuaries, we append a short description and history. For a detailed presentation, the reader is referred to any standard Bible dictionary or Bible encyclopedia.

The Tabernacle (Exod 25-31, 35-40; Heb 9:1-5)

Although the sacrificial system was instituted after the Fall (cf. Gen 4:3-5; Heb 11:4), it was not until the organization of the nation of Israel at Mount

Sinai that God directed Moses to build a tabernacle-sanctuary. Eventually, this portable "tent" was replaced by a permanent Temple of stone. At the same time God ordered the building of the tabernacle, He established a specialized priesthood to replace the role of the father or tribal elders who had previously led out in the common worship.

The appointed craftsmen, qualified by God's Spirit, completed the tabernacle and its furnishings, and the clothing for the priests in about six months. Built to meet the traveling conditions of the national migration from Egypt to Canaan, the tabernacle was made of many detachable pieces (wooden frames, rods, sockets, coverings, hangings, etc.) so that it could be quickly taken apart, transported, and reassembled at a new location.

Description of the Tabernacle

A small structure, the tabernacle measured 30 cubits in length by 10 cubits in width and height. If the craftsmen employed the Egyptian cubit (20.6 inches), the tabernacle was about 51½ feet in length and a trifle over 17 feet in width and height. A beautiful curtain, made of fine linen mixed with blue, purple, and scarlet wool, and embroidered with figures of cherubim, divided the tabernacle into two apartments. Suspended from four pillars of acacia wood overlaid with gold, this veil marked off the innermost apartment, the Most Holy Place, as a cube of 10 cubits and the first apartment or holy place as a rectangle 20 x 10 cubits. Moses pitched the tabernacle on an east-west axis with the entrance facing east. This orientation placed the worshipers in a position to pray westward toward the sanctuary.

A series of "frames" (RSV), 10 cubits high by 1½ cubits wide, fashioned from acacia wood overlaid with gold, formed the "walls" on three sides. A veil, sewn from materials similar to the inner veil, served as the doorway into the first apartment. Two tenons on the bottom of each frame projected into silver sockets which in turn functioned as the building's foundation. Bars of acacia wood—overlaid with gold and shot through gold rings attached to the frames, extended along the north, south, and west sides to hold the frames in line. Thus, the wooden structure of the tabernacle was like a large trellis—light, yet strong, and easy to assemble or to take apart.

The builders stretched four coverings over this golden trellis. The innermost (like the veils) was made of fine linen, the colored wools, and embroidered with cherubim. In this manner, the cherubim in the ceiling and in the spaces of the golden frames portrayed the heavenly dwelling of the Creator, surrounded by the shining hosts of angels.

A covering of goats' hair overlay the linen ceiling and the sides to the tabernacle down to, and including, the silver sockets. This is a scholarly opinion based on the given measurements for both coverings and the assumption that the "roof" was flat. No figures are given for the two leather coverings (rams' skins dyed red and the seal or goat skins). These may have formed a flat roof too, although some think the latter may have been pitched to form a gabled roof over the whole structure.

The tabernacle contained only four pieces of furniture. The ark of the covenant, a wooden chest overlaid with gold—a little over 4 feet in length by 2½ feet in width and depth—stood in the Most Holy Place. A gold slab functioned as its cover. On either end of this lid a golden cherub was attached. These faced each other, looking reverently downward. One wing of each cherub arched over the center of the ark; the other wing was folded over the body, symbolic of the reverence and humility of the angelic hosts toward God. The chest contained the Ten Commandments, the reason for the designation, "the ark of the covenant." Since the visible Shekinah cloud of glory hovered over the ark and between the cherubim, this whole arrangement was viewed as the Lord's throne (cf. 1 Sam 4:4; 2 Sam 6:2; Ps. 99:1, RSV).

In the holy place, immediately in front of the inner veil stood a small golden altar (1 cubit square, 2 cubits high) which was used only for the burning of incense. On the north side of the same apartment stood a golden table with 12 cakes of bread in two stacks of six each. On the south side of the room a seven-branched, solid gold lampstand with its oil lamps provided the only artificial light in the apartment.

The tabernacle stood within a large court formed by linen hangings suspended from bronzed-wooden posts, held in position by bronze sockets, ropes, and pegs. A large, hollow altar made of boards overlaid with bronze stood at a little distance from the entrance to the tabernacle. Here the sacrifices were offered and the sacred fire continuously burned the public offering which was renewed morning and evening. Designated as the "altar of burnt offering," it nevertheless was used to burn the several different kinds of sacrifices, both public and private.

Between the tabernacle and the altar of burnt offering stood a bronze laver at which the priests washed both their hands and feet before entering the tabernacle or before they approached the altar of burnt offering to present a sacrifice.

The Tabernacle's Later History

The tabernacle was taken down and set up many times throughout the long years of Israel's wandering in the wilderness. During the several years it took for Joshua to conquer western Canaan, the tabernacle remained pitched at his field camp in Gilgal, near Jericho on the west side of the Jordan. When Joshua's campaigns drew to a close, he established the tabernacle at Shiloh, a location central to the various allotments of territory made to the tribes. Here the tabernacle continued to serve as the center of Israelite worship for approximately 300 years, until the Philistines overran the armies of Israel in the days of the high priest and judge, Eli. At that time the Philistines captured the ark of the covenant, which had been carried to the field of battle by Eli's two sons, and burned Shiloh (about 1100 B.C., 1 Sam 4).

Although the Philistines returned the ark to the Israelites within seven months (1 Sam 6:1), it was never restored to its place in the tabernacle. The sacred chest remained in private Israelite homes throughout the judgeship of Samuel and the reign of king Saul. David brought it to Jerusalem in the early years of his reign and placed in a special tent. There it remained until Solomon, David's son, built the first permanent sanctuary structure and restored the ark of the covenant to its rightful position in the Most Holy Place.

Evidently before Shiloh was captured and burned, the tabernacle was quickly taken down and removed, because it next appears in the town of Nob (1 Sam 21:1-9), a village of the priests thought to have been located on Mt. Scopus, about two miles northeast of Jerusalem. After King Saul's slaughter of the high priest and his associate priests at Nob (1 Sam 22:11-19), the tabernacle was relocated once more, this time at Gibeon, the territory of Benjamin, about six miles northwest of Jerusalem (1 Kgs 3:4; 1 Chr 16:39, 40; 21:29). There it remained until replaced by Solomon's Temple on Mt. Moriah (2 Chr 1:1-6; 5:5).

If we can peg the construction of the tabernacle with a fifteenth century B.C. Exodus (about 1445 B.C.) and the completion of Solomon's Temple around 960 B.C., then we may estimate that this portable tabernacle continued to provide the center of Israelite worship for approximately 485 years, until its usable parts were assimilated into the worship of the permanent Temple structure.

Solomon's Temple (1 Kgs 5-8; 2 Chr 2-7)

David greatly desired to build a permanent temple for the worship of the true God, but he was forbidden because of his involvement in war and bloodshed (1 Chr 28:1-3). He was permitted, however, to prepare plans and materials for its erection (1 Chr 28:5-21; 29:1-9). Eventually, the national leaders and the common people added their freewill gifts to the king's store of materials. The Lord directed that Solomon, David's son, should take the throne and would build the Temple.

The site prepared for the Temple was on Mount Moriah where Abraham had built an altar to offer Isaac as a burnt sacrifice, but was permitted to offer a ram in his place. It was also the location at which David sacrificed special offerings in behalf of the nation.

Although built of stone, the walls of the two apartments were lined with cedar so that no stone surface was visible within. The floors were of cypress planks. Artisans carved figures of cherubim, palm trees, and flowers in the cedar paneling and overlaid both walls and floors with gold. Precut and prepared at the quarry, the stones that framed the Temple were moved into place without the sound of tools.

Some differences naturally appear in this larger structure as compared to the portable tabernacle. The floor dimensions of the two apartments were doubled. However, the Most Holy Place retained its cube shape (20 x 20 x 20 cubits). Two courts appear in this Temple, a "court of the priests," and a court for all the people. The altar of burnt offering was enlarged to a 20 cubit square and stood 10 cubits high. Three articles were multiplied: 10 lavers stood in the court, rather than one. Ten seven-branched lampstands and 10 golden tables stood in the 40 x 20 cubit holy place, five on each of the long sides of this apartment. But there was only one golden altar of incense, placed before the entrance to the Most Holy Place. The same ark of the covenant, which Moses had constructed, was placed in the Most Holy Place; however, it now rested beneath the outstretched wings of two larger cherubim made from olivewood overlaid with gold.

The Temple had two features altogether new to it. A huge, bronze "basin"—ten cubits in diameter—rested on the backs of 12 bronze oxen. In groups of three, the oxen faced outward toward the four points of the compass. This large "sea," as it was called, stood in the court of the priests and was restricted to priestly washings. The 10 lavers provided the necessary water for the washings performed in connection with the sacrifices. A pair of bronze pillars, 18 cubits high and 12 in circumference, were placed at the vestibule of the Temple. Highly ornamented capitals further extended their height.

The Temple actually consisted of much more than the two apartments. Three stories of chambers were built against the outside walls of these apartments on the north, west, and south sides. There may have been other construction as well, since some aspects of the description are vaguely stated. Be that as it may, the entire building complex occupied the strength and time of thousands of workers in the forests and stone quarries and on the building site. It took seven years to complete the Temple, although it did not stand as long as the portable tabernacle. In 586 B.C. this noble structure was destroyed by Nebuchadnezzar when the Babylonians overthrew the nation of Judah. Solomon's Temple stood approximately 374 years.

Zerubbabel's Temple
(Ezra 6:3, 4)

A building program to restore the Temple was started about 536 B.C. with the return of the first wave of exiles from Babylonian captivity. The newly appointed governor, Zerubbabel, with the high priest Joshua, had the oversight of the task. But many obstacles hindered the builders, and it was not until the spring of 515 B.C. that the structure was completed (Ezra 6:15).

Since no record exists regarding its features, we can only surmise that it was similar to Solomon's Temple. However, the size of the proposed complex was evidently greatly reduced, because the older citizens envisioned that the finally completed building would be as "nothing" in comparison with the previous edifice.

> Who is left among you that saw this house in its former glory? How do you see it now? Is it not in your sight as nothing? Yet now take courage, O Zerubbabel . . . take courage, O Joshua, . . . take courage, all you people of the land, says the Lord; work, for I am with you, says the Lord of hosts (Hag 2:3, 4).

"The latter splendor of this house shall be greater than the former," the Lord promised (Hag 2:9). The promise found fulfillment in the presence of Jesus Christ who taught in its courts.

Herod's Temple

No alien armies destroyed Zerubbabel's Temple, but after about 500 years it stood in need of repair. Herod the Great took on the project midway in his kingship and turned the Temple into his greatest building project. The two apartments were complete within eighteen months, and eight more years were given to constructing the surrounding complex, but the process of embellishing continued on for decades. In the time of Christ it still was incomplete after 46 years (John 2:20). Around A.D. 63 or 64 the last touches were applied, but the doomed Temple was destroyed only a few years later in A.D. 70 in the Jewish-Roman war (cf. Matt. 23:38; 24:2).

Although the Temple is not described in the NT, a fair amount of information is available from the writings of Josephus (*Ant.* xv.11; *War* v.5) and the tractate *Middoth* in the Jewish work known as the Mishna. Modern archeological data has also contributed useful information.

We may assume that the two apartments were largely the same in all the Israelite sanctuaries. But the number of outside courts changes. The tabernacle had only one court for both priests and people; Solomon's had two, one for the priests and one for the people. Herod's Temple on the other hand had four courts: a large court for non-Jews (the court of the Gentiles); a Court of the Women; a Court of Israel (that is, the Court of Man); and closest in, the Court of the Priests.

Although Herod created a magnificent house of worship, far exceeding the former Temple, the Jews always refer to it as the *second* Temple. Herod's endeavor is downgraded to a repair and remodeling program. This possibly reflects a Jewish attitude toward the king's Edomite heritage, but it may also indicate that the Temple rites never ceased while the two apartments were being rebuilt and in that sense the second Temple erected by Zerubbabel never really ceased to exist.

Neither Zerubbabel's nor Herod's Temple contained the ark of the covenant with its treasured Ten Commandments on stone. The ark disappears from history with the destruction of Solomon's Temple by the Babylonians in 586 B.C. According to Jewish tradition it was hidden in a cave by Jeremiah and other pious persons before the sack of the city.

We may assume that the rituals carried out in either tabernacle or Temple were essentially the same. We see from the biblical records that David devised a richer service to accompany the prescribed rites in terms of Levitical chanting of various psalms to the accompaniment of musical instruments. Postbiblical Jewish writings indicate a development of more complicated procedures in carrying out the proscribed Mosaic rites. However, when the inspired writer of the Epistle to the Hebrews discusses the significance of the sanctuary rites and the priesthood, his focus is always on the tabernacle and OT information, and not on the current scene in Herod's Temple.

Ezekiel's Temple (Ezek 40-48)

The vision given to the prophet Ezekiel and recorded in his book was given while the Jewish nation was in Babylonian captivity. Among other things it contains minute details for a new temple. The vision seems to foreshadow what

God proposed to do with the re-establishment of the nation after the Babylonian captivity.

However, the Jews largely failed to respond to the imposed discipline of the captivity. It is estimated that only about 58,000 returned to Palestine in the two recorded migrations combined (that of Zerubbabel and that of Ezra, 80 years later). The records also attest to the low spiritual experience of many during the first 100 years of reoccupation (see accounts in Ezra, Nehemiah, and Malachi). There is no biblical evidence that Zerubbabel's Temple matched the pattern given to Ezekiel other than at the basic points all the sanctuaries had in common. Ezekiel's Temple would only have had meaning in the postcaptivity period *before* the advent of the Messiah, the antitype of all its animal sacrifices and human priesthood. It was never built in postexilic times, and we may safely conclude (against futurist interpreters) that it will never be built. The Christian's focus is on the heavenly sanctuary and our High Priest who is now appearing in the presence of God for us (Heb 9:24).[1]

Sanctuary Personnel

While the nation of Israel encamped at Mt. Sinai, the Lord directed Moses to appoint the tribe of Levi to the service of His sanctuary. No landed inheritance was to be assigned to this tribe. The Lord would be their "inheritance" (Deut 10:8, 9).

A distinction, however, was made within the Levites themselves. Only Aaron and his direct descendants would serve as priests (Num 18:1-7). Theirs was to be a hereditary priesthood (Exod 40:15). The other Levitical families would assist the priests at their discretion (Num 3:5-10). Many Levites served the sanctuaries—both tabernacle and Temple—performing the manual labor involved with preparing the sacrifices, carrying in the needed water and wood, etc. During the wilderness travels, other Levites transported the tabernacle and its furnishings.

With the establishment of a permanent Temple, David and Solomon diversified the employment of the non-priestly Levites (cf. 1 Chr 23-26). Many, of course, continued to assist the priesthood directly in the Temple, but others were assigned to serve as singers and musicians, and Temple gatekeepers. Others were appointed over the Temple treasuries which also involved the distribution of the tithes to the priesthood (1 Chr 26:20; cf. Neh 13:13). Some Levites were selected to serve the nation as judges and officers (1 Chr 23:4), and still others as teachers of the people in the religion of the nation (cf. 2 Chr 17:7-9). It is easy to see that God intended the tribe of Levi to be a strong spiritual force in the nation.

Joshua appointed the Levitical families 48 cities to live in (Josh 21). Thirteen were allotted to the priests in the tribal areas of Judah, Simeon, and Benjamin which, as it turned out later, placed them in close proximity to the permanent Temple in Jerusalem. The balance of the cities—35—distributed the Levites like "salt" throughout the territories of the other tribes.

While the Levites drew some support from the nearby fields attached to the cities, their real support came from the tithes returned to God from all Israel. God directed that Israel's tithe would take the place of the tribe's landed inheritance (Num 18:20-24). The Levites, in turn, were to tithe what they received and to pass this "tithe of the tithe" on to the priesthood (Num 18:25-28). The priestly families also secured a portion of their income from the sacrifices and offerings which the people brought to the sanctuary in connection with their worship. In this manner the Lord designed to relieve the priests and their assistants of many secular concerns so they might devote themselves more fully to the nourishing and strengthening of the spiritual life of the nation.[2]

Just as the house of Aaron was separated from the other Levitical families to serve as priests, so the office of high priest seems to have been reserved for the eldest son in the line of Eleazar. After the early death of Nadab and Abihu, only two of Aaron's sons remained: Eleazar (the older) and Ithamar. Eleazar succeeded his father Aaron as high priest upon the latter's death (Num 20:25-29). It is thought by some commentators that the office of high priest was confirmed to his family line after his eldest son, Phinehas, in righteous indignation, executed a brazen Israelite and his pagan "amour" (Num 25:10-13).

At any rate the high priest's office apparently remained in the line of Eleazar's descendants until Eli occupied the role as high priest and judge (it may be inferred from 1 Chronicles 24:3, 6 that Eli was a descendant of Ithamar). Because of his failure to control his sons, God foretold the ruin of Eli's house (1 Sam 2:27-36; 3:1-18). The judgment fell many years later when Solomon removed the high priest Abiathar from office because of his treasonous conduct in David's old age (1 Kgs 2:26, 27). The office returned to Eleazar's line (vs. 35) until the period of Greek rule over Palestine. The Maccabean rulers—Jewish patriots—assumed the office during their short-lived monarchy. Under the succeeding Roman domination, the position of the high priest became an appointed office.

The high priest could rightfully perform all the duties required by the rites in either the tabernacle or the later temples. But, obviously, he could not personally meet the demands of the thousands of worshipers who thronged the sacred places, bringing their sacrifices. Hence, the common priests functioned as the extension of his office. It was one priesthood. Only with respect to the special rite of the Day of Atonement was the common priest restricted. The high priest alone was allowed on that day to enter the Most Holy Place to perform the required rites (cf. Lev 16; Heb 9:6, 7).

Priestly Garments (Exod 28:1-43; 39:1-31)

The clothing of the common priests consisted of four pieces: (1) linen breeches (as underclothing); (2) a linen coat or robe that extended to the foot and probably was long-sleeved; (3) a girdle or sash composed of fine linen and blue, purple, and scarlet wool, embroidered with needlework; (4) a linen miter or turban.

The high priest's clothing was similar, but in full dress he wore four additional items:

1. The robe of the ephod. This garment was blue in color, woven in one piece and sleeveless. The high priest wore it over his long linen robe. It reached below his knees. Attached to the bottom edge were pomegranates made of wool in three colors—blue, purple, and scarlet. These alternated with small golden bells. The bells' tinkling sound could be heard when the high priest walked, and when he entered the sanctuary.

2. The ephod. The ephod was a kind of jerkin or waistcoat, consisting of two pieces, one covering the front and the other the back, joined at the shoulders by two onyx stones—one on each shoulder, and held in place around the waist by a girdle/sash made of the same material as the ephod. The ephod and sash were richly designed of gold threads woven together with blue and purple and scarlet wool and fine linen.

3. The breastpiece. Attached to the ephod by golden chains and blue lace was the breastpiece, a double piece of cloth (perhaps making a pocket), about ten inches square. Attached to the breastpiece were twelve precious gems, arranged in four rows of three each, each gem engraved with the name of one of the tribes. The breastpiece was never removed from the ephod.

4. The miter/turban. A golden plate, inscribed with the Hebrew words, "Holiness to the Lord," was attached to the high priest's linen turban by a ribbon or lace of blue. This completed the high priest's full attire.

These "holy garments"—crafted "for glory and for beauty"—portrayed spiritual truth to the Israelite in his times even as it foreshadowed characteristics of the messianic High Priest who would one day come into His own Temple.

———— ◆ ————

Endnotes

1 For a diagram of Ezekiel's temple, see SDABC 4:716, or SDABD, "Temple," 1074.

2 A fine summarization in outline form of the various sacrifices, festivals, and procedures involved in the sanctuary worship system (with supporting references) may be found in SDABC 1:698-710.

Appendix D

Daniel

Chart 1

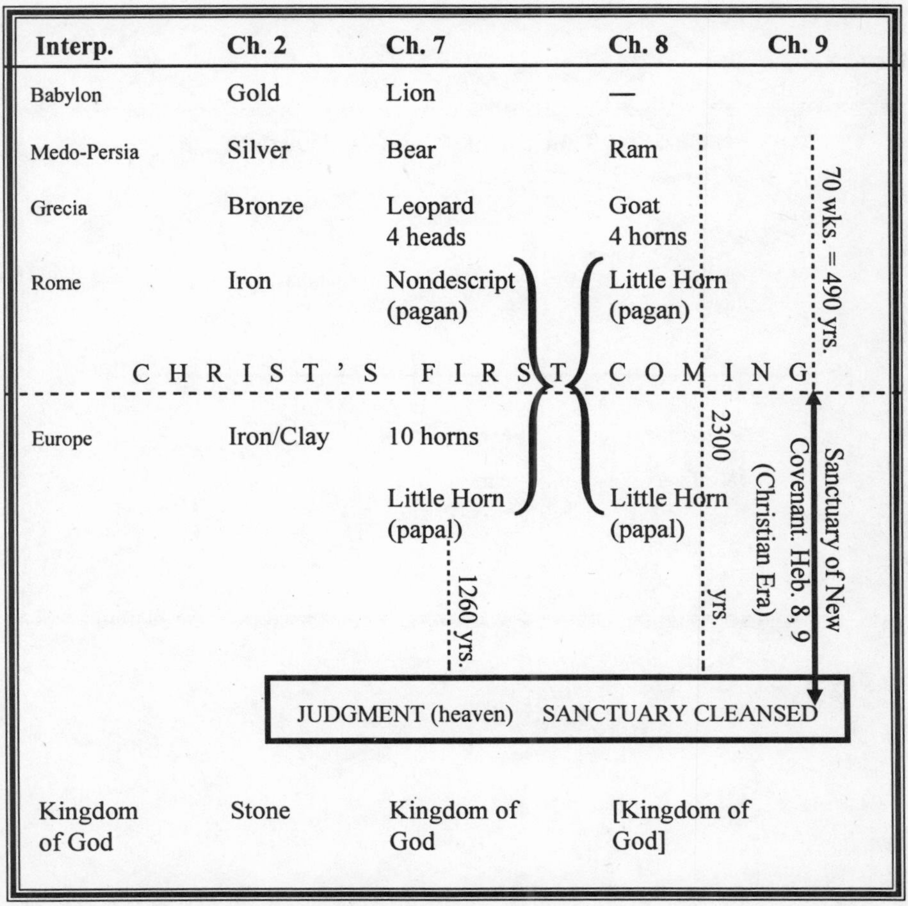

Interp.	Ch. 2	Ch. 7	Ch. 8	Ch. 9
Babylon	Gold	Lion	—	
Medo-Persia	Silver	Bear	Ram	
Grecia	Bronze	Leopard 4 heads	Goat 4 horns	
Rome	Iron	Nondescript (pagan)	Little Horn (pagan)	

70 wks. = 490 yrs.

C H R I S T ' S   F I R S T   C O M I N G

Europe	Iron/Clay	10 horns		
		Little Horn (papal)	Little Horn (papal)	

2300 yrs. (Christian Era)

Sanctuary of New Covenant. Heb. 8, 9

1260 yrs.

JUDGMENT (heaven)   SANCTUARY CLEANSED

Kingdom of God	Stone	Kingdom of God	[Kingdom of God]	

Chart 2

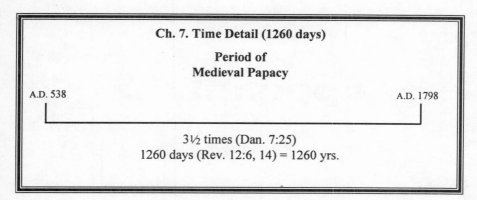

Ch. 7. Time Detail (1260 days)

**Period of
Medieval Papacy**

A.D. 538   A.D. 1798

3½ times (Dan. 7:25)
1260 days (Rev. 12:6, 14) = 1260 yrs.

Chart 3

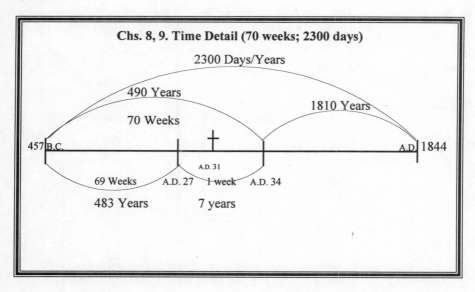

Chs. 8, 9. Time Detail (70 weeks; 2300 days)

2300 Days/Years

490 Years

70 Weeks

1810 Years

457 B.C.   A.D. 1844

A.D. 31

69 Weeks   A.D. 27   1 week   A.D. 34

483 Years   7 years

Chart 4

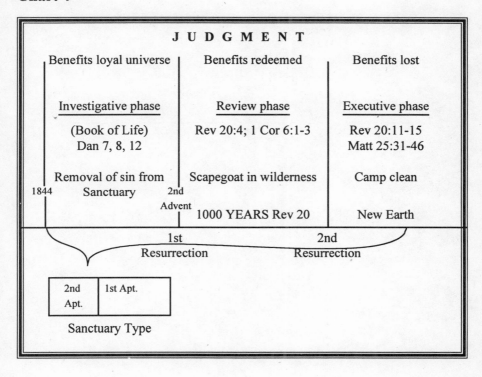

J U D G M E N T

Benefits loyal universe	Benefits redeemed	Benefits lost
Investigative phase	Review phase	Executive phase
(Book of Life) Dan 7, 8, 12	Rev 20:4; 1 Cor 6:1-3	Rev 20:11-15 Matt 25:31-46
Removal of sin from Sanctuary	Scapegoat in wilderness	Camp clean
	1000 YEARS Rev 20	New Earth

1844

2nd Advent

1st Resurrection   2nd Resurrection

2nd Apt.	1st Apt.

Sanctuary Type

Index

Ministration (Second Apartment), of
judgment and vindication, 132
sanctuary-centered, 121-134, 134
nn. 5, 6

Need, human, and divine grace, 202,
203
Niṣdaq (cleanse/restore), interpret
within sanctuary setting, 151-153

Offerings (public), morning and evening, priority of, 74, 75, 89 n. 3
private, equate with prayer, 76
accessory, 76, 77
burnt, 75
peace, 75, 76
sin/guilt, 76

Papacy, teaching of, obscures Christ's
priesthood, 146, 147, 159 n. 24
identity (little horn, Dan 7), 164,
182 n. 2
Parabolē (parable), significance for interpreting Israelite sanctuary, 35,
36
Personnel, priestly, in earthly sanctuary, 238-240
Plan of salvation, formed in eternity
past, 30 n. 1
objectives of, 67, 68, 70 n. 23
Priesthood (Christ's), doctrine of, a
construct, 46, 47
essential as His death, 15 n. 22
inauguration of, 1-13
mediatorial role exercised
through, 96
OT prophecies of, 7-13
papal attack on, 146, 147, 153
requirements for (incarnation/sacri-
ficial death), 96-99
Priesthood (Israelite), bore sins of the
people, 104, 114 n. 11
emphasized the serious chasm between God and man, 95, 96,
114 n. 9

qualifications for, 100, 101
typical systems, one of two in OT,
99
united heavenly and earthly
spheres, 99, 100
Prophecy, conditional or uncondi-
tional? 154 n. 1
Prophecies (Dan 7-9), arranged in Hebraic order: "effect to cause,"
139, 154 n. 3
Propitiation, biblical meaning of, 79,
80
Psalm (110:1, 4), exposition of, 7, 8

Qōdeš qodāšîm (most holy), meaning
of in Dan 9:24, 11-13
Questions, some, about Christ's priesthood, 185-199

Romans 5:12-19, exposition of, 63,
64, 69 n. 12

Sacrifice, every, a type of Christ's
death, 53 n. 9
Sacrifices, morning and evening, 74
private 75-77
Salvation, subject matter of the sanctuary (type/antitype), 37-39, 53 n. 6
options: by decree or by faith, 133
personal, how to obtain, 201-217
Sanctification, believer's response to
grace, 206-214
process/growth, 208-214
standing/status, 207, 208
Sanctuary (earthly), antitypical fulfillments of, major categories, 39-44
misleading interpretations of, 44-
46
principles for interpreting, 35-54
relationship to the heavenly sanctuary, 17-21
weakness of, 27-30, 33 n. 33
Sanctuary (heavenly), anointing of
predicted (Dan 9:24), 11-13
center of Christ's work, 14 n. 4